Building Trading Bots Using Java

Shekhar Varshney

Apress®

Building Trading Bots Using Java

Shekhar Varshney
Granges
Switzerland

ISBN-13 (pbk): 978-1-4842-2519-6   ISBN-13 (electronic): 978-1-4842-2520-2
DOI 10.1007/978-1-4842-2520-2

Library of Congress Control Number: 2016961228

Managing Director: Welmoed Spahr
Lead Editor: Steve Anglin
Editorial Board: Steve Anglin, Pramila Balan, Laura Berendson, Aaron Black, Louise Corrigan,
    Jonathan Gennick, Robert Hutchinson, Celestin Suresh John, Nikhil Karkal,
    James Markham, Susan McDermott, Matthew Moodie, Natalie Pao, Gwenan Spearing
Coordinating Editor: Mark Powers
Copy Editor: Kezia Endsley
Compositor: SPi Global
Indexer: SPi Global
Artist: SPi Global

Distributed to the book trade worldwide by Springer Science+Business Media New York, 233 Spring Street, 6th Floor, New York, NY 10013. Phone 1-800-SPRINGER, fax (201) 348-4505, e-mail orders-ny@springer-sbm.com, or visit www.springeronline.com. Apress Media, LLC is a California LLC and the sole member (owner) is Springer Science + Business Media Finance Inc (SSBM Finance Inc). SSBM Finance Inc is a **Delaware** corporation.

For information on translations, please e-mail rights@apress.com, or visit www.apress.com.

Apress and friends of ED books may be purchased in bulk for academic, corporate, or promotional use. eBook versions and licenses are also available for most titles. For more information, reference our Special Bulk Sales–eBook Licensing web page at www.apress.com/bulk-sales.

Any source code or other supplementary materials referenced by the author in this text are available to readers at www.apress.com. For detailed information about how to locate your book's source code, go to www.apress.com/source-code/. Readers can also access source code at SpringerLink in the Supplementary Material section for each chapter.

Printed on acid-free paper

Dedicated to the angels in my life:
my mother, my wife Preshita, and my two daughters Mihika and Anya.
Last but not the least, my college professor, Dr. Rajat Moona,
who sowed the seeds of computer programming in my DNA.

Contents at a Glance

Contents at a Glance

Contents

About the Author

Shekhar Varshney is a freelance software developer based in Switzerland with over 19 years of development experience. He started his journey with IBM mainframes, correcting COBOL programs infected with the Y2K bug. At present, his main software development focus is building enterprise services based on SOA principles.

He has a keen interest in software design and architecture. In his free time, he loves experimenting with new APIs and frameworks mostly in the Java ecosystem.

CHAPTER 1

■ ■ ■

Introduction to Trading Bot

Welcome to the world of automated trading! The fact that you are reading this book suggests that you want to probably build your own bot, which hopefully can make you some money while you are busy with your day job or, like me, want to experiment with the technology that goes into building such a bot using Java.

Automated trading has been around for a while, although it has largely been a preserve of big players such as banks and hedge funds.

This has changed in the last few years, however. Many retail investors are now able to trade on various platforms and exchanges directly, instead of using the services of a traditional broker on the phone, which means the demand has been growing to automate the task of placing orders while these investors get on with their day jobs. As a first step in automating this process, many platforms such as OANDA, LMAX, etc., provide APIs for various programming languages such as Java, Python, C#, and PHP so that the mundane tasks of watching the market, looking at charts, and doing analysis can be automated.

On this journey, we will focus not only on the concepts of automated trading, but also on writing clean, test-driven Java programs.

Toward the end, we will not only have a working trading bot that is ready to trade with any strategy, but from a technical perspective, we will have also gained an appreciation of the event-driven, multithreaded world of Java programming.

■ **Warning** Trading foreign exchange on the margin carries a high level of risk, and may not be suitable for all investors. Past performance is not indicative of future results. The high degree of leverage can work against you as well as for you. Before deciding to invest in foreign exchange, you should carefully consider your investment objectives, level of experience, and risk appetite. The possibility exists that you could sustain a loss of some or all of your initial investment and therefore you should not invest money that you cannot afford to lose. You should be aware of all the risks associated with foreign exchange trading and seek advice from an independent financial advisor if you have any doubts.

Electronic supplementary material The online version of this chapter (doi:10.1007/978-1-4842-2520-2_1) contains supplementary material, which is available to authorized users.

© Shekhar Varshney 2016
S. Varshney, *Building Trading Bots Using Java*, DOI 10.1007/978-1-4842-2520-2_1

What Is a Trading Bot?

In very simple language, a *trading bot* is a computer program that can automatically place orders to a market or exchange, without the need for human intervention. The simplest of bots could be a curl[1] POST to an OANDA REST API, such as

```
1  $curl -X POST -d "instrument=EUR_USD&units=2&side=sell&type=market"
   "https://api-fxtrade.oanda.com/v1/accounts/12345/ord\
2  ers"
```

which can be set up on a UNIX cron[2] to run every hour, during trading hours. It has no strategy, nor any external interface or dependencies. It is a one-liner to place an order, which has an equal probability to be in profit or in loss.

On the other end of the spectrum, it could be a complex program based on a distributed architecture, consuming lots of feeds from various sources, analyzing them in realtime and then placing an order. It will be highly available with extremely low latency.

The scale and scope of the bot, as we can see, is varied. To be effective, the bot should be able to accomplish the following tasks:

- Consume market data and/or external news events and social media feeds and distribute them to interested components within the system.

- Have at least one strategy that provides a trading signal.

- Based on a trading signal, place orders with the brokerage platform.

- Account management, i.e., have the ability to keep track of margin requirements, leverage, PNL, amount remaining, etc., in order to curb trading if the amount available breaches a given threshold.

- Position management, i.e., keep track of all currently active positions of various instruments, units of such positions, average price, etc.

- Have the ability to handle events which are triggered by the brokerage platform such as ORDER_FILLED, STOP_LOSS, etc., and if required take appropriate decisions for such events.

- Some basic monitoring and alerting.

- Some basic risk management. For example, loss limitation by using stop losses for orders or making sure that risk is distributed between risky and safe haven instruments. These are just examples and by no means a comprehensive list of fully managing the risk.

---

[1]https://en.wikipedia.org/wiki/CURL
[2]https://en.wikipedia.org/wiki/Cron

Why Do We Need a Trading Bot?

I believe most of services provided by exchanges/platforms revolve around the following:

- Market data subscription for instruments of choice and dissemination

- Place orders and trades

- Account and position management

- Historic market data

- Heartbeating

- Callbacks for trade, order, and account events

- Authentication

The trading bot is an attempt to generalize these tasks in a framework and provide an ability to provide the broker/exchange platform specific implementation at runtime, using a dependency injection[3] framework like Spring. Therefore, theoretically speaking, it will just be a change in the Spring configuration file, where we define our implementations for various interfaces that implement these services, and voila, we should be able to support various broker/exchange platforms.

The Capabilities of the Trading Bot

Our bot will have the following capabilities, which are discussed in detail in later chapters:

- Account management

- Integrate with realtime market data feed

- Disseminate of market data

- Place orders

- Handle order/trade and account events

- Analyze of historic prices

- Integrate with Twitter

- Develop strategies

---

[3]https://en.wikipedia.org/wiki/Dependency_injection

Design Goals

One of the key design goals, alluded to in the beginning of this chapter, is to have the ability to change the implementation of a broker/exchange platform at runtime through Spring configuration. This is possible if we can create specifications for these platform API calls, very similar to the JDBC specification. For example, a sample specification/interface defining the position management requirements are as follows:

```
1   /**
2    * A provider of services for instrument positions. A position for an
         instrument
3    * is by definition aggregated trades for the instrument with an
         average price
4    * where all trades must all be a LONG or a SHORT. It is a useful
         service to
5    * project a summary of a given instrument and also if required close
         all trades
6    * for a given instrument, ideally using a single call.
7    *
8    * The implementation might choose to maintain an internal cache of
         positions in
9    * order to reduce latency. If this is the case then it must find means
         to
10   * either 1) hook into the event streaming and refresh the cache based
         on an
11   * order/trade event or 2) regularly refresh the cache after a given
         time
12   * period.
13   *
14   * @param <M>
15   *       The type of instrumentId in class TradeableInstrument
16   * @param <N>
17   *       the type of accountId
18   *
19   * @see TradeableInstrument
20   */
21   public interface PositionManagementProvider<M, N> {
22
23       /**
24        *
25        * @param accountId
26        * @param instrument
27        * @return Position<M> for a given instrument and accountId(may
                  be null if
28        *         all trades under a single account).
29        */
```

```
30        Position<M> getPositionForInstrument(N accountId,
          TradeableInstrument<M> instrument);
31
32        /**
33         *
34         * @param accountId
35         * @return Collection of Position<M> objects for a given
             accountId.
36         */
37        Collection<Position<M>> getPositionsForAccount(N accountId);
38
39        /**
40         * close the position for a given instrument and accountId.
             This is one shot
41         * way to close all trades for a given instrument in an
             account.
42         *
43         * @param accountId
44         * @param instrument
45         * @return if the operation was successful
46         */
47        boolean closePosition(N accountId, TradeableInstrument<M>
          instrument);
48
49  }
```

If we create such specifications/interfaces for each aspect of the platform interaction, we can in theory create providers for these services and swap them when required, through the Spring configuration. From code organization perspective, all these interfaces, therefore, go in a project that forms part of the core API. This project will therefore be broker/exchange provider-agnostic and will comprise such interfaces and services.

- Write services that solve a single business problem or a collection of related problems. These services lend themselves to easy unit testability and code reuse that eventually leads to better software quality.

- Loosely couple services. This enables reducing system dependencies and as a result results in more maintainable software. Our software will be continuously evolving as one might decide to integrate more social media feeds or add more complex strategies. Writing loosely coupled components ensures that we have little knockon effect on already working code.

- High unit test coverage. It is extremely important that we aim to have a high unit test coverage. When used in a production environment where real money could be involved, large unit tests coverage will ensure that we catch regressions and bugs early on and prevent the manifestation of bugs as much as possible in the production environment.

Code Organization and Software Stack Used

Following on from our discussion of design goals in the previous sections, the code will be organized in at least three different projects. That means at least three JAR files will be produced from the build. Why are we saying at least three? Remember from our earlier discussion, that one of the key design goals is to be able to switch provider implementation at runtime. Since we could have more than one provider from which we can decide, there will be at least three JAR files (see Figure 1-1). We are going to discuss only one implementation in the book, i.e., the OANDA REST API implementation. Developers who use the framework are encouraged to develop more provider implementations:

- trading-core is the core of the project. It comprises all the specifications/interfaces that must be implemented. It also comprises all the generic services that use the core interfaces and provide additional useful API methods.

- oanda-restapi is our reference implementation for the specification and will be discussed in the book. You are more than welcome to swap this with your own.

- tradingbot-app is the main application that uses Spring to inject the provider API at runtime. It is also the project where we define our strategies and can implement app-specific stuff. Later in the book, we are going to talk about integration with social media, especially Twitter, which we will implement in this project.

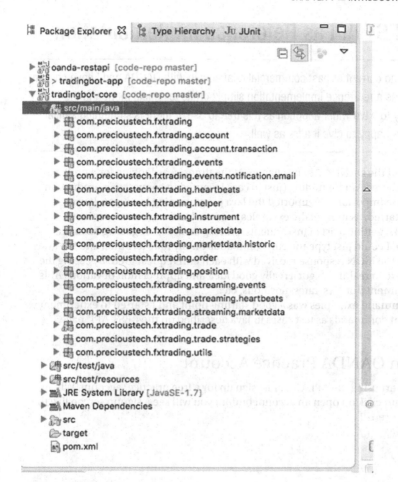

Figure 1-1. Java projects

To build our bot we are going to use the following set of software and tools:

- Java SDK 1.7+

- Spring Framework 4.1, Spring Social 1.1 (dependency in the tradingbot-app project only)

- Guava 18.0

- HttpClient 4.3

- Maven 3.2.5

- Eclipse IDE

OANDA REST API as Reference Implementation

■ **Note**   I have no current or past commercial relationship with OANDA and I have chosen OANDA REST API as a reference implementation simply on its technical merit and the fact that it is likely to have wider adoption as it is free to use. If there is something similar around, I would be happy to give it a try as well.

I encountered the OANDA API by chance. At the time, I was looking for a broker who was offering a free API for trading (just in case I wanted to convert to a production account) and more importantly supported the Java programming language. It was very easy to get started, as most of the examples used curl to demonstrate various trading actions like getting a list of instruments, placing an order, or getting historical candlesticks data. I could just type the curl commands on my Mac terminal and fire away. I could easily see the JSON response received with each curl request fired. By seeing the responses and data in realtime, I got a really good idea and appreciation of various APIs supporting instruments, orders, rates, positions, etc.

The curl command examples was a good starting point and I started to experiment writing equivalent commands as test cases in Java described on the REST API[4] page.

Opening an OANDA Practice Account

Before you can start using the API, you must sign up for a free practice[5] account. When you head there and click on open an account button, you will see a signup screen like the one shown in Figure 1-2.

---

[4]http://developer.oanda.com/rest-live/introduction/
[5]http://fxtrade.oanda.com

中文 | De | En | Es | Fr | It | Pt | Py

Sign Up In Minutes

Open an fxTrade Practice account today and experience OANDA's award-winning platforms - fxTrade, MT4, and Mobile. Trade confidently with OANDA's competitive spreads and exceptional execution.

Name	First Name
	Last Name
Email	Email
Username	Username
	Must be 2-50 alphanumeric characters
Password	Password
	Must be 8-15 characters in length
Phone	☐▾ • Primary Phone Number

By clicking **Sign Up** I confirm that:

I agree that OANDA may contact me to provide information on its products and services and to assist me in using fxTrade Practice.

Sign Up

Risk Warning
Leveraged trading is high risk and may not be suitable

∞ **Unlimited Virtual Funds**
Use virtual funds to gain insight only trading experience can provide.

⟳ **Never Expires**
Trade under real market conditions with live prices and spreads, for as long as you want.

▢ **Five Trading Platforms**
Choose the trading platform that suits you and your investing.

Figure 1-2. Oanda account signup

Once you have successfully signed up, you are now ready to sign in to your practice account. You will see the login screen shown in Figure 1-3 when you are ready to log in.

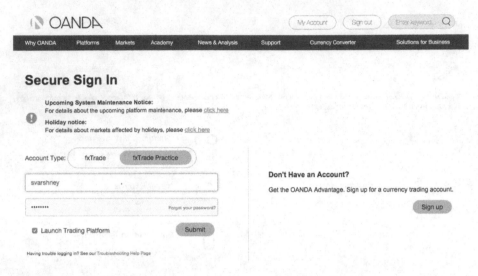

Figure 1-3. Oanda account login

After a successful sign on, you are taken to the account home page, which looks like the screen in Figure 1-4.

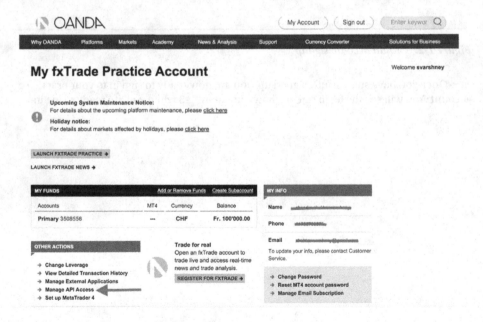

Figure 1-4. Oanda account dashboard

In order to commence API trading, we need to first generate a personal API token, which will be used by the OANDA platform to authenticate the request. You need to click on the Manage API Access link, highlighted by a arrow in Figure 1-4. You will next be taken to the screen shown in Figure 1-5.

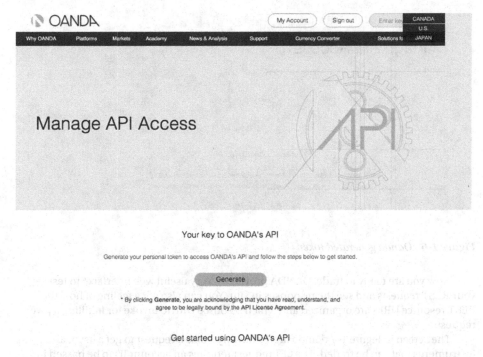

Figure 1-5. *Oanda generate API token*

When you click Generate, the platform will generate a token with you, which must be included in every request you make to the platform that hosts your practice account. The token generated will be presented and you must make a note of it (see Figure 1-6).

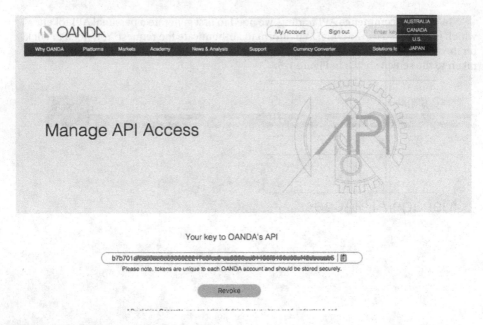

Figure 1-6. *Oanda generated token*

Now you are ready to trade. OANDA provides a very useful web interface[6] to test your REST requests and see the responses in situ. You can also get a feeling of how the REST resource URLs are organized and which resource URL to invoke for fulfilling a given request.

The screen in Figure 1-7 demonstrates how we make a request to get a list of all instruments that can be traded. The GET request requires an account ID to be passed in (this is the ID that you can find on the account page and for a practice account, comes loaded with 100,000 units of the account currency). It is imperative to provide the header as well and can be specified as Bearer <Your API Token goes here> (see Figure 1-8).

---

[6]http://developer.oanda.com/rest-live/console/
??utm_source=oandaapi&utm_medium=link&utm_campaign=accesstoken_email

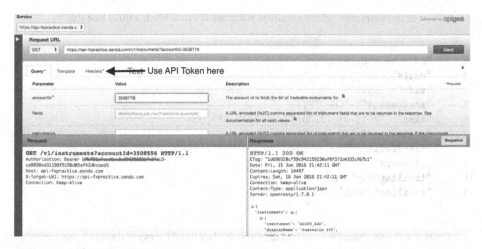

Figure 1-7. *Oanda dev API console*

Figure 1-8. *Oanda dev API console-headers tab*

OANDA JSON Keys

The OANDA JSON responses use a set of standard keys. For example, to denote a currency pair in a response, the key `instrument` is used, whether it's a streaming response for tick or candlestick information. A tick in the live stream would look like this:

```
1   {"tick":{"instrument":"AUD_CAD","time":"1401919217201682","bid":1.01484
    ,"ask":1.01502}}
```

Whereas the response, when a trade is successfully modified, would like this:

```
1   {
2      "id": 1800805337,
3      "units": 3000,
4      "side": "sell",
5      "instrument": "CHF_JPY",
6      "time": "2015-03-18T06:33:36.000000Z",
7      "price": 120.521,
8      "takeProfit": 110,
9      "stopLoss": 150,
10     "trailingStop": 0,
11     "trailingAmount": 0
12  }
```

From these two examples, we can also see the key used for event date is time. Since the same keys are used to denote a given attribute, we can create public static final String variables for these keys. So therefore the concept of the class OandaJsonKeys was born. Instead of polluting the code with these lines in many classes

```
1   String instrument = (String) instrumentJson.get("instrument");
```

it is much better practice to create a constant and use that instead. The same code snippet would look like this:

```
1   String instrument = (String) instrumentJson.get(OandaJsonKeys.
instrument);
```

There are a lot of keys, but most of the keys that we use in our trading bot are captured in the OandaJsonKeys class.

```
1   public class OandaJsonKeys {
2
3       private OandaJsonKeys() {
4       }
5
6       public static final String accounts = "accounts";
7       public static final String accountId = "accountId";
8       public static final String accountCurrency = "accountCurrency";
9       public static final String marginRate = "marginRate";
10      public static final String marginUsed = "marginUsed";
11      public static final String marginAvail = "marginAvail";
12      public static final String balance = "balance";
13      public static final String unrealizedPl = "unrealizedPl";
14      public static final String realizedPl = "realizedPl";
15      public static final String openTrades = "openTrades";
16      public static final String instruments = "instruments";
17      public static final String instrument = "instrument";
18      public static final String interestRate = "interestRate";
```

```
19        public static final String disconnect = "disconnect";
20        public static final String pip = "pip";
21        public static final String bid = "bid";
22        public static final String ask = "ask";
23        public static final String heartbeat = "heartbeat";
24        public static final String candles = "candles";
25        public static final String openMid = "openMid";
26        public static final String highMid = "highMid";
27        public static final String lowMid = "lowMid";
28        public static final String closeMid = "closeMid";
29        public static final String time = "time";
30        public static final String tick = "tick";
31        public static final String prices = "prices";
32        public static final String trades = "trades";
33        public static final String tradeId = "tradeId";
34        public static final String price = "price";
35        public static final String avgPrice = "avgPrice";
36        public static final String id = "id";
37        public static final String stopLoss = "stopLoss";
38        public static final String takeProfit = "takeProfit";
39        public static final String units = "units";
40        public static final String side = "side";
41        public static final String type = "type";
42        public static final String orders = "orders";
43        public static final String orderId = "orderId";
44        public static final String positions = "positions";
45        public static final String expiry = "expiry";
46        public static final String tradeOpened = "tradeOpened";
47        public static final String orderOpened = "orderOpened";
48        public static final String transaction = "transaction";
49        public static final String pl = "pl";
50        public static final String interest = "interest";
51        public static final String accountBalance = "accountBalance";
52    }
```

In all our OANDA API implementations, which will be discussed in the subsequent chapters, we directly use this class and statically importing constants instead of hardcoding the string literals for a given JSON key.

Constructor Dependencies for OANDA Implementations

All OANDA implementations of the core API specifications have constructors that accept the following:

- API URL
- Username
- Access token

As we know, OANDA has different environments where we can run our bot, such as sandpit, practice, and live. These environments have different URLs and access tokens and can have different usernames for the same individual. These external configuration properties are passed in as constructor parameters for various OANDA implementations. For example:

```
1   public OandaAccountDataProviderService(final String url, final String
    userName, final String accessToken) {
2           this.url = url;
3           this.userName = userName;
4           this.authHeader = OandaUtils.createAuthHeader(accessToken);
5   }
```

The parameters are passed to this implementation in the Spring configuration, as shown here:

```
1   <bean id="accountDataProvider" class="com.precioustech.fxtrading.oanda.
    restapi.account.OandaAccountDataProviderService">
2                   <constructor-arg index="0" value="${oanda.url}"/>
3                   <constructor-arg index="1" value="${oanda.userName}"/>
4                   <constructor-arg index="2" value="${oanda.
                    accessToken}"/>
5   </bean>
```

Since these variables are provided in a property file, we can easily change them at runtime, without having to do a new build or change code. It would be sufficient to just change the property file. We will cover this topic in more detail in later chapters when we talk about configuration in detail.

Event-Driven Architecture

The soul of any trading system is its event-driven architecture. The system must react to market events, social media events, user events, and maybe a plethora of other events coming from external/internal sources. These events could further trigger a chain reaction of events, resulting in state changes of various business/domain objects in the system. The real technical challenge is to make sure that these state transitions happen in a thread-safe way, backed by a transaction wherever required.

At the heart of an event-driven system are one or more event loops. These event loops typically run in an infinite while loop and wait on an event to come from a queue or a live stream. For an Oanda market data tick event, we have an event loop as following:

```
1   this.streamThread = new Thread(new Runnable() {
2
3   @Override
4   public void run() {
5     CloseableHttpClient httpClient = getHttpClient();
6       try {
```

```
 7      BufferedReader br = setUpStreamIfPossible(httpClient);
 8      if (br != null) {
 9        String line;
10        while ((line = br.readLine()) != null && serviceUp) {
11          Object obj = JSONValue.parse(line);
12          JSONObject instrumentTick = (JSONObject) obj;
13          ...
14          ...
```

In this code snippet, we have an infinite while loop that listens on new ticks being pushed on to the live stream by the OANDA platform. When a tick JSON payload is received, it is parsed and further disseminated via a queue or an event bus (see Figure 1-9).

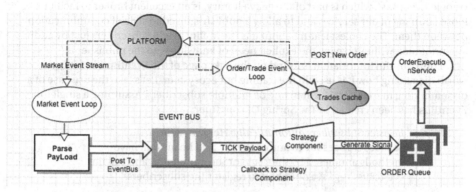

Figure 1-9. *Typical Event Chain*

Figure 1-9 depicts a typical chain of events that might be triggered by a single event.

1. Tick event is received from the stream.

2. Event is parsed and sent to an event bus.

3. The strategy component has a subscription for this event and gets a callback from an event bus.

4. The strategy component decides to generate a trading signal based on the latest tick data event and places the signal on an OrderQueue.

5. The OrderExecutionService picks up this signal, creates a new order payload, and posts it to the platform.

6. The platform executes the order and sends an event down the order event loop.

7. This event can further trigger an update of, say, the trades cache.

This basically is the essence of an *event-driven architecture*. Since we could have many components at play at the same time, it is extremely important that we decouple components as much as possible, so that new publishers and subscribers can be added with zero or minimal changes. This architecture lends itself to take advantage of Java multithreaded programming capabilities. However, by the same token, it dictates the developer to exercise great caution when performing state changes of business objects present in caches, for example, the *trades cache* in our example. We must put adequate synchronization and locking in place to make sure that the observed state of a shared object is always consistent.

Google EventBus

Google EventBus[7], which is part of the guava library, is an excellent broker to facilitate loose coupling of our services and to allow a publish-subscribe style of communication between them. The coolest feature about it is the ability to add subscribers just by adding an annotation without having the explicit need of knowing who the publisher is.

Lots of useful information is found on the wiki page of the EventBus, but it is worth discussing how it is used in the trading bot ecosystem. Let's take the use case of a disseminating market data event to one or multiple subscribers. Assuming a singleton EventBus has been created by the Spring DI container:

- *Register Subscribers automatically:* Here we write a BeanBostProcessor to automatically find beans that have methods annotated by the @Subscribe annotation and call the eventBus.register method to register the subscribers.

```
1   public class FindEventBusSubscribers implements BeanPostProcessor {
2
3   @Autowired
4   private EventBus eventBus;
5   private static final Logger LOG = Logger.getLogger(FindEventBusSubscri
    bers.class);
6
7   @Override
8   public Object postProcessAfterInitialization(Object bean, String
    beanName) throws BeansException {
9    Method[] beanMethods = bean.getClass().getMethods();
10   for (Method beanMethod: beanMethods) {
11    if (beanMethod.isAnnotationPresent(Subscribe.class)) {
12     eventBus.register(bean);
13     LOG.info(
14      String.format("Found event bus subscriber class %s. Subscriber
       method name=%s",
15       bean.getClass().getSimpleName(),  beanMethod.getName()));
16     break;
```

---

[7] https://code.google.com/p/guava-libraries/wiki/EventBusExplained

```
17      }
18    }
19    return bean;
20    }
21
22    @Override
23    public Object postProcessBeforeInitialization(Object bean, String
      beanName) throws BeansException {
24    return bean;
25    }
26
27    }
```

- *Create publisher:* It is sufficient to just call post(Object payload) to post it to the EventBus.

```
1    public MarketEventHandlerImpl(EventBus eventBus) {
2      this.eventBus = eventBus;
3    }
4    public void onMarketEvent(TradeableInstrument < T > instrument, double
      bid, double ask, DateTime eventDate) {
5      MarketDataPayLoad < T > payload = new MarketDataPayLoad < T >
        (instrument, bid, ask, eventDate);
6      eventBus.post(payload);
7    }
```

- *Consume payload:* The EventBus finds the appropriate subscriber by matching the method signature based on the input type passed into the method and annotated by the @Subscribe annotation. This method must have one and only one input parameter. There is a choice to go as fine-grained or coarse-grained as possible. In the case of coarse-grained subscription, we have the input parameter as an object, which is the super class of all known payloads in the system. The worst case being the payload java. lang.Object, in which case the subscription is the most coarse-grained. This method will be called for every eventBus.post performed in the system. On the other hand, using individual subtypes as input parameters to methods makes it extremely fine-grained. In the following example, handleMarketDataEvent will only be called by the EventBus if the payload is of the type MarketDataPayLoad or any of its subtypes.

```
1    @Subscribe
2    @AllowConcurrentEvents
3    public void handleMarketDataEvent(MarketDataPayLoad<T>
      marketDataPayLoad) {
```

```
4               if (instrumentRecentPricesCache.containsKey
                (marketDataPayLoad.getInstrument()))) {
5                   instrumentRecentPricesCache.get(
6                   marketDataPayLoad.getInstrument())
7                   .put(marketDataPayLoad.getEventDate(),marketDataPayLoad);
8           }
9   }
```

Provider Helper Interface

Often different platform providers have different notations for denoting a currency pair. *Cable* can be denoted in the following ways:

- GBP_USD

- GBPUSD

- GBP/USD

- GBP-USD

Similarly, the act of buying a currency pair could be denoted by:

- buy

- long

- +1 (or any other positive number)

- Platform specific enum, for example, TRADEACTION.BUY

In order to deal with such variances in notation provided by different providers, we need to create an interface that provides methods to address these differences. It looks like this:

```
1   /**
2    *
3    * @param <T>
4    *           The type of Long/Short notation
5    */
6   public interface ProviderHelper < T > {
7
8       /**
9        *
10       * @param instrument
11       *           in ISO currency standard, such as GBPUSD
12       * @return currency pair denoted in the platform specific format
13       */
14      String fromIsoFormat(String instrument);
15
16      /**
```

```
17      *
18      * @param instrument
19      *              in platform specific format such as GBP_USD
20      * @return currency pair denoted in ISO format
21      */
22     String toIsoFormat(String instrument);
23
24     /**
25      *
26      * @param instrument
27      *              in a 7 character format, separated by an arbitrary
                       separator
28      *              character like -,/,_
29      * @return currency pair denoted in the platform specific format
30      */
31     String fromPairSeparatorFormat(String instrument);
32
33     /**
34      *
35      * @param instrument
36      *              denoted as a hashtag, for e.g. #GBPUSD
37      * @return currency pair denoted in the platform specific format
38      */
39     String fromHashTagCurrency(String instrument);
40
41     /**
42      *
43      * @return T that denotes the action of Buying the currency pair on the
44      *          platform
45      */
46     T getLongNotation();
47
48     /**
49      *
50      * @return T that denotes the action of Selling the currency pair on
        the
51      *          platform
52      */
53    T getShortNotation();
54    }
```

The need for this interface was felt, when I was consuming data from external sources like Twitter and sites that publish economic events. Various Twitter users and external sites had their own way of denoting currency pairs and long/short trades. In order to deal with this plethora of conventions, the need for such interface was strongly felt. I am pretty sure that there will be many more, which need to be interpreted in platform-specific ways and should therefore be added to this interface.

TradingConfig Class

The class TradingConfig holds all the parameters that are configured at runtime. These parameters are required by various core APIs. Some examples include

- Maximum value of an order to be placed

- Maximum allowed contracts for a currency

As different users may have different runtime values, these values form part of the external configuration. These need to be configured in the Spring configuration (we will discuss it in detail when we talk about configuration and deployment). It is strongly recommended to configure as much as possible instead of hardcoding them inside various services.

Let's check out how the code looks:

```
1   public class TradingConfig extends BaseTradingConfig {
2
3     private String mailTo;
4     private int fadeTheMoveJumpReqdToTrade;
5     private int fadeTheMoveDistanceToTrade;
6     private int fadeTheMovePipsDesired;
7     private int fadeTheMovePriceExpiry;
8
9     public int getFadeTheMovePriceExpiry() {
10      return fadeTheMovePriceExpiry;
11    }
12
13    public void setFadeTheMovePriceExpiry(int fadeTheMovePriceExpiry) {
14      this.fadeTheMovePriceExpiry = fadeTheMovePriceExpiry;
15    }
16
17    public String getMailTo() {
18      return mailTo;
19    }
20
21    public void setMailTo(String mailTo) {
22      this.mailTo = mailTo;
23    }
24
25    public int getFadeTheMoveJumpReqdToTrade() {
26      return fadeTheMoveJumpReqdToTrade;
27    }
28
29    public void setFadeTheMoveJumpReqdToTrade(int
      fadeTheMoveJumpReqdToTrade) {
30      this.fadeTheMoveJumpReqdToTrade = fadeTheMoveJumpReqdToTrade;
31    }
32
```

```java
33    public int getFadeTheMoveDistanceToTrade() {
34     return fadeTheMoveDistanceToTrade;
35    }
36
37    public void setFadeTheMoveDistanceToTrade(int
      fadeTheMoveDistanceToTrade) {
38     this.fadeTheMoveDistanceToTrade = fadeTheMoveDistanceToTrade;
39   }
40
41    public int getFadeTheMovePipsDesired() {
42     return fadeTheMovePipsDesired;
43    }
44
45    public void setFadeTheMovePipsDesired(int fadeTheMovePipsDesired) {
46     this.fadeTheMovePipsDesired = fadeTheMovePipsDesired;
47    }
48
49   }
50
51   public class BaseTradingConfig {
52     private double minReserveRatio;
53     private double minAmountRequired;
54
55     private int maxAllowedQuantity;
56     private int maxAllowedNetContracts;
57     private double max10yrWmaOffset;
58
59     public double getMinAmountRequired() {
60       return minAmountRequired;
61   }
62
63     public void setMinAmountRequired(double minAmountRequired) {
64       this.minAmountRequired = minAmountRequired;
65   }
66
67     public double getMax10yrWmaOffset() {
68      return max10yrWmaOffset;
69   }
70
71     public void setMax10yrWmaOffset(double max10yrWmaOffset) {
72       this.max10yrWmaOffset = max10yrWmaOffset;
73   }
74
75     public int getMaxAllowedNetContracts() {
76       return maxAllowedNetContracts;
77   }
78
```

```
79    public void setMaxAllowedNetContracts(int maxAllowedNetContracts) {
80     this.maxAllowedNetContracts = maxAllowedNetContracts;
81    }
82
83    public double getMinReserveRatio() {
84     return minReserveRatio;
85    }
86
87    public void setMinReserveRatio(double minReserveRatio) {
88     this.minReserveRatio = minReserveRatio;
89    }
90
91    public int getMaxAllowedQuantity() {
92     return maxAllowedQuantity;
93    }
```

Some of these member variables may not make sense now, but all will fall into place in later chapters.

Obtaining the Source Code

All source code can be obtained at *GitHub*. The following git command will clone the repository locally on your machine:

```
1    git clone https://github.com/shekharvarshney/book-code.git
```

We will discuss how this code can be built and run locally in later chapters.

Try It Yourself Section

At the end of each chapter, we include a small program/programs (wherever appropriate) that demonstrate the concepts discussed in the chapter and for you to experiment and see the concepts in action straightaway. These small standalone programs are for demonstration purposes only and may not be part of the code that runs the bot eventually. This is to get a flavor of things that make up a component of the bot.

We will run these programs inside the eclipse IDE so that, if need be, you can debug and see what is happening inside the services used in the bot. These programs reside in a separate project called tradingbot-demo-programs, whose pom.xml file looks like the following

```
1    <project xmlns="http://maven.apache.org/POM/4.0.0"
2            xmlns:xsi="http://www.w3.org/2001/XMLSchema-instance"
3            xsi:schemaLocation="http://maven.apache.org/POM/4.0.0
4                    http://maven.apache.org/xsd/maven-4.0.0.xsd">
5      <modelVersion>4.0.0</modelVersion>
6      <groupId>com.precioustech</groupId>
```

```
 7    <artifactId>tradingbot-demo-programs</artifactId>
 8    <version>1.0</version>
 9    <properties>
10      <project.build.sourceEncoding>UTF-8</project.build.sourceEncoding>
11      <spring.framework.version>4.1.1.RELEASE</spring.framework.version>
12      <spring.framework.social.version>1.1.0.RELEASE</spring.framework.
        social.version>
13    </properties>
14    <dependencies>
15          <dependency>
16                  <groupId>com.precioustech</groupId>
17                  <artifactId>tradingbot-core</artifactId>
18                  <version>1.0</version>
19          </dependency>
20          <dependency>
21                  <groupId>com.precioustech.fxtrading</groupId>
22                  <artifactId>tradingbot-app</artifactId>
23                  <version>1.0</version>
24          </dependency>
25          <dependency>
26                  <groupId>com.precioustech</groupId>
27                  <artifactId>oanda-restapi</artifactId>
28                  <version>1.0</version>
29          </dependency>
30
31    </dependencies>
32  </project>
```

This demo project has a very simple dependency requirement on the three projects that comprise the bot.

CHAPTER 2

■ ■ ■

Account Management

The ability to manage the account is probably the first thing we need to build into our bot. When you open a trading account with a brokerage/exchange, an account is created that can be funded directly by bank transfer, credit card, PayPal, etc. An account has a base currency, which is normally the currency of the funding source. For example, if you are based in the UK and have an account with one of the UK banks used to fund the trading account, then the trading account will have a base currency of GBP (British pounds).

However, some platforms give you the option to create other currency accounts, even though you may not have a funding source set up for them. For example, after being assigned a GBP account as a result of funding from UK bank, you can create an additional USD (U.S. dollars) account, even if you don't have a USD funding source. The USD account can be funded however by transferring an amount of GBP from the main account, effectively selling GBPUSD. This exercise can be repeated for other currency accounts like CAD, EUR, etc.

All accounts on most brokerage platforms, have the following attributes that can be queried:

- An account ID
- Base currency
- Total amount
- Balance remaining to trade
- Leverage

Other optional information might include:

- Realized PNL
- Unrealized PNL
- Margin used
- Open trades
- Open orders

S. Varshney, *Building Trading Bots Using Java*, DOI 10.1007/978-1-4842-2520-2_2

We begin by capturing all this information and creating an account POJO. Listing 2-1 shows how to provide two constructors, one with minimum attributes required to construct the object based on this discussion.

Listing 2-1. Definition of Account POJO

```
1   /**
2    * A POJO that holds account information. No setters are provided as
3    * it is envisaged that the final member variables will be initialized
4    * through the constructor(s).
5    *
6    * @param <T>
7    *            the type of accountId
8    */
9   public class Account < T > {
10
11      private final double totalBalance;
12      private final double unrealisedPnl;
13      private final double realisedPnl;
14      private final double marginUsed;
15      private final double marginAvailable;
16      private final double netAssetValue;
17      private final long openTrades;
18      private final String currency;
19      private final T accountId;
20      private final String toStr;
21      private final double amountAvailableRatio; /*The amount available to
        trade as a fraction of total amount*/
22      private final double marginRate; /*The leverage offered on this
        account. for e.g. 0.05, 0.1 etc*/
23      private final int hash;
24
25      public Account(final double totalBalance, double marginAvailable,
        String currency,
26       T accountId, double marginRate) {
27       this(totalBalance, 0, 0, 0, marginAvailable, 0, currency, accountId,
         marginRate);
28      }
29
30      public Account(final double totalBalance, double unrealisedPnl,
        double realisedPnl,
31       double marginUsed, double marginAvailable, long openTrades, String
         currency,
32       T accountId, double marginRate) {
33       this.totalBalance = totalBalance;
34       this.unrealisedPnl = unrealisedPnl;
35       this.realisedPnl = realisedPnl;
36       this.marginUsed = marginUsed;
```

```
37     this.marginAvailable = marginAvailable;
38     this.openTrades = openTrades;
39     this.currency = currency;
40     this.accountId = accountId;
41     this.amountAvailableRatio = this.marginAvailable / this.
       totalBalance;
42     this.netAssetValue = this.marginUsed + this.marginAvailable;
43     this.marginRate = marginRate;
44     this.hash = calcHashCode();
45     //Create toString here as all variables are final
46     toStr = String.format("Currency=%s,NAV=%5.2f,Total Balance=%5.2f,
       UnrealisedPnl=%5.2f, " + "RealisedPnl=%5.2f, MarginU\
47 sed=%5.2f, MarginAvailable=%5.2f," + " OpenTrades=%d,
   amountAvailableRatio=%1.2f, marginRate=%1.2f", currency,
48       netAssetValue, totalBalance, unrealisedPnl, realisedPnl,
         marginUsed, marginAvailable,
49       openTrades, this.amountAvailableRatio, this.marginRate);
50     }
51
52     public double getAmountAvailableRatio() {
53       return amountAvailableRatio;
54     }
55
56     public double getMarginRate() {
57       return marginRate;
58     }
59
60     @Override
61     public String toString() {
62       return this.toStr;
63     }
64
65     public T getAccountId() {
66       return accountId;
67     }
68
69     public String getCurrency() {
70       return currency;
71     }
72
73     public double getNetAssetValue() {
74       return  this.netAssetValue;
75     }
76
77     public double getTotalBalance() {
78       return totalBalance;
79     }
80
```

```
81    public double getUnrealisedPnl() {
82     return  unrealisedPnl;
83    }
84
85    public double getRealisedPnl() {
86     return realisedPnl;
87    }
88
89    public double getMarginUsed() {
90     return marginUsed;
91    }
92
93    @Override
94    public int hashCode() {
95     return this.hash;
96    }
97
98    private int calcHashCode() {
99     final int prime = 31;
100    int result = 1;
101    result = prime * result + ((accountId == null) ? 0 : accountId.
       hashCode());
102    return result;
103    }
104
105    @Override
106    public boolean equals(Object obj) {
107     if (this == obj)
108      return true;
109     if (obj == null)
110      return false;
111     if (getClass() != obj.getClass())
112      return false;
113     @SuppressWarnings("unchecked")
114     Account < T > other = (Account < T > ) obj;
115     if (accountId == null) {
116      if (other.accountId != null)
117       return false;
118     } else  if  (!accountId.equals(other.accountId))
119      return false;
120     return true;
121    }
122
123    public double getMarginAvailable() {
124     return  marginAvailable;
125    }
126
```

```
127    public long getOpenTrades() {
128      return openTrades;
129    }
130
131  }
```

Looking at Listing 2-1, we can do a couple of small optimizations. All member variables are *final*, which means they are immutable. We can therefore calculate the hashCode() and toString() values upfront in the constructors and store them in final variables. Any call to toString() or hashCode() will return the pre-calculated values.

Account Provider Interface

We now need to specify our account data interface that defines what we expect our provider (aka implementation) to provide. We would not be interested in doing any account updates such as changing the leverage etc. but just interested in read-only information. Therefore, we require the provider to either give us a *collection* of all accounts or an account if the *accountId* is provided. Our interface would look something like Listing 2-2.

Listing 2-2. AccountDataProvider Interface Definition

```
1    /**
2     * A provider of Account information. An account information might
3     * typically include base currency, leverage, margin available, PNL
4     * information etc. Some brokerages allow the creation of various sub
5     * accounts or currency wallets. The idea is to give ability to fund
6     * these accounts from various currency denominated bank accounts.
7     * So for e.g. a user in Switzerland might have a CHF current account
8     * but also a EUR savings account. One can then open 2 currency
9     * accounts or wallets on the brokerage, denominated in CHF and EUR
10    * and these can then be funded by the real bank accounts.
11    * Alternatively, one can also just create these multiple currency
12    * wallets even if they have just a single source funding currency.
13    * When the primary account is funded, a transfer trade can be
14    * executed to fund the other currency wallet. For e.g. a user in
15    * United Kingdom who just has a GBP account, can open a USD
16    * wallet, fund the GBP account and then execute a transfer of a
17    * given units of GBP into USD.
15    *
16    * @param <T>
17    *           The type of accountId
18    *
19    * @see Account
20    */
```

```
21   public interface AccountDataProvider < T > {
22
23   /**
24    *
25    * @param accountId
26    * @return Account information for the given accountId
27    */
28   Account < T > getLatestAccountInfo(T accountId);
29
30   /**
31    *
32    * @return A collection of ALL accounts available
33    */
34   Collection < Account < T >> getLatestAccountInfo();
35   }
```

This interface is pretty straightforward. We are just interested in a single account or a collection of accounts. We will see later in this chapter how this can be used in a service to do some advanced account-related operations/calculations.

A Concrete Implementation for AccountDataProvider

Our next task is to provide an OANDA implementation that achieves this. We begin by first statically importing all the relevant JSON keys that we expect to find in our payload. A sample response returned for account 123456 would look something like Listing 2-3.

Listing 2-3. Sample JSON Payload for an Account

```
1    {
2       "accountId" : 123456,
3       "accountName" : "main",
4       "balance" : 20567.9,
5       "unrealizedPl" : -897.1,
6       "realizedPl" : 1123.65,
7       "marginUsed" : 89.98,
8       "marginAvail" : 645.3,
9       "openTrades" : 5,
10      "openOrders" : 0,
11      "marginRate" : 0.05,
12      "accountCurrency" : "CHF"
13   }
```

Listing 2-4. Import JSON Keys Statically

```
1  import static com.precioustech.fxtrading.oanda.restapi.OandaJsonKeys.
   accountCurrency;
2  import static com.precioustech.fxtrading.oanda.restapi.OandaJsonKeys.
   accountId;
3  import static com.precioustech.fxtrading.oanda.restapi.OandaJsonKeys.
   balance;
4  import static com.precioustech.fxtrading.oanda.restapi.OandaJsonKeys.
   marginAvail;
5  import static com.precioustech.fxtrading.oanda.restapi.OandaJsonKeys.
   marginRate;
6  import static com.precioustech.fxtrading.oanda.restapi.OandaJsonKeys.
   marginUsed;
7  import static com.precioustech.fxtrading.oanda.restapi.OandaJsonKeys.
   openTrades;
8  import static com.precioustech.fxtrading.oanda.restapi.OandaJsonKeys.
   realizedPl;
9  import static com.precioustech.fxtrading.oanda.restapi.OandaJsonKeys.
   unrealizedPl;
```

Since the OANDA account ID is a long, substituting long for T becomes

```
1  public class OandaAccountDataProviderService implements
AccountDataProvider<Long> {
```

We provide the OANDA URL, the username and access token in the constructor, which looks like Listing 2-5.

Listing 2-5. Constructor Definition

```
1   private final String url;
2   private final String userName;
3   private final BasicHeader authHeader;
4
5   public OandaAccountDataProviderService(final String url, final String
    userName,
6    final String accessToken) {
7    this.url = url; //OANDA REST service base url
8    this.userName = userName; //OANDA account user name
9    this.authHeader = OandaUtils.createAuthHeader(accessToken);
10   }
```

We now turn our attention to first of the implementations of the interface, which is to get information for a single account ID provided. Before we get to that, we must prepare the URL to send across to OANDA. The REST request must go to the ACCOUNTS_RESOURCE, which is defined as follows:

```
1  public static final String ACCOUNTS_RESOURCE = "/v1/accounts";
```

Therefore our function to construct the full URL to get account information would look like this:

```
1  String getSingleAccountUrl(Long accountId) {
2   return url + ACCOUNTS_RESOURCE + TradingConstants.FWD_SLASH +
    accountId;
3  }
```

If we pass account ID 123456 to this function and, assuming the base URL is https://api-fxtrade.oanda.com, then this function would return https://api-fxtrade.oanda.com/v1/accounts/123456. Getting back to the implementation of the method that retrieves information for a single account, which would look something like Listing 2-6.

Listing 2-6. Single Account Fetch Implementation

```
1   @Override
2   public Account < Long > getLatestAccountInfo(final Long accountId) {
3    CloseableHttpClient httpClient = getHttpClient();
4    try {
5     return getLatestAccountInfo(accountId, httpClient);
6    } finally {
7     TradingUtils.closeSilently(httpClient);
8    }
9   }
10
11
12  private Account < Long > getLatestAccountInfo(final Long accountId,
    CloseableHttpClient httpClient) {
13   try {
14    HttpUriRequest httpGet = new HttpGet(getSingleAccountUrl(accountId));
15    httpGet.setHeader(authHeader);
16
17    LOG.info(TradingUtils.executingRequestMsg(httpGet));
18    HttpResponse httpResponse = httpClient.execute(httpGet);
19    String strResp = TradingUtils.responseToString(httpResponse);
20    if (strResp != StringUtils.EMPTY) {
21     Object obj = JSONValue.parse(strResp);
22     JSONObject accountJson = (JSONObject) obj;
23
```

```
24      /*Parse JSON response for account information*/
25      final double accountBalance = ((Number) accountJson.get(balance)).
        doubleValue();
26      final double accountUnrealizedPnl =
27      ((Number) accountJson.get(unrealizedPl)).doubleValue();
28      final double accountRealizedPnl =
29      ((Number) accountJson.get(realizedPl)).doubleValue();
30      final double accountMarginUsed =
31      ((Number) accountJson.get(marginUsed)).doubleValue();
32      final double accountMarginAvailable =
33      ((Number) accountJson.get(marginAvail)).doubleValue();
34      final Long accountOpenTrades = (Long) accountJson.get(openTrades);
35      final String accountBaseCurrency = (String) accountJson.
        get(accountCurrency);
36      final Double accountLeverage = (Double) accountJson.get(marginRate);
37
38      Account < Long > accountInfo = new Account < Long > (accountBalance,
        accountUnrealizedPnl,
39       accountRealizedPnl, accountMarginUsed, accountMarginAvailable,
        accountOpenTrades,
40       accountBaseCurrency, accountId, accountLeverage);
41      return accountInfo;
42      } else {
43      TradingUtils.printErrorMsg(httpResponse);
44      }
45      } catch (Exception e) {
46      LOG.error(e);
47      }
48      return null;
49      }
```

The public method actually delegates to a private method where the main action happens. The processing starts by invoking the getSingleAccountUrl() method to prepare the URL to be sent to the OANDA REST API. We then instantiate an HttpGet request providing the URL to fetch information from. Before we trigger the request, we must not forget to set the authentication header without which the request will not be successful. After httpGet.setHeader(authHeader), we are now set to make the request. Using the httpClient object, we can now fire off our GET request. If HTTP 200 is returned and TradingUtils.responseToString is able to convert the response to String, we should now have a valid JSON string payload something similar to Listing 2-3. Now all that is left is to parse this payload and construct the account POJO. You may be wondering why, in this peculiar code:

```
1    final double accountBalance = ((Number) accountJson.get(balance)).
     doubleValue();
```

Why do we have the cast this to a Number object and then call doubleValue() instead of just casting to the Double object? The answer is that for some keys, which are presumed double, if the value is a whole number, the JSON response will not have a decimal value; instead it will have a Long. So for example, let's say that the account balance is at a given time 3000.00. The value in the response will be something like this:

```
1   "balance" : 3000
```

The cast to Double directly will fail with a ClassCastException, hence we use this workaround to circumvent this subtlety in parsing.

We must now provide an implementation for getting a collection of available accounts as per the interface contract.

Listing 2-7. Fetch All Accounts Implementation

```
1   @Override
2   public Collection < Account < Long >> getLatestAccountInfo() {
3     CloseableHttpClient httpClient = getHttpClient();
4     List < Account < Long >> accInfos = Lists.newArrayList();
5     try {
6       HttpUriRequest httpGet = new HttpGet(getAllAccountsUrl());
7       httpGet.setHeader(this.authHeader);
8
9       LOG.info(TradingUtils.executingRequestMsg(httpGet));
10      HttpResponse resp = httpClient.execute(httpGet);
11      String strResp = TradingUtils.responseToString(resp);
12      if (strResp != StringUtils.EMPTY) {
13        Object jsonObject = JSONValue.parse(strResp);
14        JSONObject jsonResp = (JSONObject) jsonObject;
15        JSONArray accounts = (JSONArray) jsonResp.get(OandaJsonKeys.
          accounts);
16        /*
17         * We are doing a per account json request because not all
18         information is returned in the array of results
19         */
20        for (Object o: accounts) {
21          JSONObject account = (JSONObject) o;
22          Long accountIdentifier = (Long) account.get(accountId);
23          Account < Long > accountInfo = getLatestAccountInfo
            (accountIdentifier, httpClient);
24          accInfos.add(accountInfo);
25        }
26      } else {
27        TradingUtils.printErrorMsg(resp);
28      }
29
```

```
30    } catch (Exception e) {
31      LOG.error(e);
32    } finally {
33      TradingUtils.closeSilently(httpClient);
34    }
35    return accInfos;
36  }
```

The OANDA REST API has an endpoint to retrieve all account information in a single request:

```
1   GET v1/accounts
```

However, looking at Listing 2-7, we still call the function that provides all account information for a single account iteratively. Why do we do this? The reason is that when we request information for all accounts using the endpoint v1/accounts, OANDA does not provide all information we need to construct our account POJO, as is evident from this response:

```
1   {
2     "accounts": [
3       {
4         "accountId" : 1234567,
5         "accountName" : "Primary",
6         "accountCurrency" : "GBP",
7         "marginRate" : 0.05
8       },
9       {
10        "accountId"    : 2345678,
11        "accountName"   : "EUR Account",
12        "accountCurrency"  : "EUR",
13        "marginRate"    : 0.1
14      }
15    ]
16  }
```

Encapsulating Everything Behind a Generic AccountInfoService

As previously discussed, one of our key design objectives is to be able to encapsulate providers behind meaningful services so that if required, we can switch provider implementations and change from provider OANDA to say provider LMAX without having to change a single line of compiled code. Changes in the Spring configuration will hopefully help us make this transition smoothly. AccountInfoService, in addition to providing a facade for all the AccountDataProvider methods, has three additional useful methods:

```
1    public Collection<K> findAccountsToTrade();
2
3    public double calculateMarginForTrade(K accountId,
     TradeableInstrument<N>
4            instrument, int units);
5
6    public double calculateMarginForTrade(Account<K> accountInfo,
7           TradeableInstrument<N> instrument, int units);
```

Before discussing these, let's quickly glance over the constructor that defines the dependencies of the service.

```
1    /**
2     *
3     * @param <K>
4     *            type of accountId
5     * @param <N>
6     *            type of The type of instrumentId in class
                   TradeableInstrument
7     * @see TradeableInstrument
8     */
9    public class AccountInfoService<K, N> {
10
11           private final AccountDataProvider<K> accountDataProvider;
12           private final BaseTradingConfig baseTradingConfig;
13           private final CurrentPriceInfoProvider<N>
               currentPriceInfoProvider;
14           private final ProviderHelper providerHelper;
15           private Comparator<Account<K>> accountComparator = new MarginAv
               ailableComparator<K>();
16
17           public AccountInfoService(AccountDataProvider<K>
               accountDataProvider,
18                   CurrentPriceInfoProvider<N> currentPriceInfoProvider,
19                   BaseTradingConfig baseTradingConfig, ProviderHelper
                       providerHelper) {
20                   this.accountDataProvider = accountDataProvider;
21                   this.baseTradingConfig = baseTradingConfig;
22                   this.currentPriceInfoProvider =
                       currentPriceInfoProvider;
23                   this.providerHelper = providerHelper;
24           }
```

- AccountDataProvider is the obvious one, as the service needs to be able to provide information for an individual account ID and all available accounts.

- CurrentPriceInfoProvider is a provider of current prices for a given set of instruments and will be discussed in later chapters.

- `BaseTradingConfig`, as discussed earlier, is an object that holds all the configuration parameters.

- `ProviderHelper`, also discussed previously, provides helper methods to deal with provider related data transformations.

We now turn our attention to the discussion of the `findAccountsToTrade()` method. As the name suggests, this method tries to find available accounts to trade, given certain conditions are met. Often, before placing a trade/order, the first exercise is to find a suitable account. Of course, this discussion does not apply to platforms where there is only a single account to trade, because all trades executed by default belong to this account.

```
1   public Collection < K > findAccountsToTrade() {
2     List < Account < K >> accounts = Lists.newArrayList(getAllAccounts());
3     Collection < K > accountsFound = Lists.newArrayList();
4     Collections.sort(accounts,  accountComparator);
5     for (Account < K > account: accounts) {
6       if (account.getAmountAvailableRatio() >= baseTradingConfig.
        getMinReserveRatio() && account.getNetAssetValue() >= baseT\
7   radingConfig.getMinAmountRequired()) {
8         accountsFound.add(account.getAccountId());
9       }
10    }
11    return  accountsFound;
12  }
```

The method first fetches all available accounts by calling `getAllAccounts()`, which just delegates to the `accountProvider`:

```
1   public Collection<Account<K>> getAllAccounts() {
2     return this.accountDataProvider.getLatestAccountInfo();
3   }
```

Next, it tries to sort the accounts available, in decreasing order of margin availability using the `MarginAvailableComparator`. This comparator places the account with the maximum margin at the top of list and so on. The idea is to pick the account with maximum margin available. Of course, this is just a strategy to find an account when the accounts with denominated currencies are comparable in exchange rates. For example, if you have three accounts denominated in currencies CHF, EUR, USD, then this works because EURCHF ~= 1.08, USDCHF ~=1.0, and EURUSD ~= 1.0 (rates at the time of writing). This should fulfill the strategy of the account with the maximum available margin; however, it will fail miserably, if for example, one of the currencies is JPY instead of EUR. Since CHFJPY and USDJPY at the time of writing ~= 122.0, this is not ideal as most of the time the JPY account will be picked.

```
1   static class MarginAvailableComparator < K > implements Comparator <
    Account < K >> {
2
3    @Override
4    public int compare(Account < K > ai1, Account < K > ai2) {
5     if (ai1.getMarginAvailable() > ai2.getMarginAvailable()) {
6      return -1;
7     } else if (ai1.getMarginAvailable() < ai2.getMarginAvailable()) {
8      return 1;
9     }
10     return 0;
11   }
12
13  }
```

Next, the account is selected to place an order/trade only if the following condition is met:

```
1   if (account.getAmountAvailableRatio() >= baseTradingConfig.
    getMinReserveRatio()
2       && account.getNetAssetValue() >= baseTradingConfig.
        getMinAmountRequired()) {
3    accountsFound.add(account.getAccountId());
4   }
```

Assuming that

```
1   minReserveRatio=0.2
2   minAmountRequired=50.0
```

A minimum reserve ratio of 0.2 is a metric that stipulates that if a GBP account has total amount of £1000, then we must only select this account to trade if the amount available to trade > 0.2 x £1000(£200). I would strongly recommend having this validation in place, simply because this leaves the account with a decent buffer and prevents the NAV going negative, in case of wild swings in prices. This ought to be a higher value if the account leverage is quite high, say 1:50.

The minimum amount required is a metric that stipulates that an account must have a minimum net asset value to be considered for trading. In this case, we must have at least £50 in NAV to be eligible to trade.

Next we discuss the two overloaded methods calculateMarginForTrade. As the name suggests, these methods calculate the margin requirement for a given trade/order. These methods prove very useful in situations where we want to place bulk orders for various instruments and want to get an idea of margin requirements for them. These methods are also used a prevalidation check before sending the order to the platform, making sure that margin requirement for the given order is less than the amount available.

```
1   /*
2           * ({BASE} / {Home Currency}) * units) / (margin ratio)
3           For example, suppose:
4           Home Currency = USD
5           Currency Pair = GBP/CHF
6           Base = GBP; Quote = CHF
7           Base / Home Currency = GBP/USD = 1.5819
8           Units = 1000
9           Margin Ratio = 20:1
10          Then, margin used:
11          = (1.5819 * 1000) / 20
12          = 79.095 USD
13  */
14  @SuppressWarnings("unchecked")
15  public double calculateMarginForTrade(Account < K > accountInfo,
    TradeableInstrument < N > instrument, int units) {
16    String tokens[] = TradingUtils.splitInstrumentPair(instrument.
      getInstrument());
17    String baseCurrency = tokens[0];
18    double  price = 1.0;
19
20    if (!baseCurrency.equals(accountInfo.getCurrency())) {
21      String currencyPair = this.providerHelper.fromIsoFormat(baseCurrency +
        accountInfo.getCurrency());
22
23      Map < TradeableInstrument < N > , Price < N >> priceInfoMap = this.
        currentPriceInfoProvider
24        .getCurrentPricesForInstruments(Lists.newArrayList(
25        new TradeableInstrument < N > (currencyPair)));
26      if (priceInfoMap.isEmpty()) { /*this means we got the currency pair
        inverted*/
27        /*example when the home currency is GBP and instrument is USDJPY*/
28        currencyPair = this.providerHelper.fromIsoFormat(
29          accountInfo.getCurrency() + baseCurrency);
30        priceInfoMap = this.currentPriceInfoProvider.getCurrentPricesForInst
          ruments(Lists
31        .newArrayList(new TradeableInstrument < N > (currencyPair)));
32        if (priceInfoMap.isEmpty()) { // something else is wrong here
33          return  Double.MAX_VALUE;
34        }
35        Price < N > priceInfo = priceInfoMap.values().iterator().next();
36        /*take avg of bid and ask prices*/
37        price = 1.0 / ((priceInfo.getBidPrice() + priceInfo.getAskPrice()) /
          2.0);
38      } else {
39        Price < N > priceInfo = priceInfoMap.values().iterator().next();
```

```
40      /*take avg of bid and ask prices*/
41      price = (priceInfo.getBidPrice() + priceInfo.getAskPrice()) / 2.0;
42    }
43
44  }
45  return price * units * accountInfo.getMarginRate();
46  }
47
48  public double calculateMarginForTrade(K accountId, TradeableInstrument
    < N > instrument, int units) {
49  return calculateMarginForTrade(getAccountInfo(accountId), instrument,
    units);
50  }
```

Before we discuss the logic in the method, let's first highlight the variables that affect the calculations, which are:

- The denominated or base currency (GBP in pair GBPUSD)

- The quoted currency (USD in pair GBPUSD)

- The account currency (e.g., CHF)

- The margin rate or leverage (0.05 or 1:20)

The easiest case is when the denominated currency is the same as the account currency. For example, if we want to place a buy order for 3000 units for instrument EURAUD and the account currency is EUR, then the calculation is 3000*0.05 = €150. The next case is where the base currency, quoted currency, and account currency are all different. Here we need to effectively get the current price for {BASE ccy}/{ACCOUNT ccy} and then multiply the price with units and margin rate. For example, if we want to buy 3000 units of GBPUSD and account currency is CHF, we need to effectively get the price of GBPCHF first and then do the rest of the multiplication. Assuming the GBPCHF price is 1.54, the margin requirement is

```
1   double marginRequired = 1.54 * 3000 * 0.05 //231 CHF
```

The last case is a derivative of the previous case with the difference being that the valid currency pair is {ACCOUNT ccy}/{BASE ccy}. In such a case we have to divide the {ACCOUNT ccy}/{BASE ccy} price. Assuming we want to buy 3000 units of USDCHF and the account currency is GBP and the GBPUSD price is 1.53, then the margin required is

```
1   double marginRequired = 3000 * 0.05/1.53 //98.03 GBP
```

This service concludes our discussion of pretty much everything you need to learn about account management.

Try It Yourself

In this section, we are going to create a demo program that will invoke some of the methods of AccountInfoService and print output to the console. See Figures 2-1 and 2-2.

```
1    package com.precioustech.fxtrading.account;
2
3    import java.util.Collection;
4
5    import org.apache.log4j.Logger;
6
7    import com.precioustech.fxtrading.BaseTradingConfig;
8    import com.precioustech.fxtrading.helper.ProviderHelper;
9    import com.precioustech.fxtrading.instrument.TradeableInstrument;
10   import com.precioustech.fxtrading.marketdata.CurrentPriceInfoProvider;
11   import com.precioustech.fxtrading.oanda.restapi.account.
     OandaAccountDataProviderService;
12   import com.precioustech.fxtrading.oanda.restapi.helper.
     OandaProviderHelper;
13   import com.precioustech.fxtrading.oanda.restapi.marketdata.
     OandaCurrentPriceInfoProvider;
14
15   public class AccountInfoServiceDemo {
16
17     private static final Logger LOG = Logger.getLogger(AccountInfoService
       Demo.class);
18
19     private static void usage(String[] args) {
20       if (args.length != 3) {
21         LOG.error("Usage: AccountInfoServiceDemo <url> <username>
           <accesstoken>");
22         System.exit(1);
23       }
24     }
25
26     public static void main(String[] args) {
27       usage(args);
28       String url = args[0];
29       String userName = args[1];
30       String accessToken = args[2];
31
32       // initialise the dependencies
33       AccountDataProvider < Long > accountDataProvider = new OandaAccountDa
         taProviderService(url, userName,
34         accessToken);
```

```
35    CurrentPriceInfoProvider < String > currentPriceInfoProvider = new Oa
      ndaCurrentPriceInfoProvider(url,
36     accessToken);
37    BaseTradingConfig tradingConfig = new BaseTradingConfig();
38    tradingConfig.setMinReserveRatio(0.05);
39    tradingConfig.setMinAmountRequired(100.00);
40    ProviderHelper < String > providerHelper = new OandaProviderHelper();
41
42    AccountInfoService < Long, String > accountInfoService = new
      AccountInfoService < Long, String > (
43     accountDataProvider,
44     currentPriceInfoProvider, tradingConfig, providerHelper);
45
46    Collection < Account < Long >> accounts = accountInfoService.
      getAllAccounts();
47    LOG.info(String.format("Found %d accounts to trade for user %s",
      accounts.size(), userName));
48    LOG.info("++++++++++++++++++++++++++++++++ Dumping Account Info ++++++
      +++++++++++++++++++++++++");
49    for (Account < Long > account: accounts) {
50    LOG.info(account);
51    }
52    LOG.info("++++++++++++++++++++++++ Finished Dumping Account Info ++++++
      +++++++++++++++++++++++++");
53    Account < Long > sampleAccount = accounts.iterator().next();
54    final int units = 5000;
55    TradeableInstrument < String > gbpusd = new  TradeableInstrument <
      String > ("GBP_USD");
56    TradeableInstrument < String > eurgbp = new  TradeableInstrument <
      String > ("EUR_GBP");
57    double gbpusdMarginReqd = accountInfoService.calculateMarginForTrade(
      sampleAccount, gbpusd, units);
58    double eurgbpMarginReqd = accountInfoService.calculateMarginForTrade(
      sampleAccount, eurgbp, units);
59    LOG.info(String.format("Margin requirement for trading pair %d units
      of %s is %5.2f %s ", units,
60     gbpusd.getInstrument(), gbpusdMarginReqd, sampleAccount.
      getCurrency()));
61    LOG.info(String.format("Margin requirement for trading pair %d units
      of %s is %5.2f %s ", units,
62     eurgbp.getInstrument(),  eurgbpMarginReqd,  sampleAccount.
      getCurrency()));
63    }
64
65    }
```

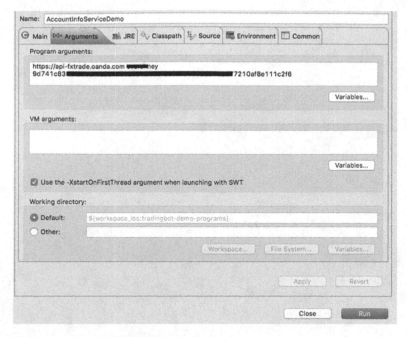

Figure 2-1. *Launch configuration*

```
<terminated> AccountInfoServiceDemo [Java Application] /Library/Java/JavaVirtualMachines/jdk1.7.0_71.jdk/Contents/Home/bin/java (26 Jan 2016 19:55:45)
2016-01-26 19:55:46,445 INFO  [main] - Executing request : GET https://api-fxtrade.oanda.com/v1/accounts?username=cvarshney HTTP/1.1
2016-01-26 19:55:47,870 INFO  [main] - Executing request : GET https://api-fxtrade.oanda.com/v1/accounts/▓▓▓▓ HTTP/1.1
2016-01-26 19:55:48,120 INFO  [main] - Executing request : GET https://api-fxtrade.oanda.com/v1/accounts/▓▓▓▓ HTTP/1.1
2016-01-26 19:55:48,247 INFO  [main] - Executing request : GET https://api-fxtrade.oanda.com/v1/accounts/▓▓▓▓ HTTP/1.1
2016-01-26 19:55:48,353 INFO  [main] - Executing request : GET https://api-fxtrade.oanda.com/v1/accounts/▓▓▓▓ HTTP/1.1
2016-01-26 19:55:48,457 INFO  [main] - Executing request : GET https://api-fxtrade.oanda.com/v1/accounts/▓▓▓▓ HTTP/1.1
2016-01-26 19:55:48,575 INFO  [main] - Executing request : GET https://api-fxtrade.oanda.com/v1/accounts/▓▓▓▓ HTTP/1.1
2016-01-26 19:55:48,688 INFO  [main] - Found 6 accounts to trade for user ▓▓▓▓ney
2016-01-26 19:55:48,688 INFO  [main] - ++++++++++++++++++++++++++++++ Dumping Account Info +++++++++++++++++++++++++++++++
2016-01-26 19:55:48,688 INFO  [main] - Currency=CHF,NAV=187▓▓▓,Total Balance=▓▓▓▓▓, UnrealisedPnl=▓▓▓▓, RealisedPnl=7▓▓▓, MarginUsed=1101.97, MarginAvailable=▓▓▓
2016-01-26 19:55:48,688 INFO  [main] - Currency=GBP,NAV= 0.00,Total Balance= 0.00, UnrealisedPnl= 0.00, RealisedPnl=▓▓▓.▓▓, MarginUsed= 0.00, MarginAvailable= 0.00, OpenTrc
2016-01-26 19:55:48,689 INFO  [main] - Currency=EUR,NAV=▓▓▓▓,Total Balance=▓▓▓▓, UnrealisedPnl=▓▓▓.▓▓, RealisedPnl=-82.06, MarginUsed=186.98, MarginAvailable=▓▓▓.▓▓, Op
2016-01-26 19:55:48,689 INFO  [main] - Currency=USD,NAV= 0.01,Total Balance= 0.01, UnrealisedPnl= 0.00, RealisedPnl= 0.00, MarginUsed= 0.00, MarginAvailable= 0.01, OpenTrc
2016-01-26 19:55:48,689 INFO  [main] - Currency=AUD,NAV=▓▓▓▓,Total Balance=▓▓▓▓▓, UnrealisedPnl=▓▓▓.▓▓, RealisedPnl=▓▓▓.11, MarginUsed=▓▓▓▓▓, MarginAvailable=147
2016-01-26 19:55:48,689 INFO  [main] - Currency=CAD,NAV= 0.00,Total Balance= 0.00, UnrealisedPnl= 0.00, RealisedPnl= 0.00, MarginUsed= 0.00, MarginAvailable= 0.00, OpenTrc
2016-01-26 19:55:48,755 INFO  [main] - ++++++++++++++++++++++++++++++ Finished Dumping Account Info +++++++++++++++++++++++++++++++
2016-01-26 19:55:48,755 INFO  [main] - Executing request : GET https://api-fxtrade.oanda.com/v1/prices?instruments=GBP_CHF HTTP/1.1
2016-01-26 19:55:49,323 INFO  [main] - Executing request : GET https://api-fxtrade.oanda.com/v1/prices?instruments=EUR_CHF HTTP/1.1
2016-01-26 19:55:49,792 INFO  [main] - Margin requirement for trading pair 5000 units of GBP_USD is 365.45 CHF
2016-01-26 19:55:49,793 INFO  [main] - Margin requirement for trading pair 5000 units of EUR_GBP is 276.21 CHF
```

Figure 2-2. *Sample output*

CHAPTER 3

■ ■ ■

Tradeable Instruments

In this chapter we will focus our attention on instruments available to trade on the brokerage platform. The instrument entity is pretty much the core of a trading platform, as everything revolves around it. From obtaining prices, to placing orders/trades, the instrument is what is the principal actor. Before much further ado, let's dive into the POJO, which describes the tradeable instrument.

Listing 3-1. TradeableInstrument POJO Definition

```
1    /**
2     *
3     * @param <T>
4     *              the type of instrumentId
5     */
6    public class TradeableInstrument < T > {
7      private final String instrument;
8      private final String description;
9      private final T instrumentId;
10     private final double pip;
11     private final int hash;
12     private InstrumentPairInterestRate instrumentPairInterestRate;
13
14     public TradeableInstrument(String instrument) {
15       this(instrument, null);
16     }
17
18     public TradeableInstrument(String instrument, String description) {
19       this(instrument, null, description);
20     }
21
22     public TradeableInstrument(String instrument, T instrumentId, String description) {
23       this(instrument, instrumentId, 0, null);
24     }
25
```

© Shekhar Varshney 2016

S. Varshney, *Building Trading Bots Using Java*, DOI 10.1007/978-1-4842-2520-2_3

```
26    public TradeableInstrument(final String instrument, final double pip,
27     InstrumentPairInterestRate instrumentPairInterestRate, String
       description) {
28     this(instrument, null, pip, instrumentPairInterestRate, description);
29
30    }
31
32    public TradeableInstrument(final String instrument, T instrumentId,
       final double pip,
33     InstrumentPairInterestRate instrumentPairInterestRate) {
34     this(instrument, instrumentId, pip, instrumentPairInterestRate, null);
35    }
36
37    public TradeableInstrument(final String instrument, T instrumentId,
       final double pip,
38     InstrumentPairInterestRate instrumentPairInterestRate, String
       description) {
39     this.instrument = instrument;
40     this.pip = pip;
41     this.instrumentPairInterestRate = instrumentPairInterestRate;
42     this.instrumentId = instrumentId;
43     this.description = description;
44     this.hash = calcHashCode();
45    }
46
47    private int calcHashCode() {
48     final int prime = 31;
49     int result = 1;
50     result = prime * result + ((instrument == null) ? 0 : instrument.
       hashCode());
51     result = prime * result + ((instrumentId == null) ? 0 :
       instrumentId.hashCode());
52     return result;
53    }
54
55    public T getInstrumentId() {
56     return this.instrumentId;
57    }
58
59    public String getDescription() {
60     return description;
61    }
62
63    @Override
64    public int hashCode() {
65     return hash;
66    }
67
```

```java
68    @Override
69    public boolean equals(Object obj) {
70     if (this == obj)
71      return true;
72     if (obj == null)
73      return false;
74     if (getClass() != obj.getClass())
75      return false;
76     @SuppressWarnings("unchecked")
77     TradeableInstrument < T > other = (TradeableInstrument < T > ) obj;
78     if (instrument == null) {
79      if (other.instrument != null) {
80       return false;
81      }
82     } else if (!instrument.equals(other.instrument)) {
83      return false;
84     }
85     if (instrumentId == null) {
86      if (other.instrumentId != null) {
87       return false;
88      }
89     } else if (!instrumentId.equals(other.instrumentId)) {
90      return false;
91     }
92     return true;
93    }
94
95    public InstrumentPairInterestRate getInstrumentPairInterestRate() {
96     return instrumentPairInterestRate;
97    }
98
99    public void setInstrumentPairInterestRate(InstrumentPairInterestRate
      instrumentPairInterestRate) {
100    this.instrumentPairInterestRate = instrumentPairInterestRate;
101   }
102
103   @Override
104   public String toString() {
105    return "TradeableInstrument [instrument=" + instrument + ",
       description=" + description + ", instrumentId=" + instrume\
106   ntId + ", pip=" + pip + ", instrumentPairInterestRate=" +
      instrumentPairInterestRate + "]";
107   }
108
109   public String getInstrument() {
110    return instrument;
111   }
112
```

```
113    public double getPip() {
114      return pip;
115    }
116  }
```

The `TradeableInstrument` definition is fairly straightforward but has a generic T parameter, to cater to different types of instrument IDs on different brokerage platforms. We also provide several constructors to construct our POJO. The minimum attribute required to construct our POJO is attribute `instrument`.

The POJO comprises these attributes:

```
1    private final String instrument;
2    private final String description;
3    private final T instrumentId;
4    private final double pip;
5    private InstrumentPairInterestRate instrumentPairInterestRate;
```

The first two attributes are fairly self explanatory. Instrument ID represents an internal identifier for that instrument on the given platform. This may be required on some platforms to be passed in instead of the actual instrument code (like GBP_USD) for placing an order/trade. It, along with `instrument` attribute, participates in the definition of `hashCode()` and `equals()`.

The *pip*[1] is, as far as I understand, is the lowest precision at which the given instrument ticks. For example, the pip value for USDJPY is 0.001, which means the minimum change in price for USDJPY would be 0.001. If the current USDJPY price is 123.462, then at minimum the next price change would be to either 123.461 or 123.463.

The `instrumentPairInterestRate` is an interesting attribute that may or may not be available on all platforms. As seen in its definition, it can capture some important information like what the charges for a given instrument are likely to be, both in the cases of buying and selling it. The finance charge,[2] in brief, is an amount of currency paid by brokerage platform or due to it, for holding a trade for given pair. For example, at the time of writing a certain amount will be due to the holder of long NZDCHF trade, but vice versa an amount liable for short NZDCHF trade. This value arises from the interest rate differentials of the two currencies in question (NZD base rate=3%, CHF base rate=0%).

Listing 3-2. InstrumentPairInterestRate POJO Definition

```
1    package com.precioustech.fxtrading.instrument;
2
3    public class InstrumentPairInterestRate {
4
5      private final Double baseCurrencyBidInterestRate;
6      private final Double baseCurrencyAskInterestRate;
7      private final Double quoteCurrencyBidInterestRate;
8      private final Double quoteCurrencyAskInterestRate;
9
```

---

[1]http://fxtrade.oanda.com/learn/intro-to-currency-trading/conventions/pips
[2]http://fxtrade.oanda.ca/learn/intro-to-currency-trading/conventions/rollovers

```
10    public InstrumentPairInterestRate() {
11     this(null, null, null, null);
12    }
13
14    public InstrumentPairInterestRate(Double baseCurrencyBidInterestRate,
15     Double baseCurrencyAskInterestRate, Double
       quoteCurrencyBidInterestRate,
16    Double quoteCurrencyAskInterestRate) {
17    this.baseCurrencyBidInterestRate = baseCurrencyBidInterestRate;
18    this.baseCurrencyAskInterestRate = baseCurrencyAskInterestRate;
19    this.quoteCurrencyBidInterestRate = quoteCurrencyBidInterestRate;
20    this.quoteCurrencyAskInterestRate = quoteCurrencyAskInterestRate;
21    }
22
23    public Double getBaseCurrencyBidInterestRate() {
24     return baseCurrencyBidInterestRate;
25    }
26
27    public Double getBaseCurrencyAskInterestRate() {
28     return baseCurrencyAskInterestRate;
29    }
30
31    public Double getQuoteCurrencyBidInterestRate() {
32     return quoteCurrencyBidInterestRate;
33    }
34
35    public Double getQuoteCurrencyAskInterestRate() {
36     return quoteCurrencyAskInterestRate;
37    }
38
39    @Override
40    public String toString() {
41     return "InstrumentPairInterestRate [baseCurrencyBidInterestRate=" +
       baseCurrencyBidInterestRate + ", baseCurrencyAskIn\
42    terestRate=" + baseCurrencyAskInterestRate + ", quoteCurrency
       BidInterestRate=" + quoteCurrencyBidInterestRate + ", quote\
43    CurrencyAskInterestRate=" + quoteCurrencyAskInterestRate + "]";
44     }
45    }
```

Instrument Provider Interface

We must now define the interface that the provider must implement to get instrument data. Like with the accounts, we are only interested in read-only data, as there is nothing that we can create, update, or delete regarding instruments on the brokerage platform. It is a very simple case of getting immutable data, which probably never changes, at least during trading hours. There may be rare occasions where certain instruments are no longer supported, but most of the time, the observation is that new instruments are added to be traded. Something that might change more frequently but only during the rollover window is the interest rate for various currencies. As seen in Listing 3-3, the interface is extremely straightforward.

Listing 3-3. InstrumentDataProvider Interface Definition

```
1    /**
2     * A provider of tradeable instrument data information. At the very
3     * minimum the provider must provide the instrument name and pip
4     * value for each instrument. Since the instrument data almost never
5     * changes during trading hours, it is highly recommended that the
6     * data returned from this provider is cached in an immutable
7     * collection.
8     * @param <T>The type of instrumentId in class TradeableInstrument
9     * @see TradeableInstrument
10    * /
11   public interface InstrumentDataProvider < T > {
12   /**
13    *
14    * @return a collection of all TradeableInstrument available to trade
         on the
15    *          brokerage platform.
16    */
17   Collection < TradeableInstrument < T >> getInstruments();
18   }
```

A Concrete Implementation for InstrumentDataProvider

Before we dive into detailed discussion of the OANDA implementation of the interface, let's quickly look at an extract of sample JSON that is returned when we request a list of all tradeable instruments. The actual JSON would contain many instruments.

Listing 3-4. Sample JSON Payload for Instruments

```
1    {
2       "instruments": [
3          {
4             "instrument": "AUD_CAD",
5             "pip": "0.0001",
6             "interestRate": {
7                "AUD": {
8                   "bid": 0.0164,
9                   "ask": 0.0274
10                  },
```

```
11            "CAD": {
12              "bid": 0.002,
13              "ask": 0.008
14            }
15         }
16      },
17      {
18         "instrument": "AUD_CHF",
19         "pip": "0.0001",
20         "interestRate": {
21            "AUD": {
22              "bid": 0.0164,
23              "ask": 0.0274
24            },
25            "CHF": {
26              "bid": -0.013,
27              "ask": 0.003
28            }
29         }
30      }
31   ]
32 }
```

As usual we begin our code discussion by listing all the JSON keys that will be used:

```
1  import static com.precioustech.fxtrading.oanda.restapi.OandaJsonKeys.ask;
2  import static com.precioustech.fxtrading.oanda.restapi.OandaJsonKeys.bid;
3  import static com.precioustech.fxtrading.oanda.restapi.OandaJsonKeys.
   instruments;
4  import static com.precioustech.fxtrading.oanda.restapi.OandaJsonKeys.
   interestRate;
```

Since OANDA currently does not have an internal identifier for an instrument, we use the instrument name as the identifier. So replacing the T param type with String gives us:

```
1  public class OandaInstrumentDataProviderService implements
InstrumentDataProvider<String> {
```

For the constructor definition, we provide the OANDA URL, a valid account ID, and an access token. Please bear in mind that the account ID should be a valid account for the user associated with the access token.

```
1  public OandaInstrumentDataProviderService(String url, long accountId,
   String accessToken) {
2    this.url = url; // OANDA REST service base url
3    this.accountId = accountId; // OANDA valid account id
4    this.authHeader = OandaUtils.createAuthHeader(accessToken);
5  }
```

The instruments resource endpoint is

```
1   public static final String INSTRUMENTS_RESOURCE = "/v1/instruments";
```

Therefore our function to compute the URL to get all tradeable instruments from OANDA would look like this:

```
1   static final String fieldsRequested = "instrument%2Cpip%2CinterestRate"
    //URL encoded csv list of fields;
2
3   String getInstrumentsUrl() {
4     return this.url + OandaConstants.INSTRUMENTS_RESOURCE + "?accountId=" +
5     this.accountId + "&fields=" + fieldsRequested;
6   }
```

A note about the variable fieldsRequested. By default, if this request param is not part of the URL then OANDA returns by default fields instrument, displayName, pip, and maxTradeUnits, as seen in the following sample JSON response:

```
1   {
2     "instruments" : [
3       {
4         "instrument" : "AUD_CAD",
5         "displayName" : "AUD\/CAD",
6         "pip" : "0.0001",
7         "maxTradeUnits" : 10000000
8       },
9       {
10        "instrument"   : "AUD_CHF",
11        "displayName"  : "AUD\/CHF",
12        "pip"   : "0.0001",
13        "maxTradeUnits"   : 10000000
14      }
15    ]
16  }
```

Since interestRate is not in the default field list, we have to explicitly request it using the fieldsRequested query param, along with every field that we want in the response. Now let's move on to the main implementation of the interface, which looks like Listing 3-5.

Listing 3-5. getInstruments() Implementation

```
1   @Override
2   public Collection < TradeableInstrument < String >> getInstruments() {
3     Collection < TradeableInstrument < String >> instrumentsList = Lists.
      newArrayList();
4     CloseableHttpClient httpClient = getHttpClient();
```

```
5    try {
6    HttpUriRequest httpGet = new HttpGet(getInstrumentsUrl());
7    httpGet.setHeader(authHeader);
8    LOG.info(TradingUtils.executingRequestMsg(httpGet));
9    HttpResponse resp = httpClient.execute(httpGet);
10   String strResp = TradingUtils.responseToString(resp);
11   if (strResp != StringUtils.EMPTY) {
12    Object obj = JSONValue.parse(strResp);
13    JSONObject jsonResp = (JSONObject) obj;
14    JSONArray instrumentArray = (JSONArray) jsonResp.get(instruments);
15
16     for (Object o: instrumentArray) {
17     JSONObject instrumentJson = (JSONObject) o;
18     String instrument = (String) instrumentJson.get(OandaJsonKeys.
       instrument);
19     String[] currencies = OandaUtils.splitCcyPair(instrument);
20     Double pip = Double.parseDouble(instrumentJson.get(OandaJsonKeys.
       pip).toString());
21     JSONObject interestRates = (JSONObject) instrumentJson.
       get(interestRate);
22     if (interestRates.size() != 2) {
23      throw new IllegalArgumentException();
24     }
25
26     JSONObject currency1Json = (JSONObject) interestRates.
       get(currencies[0]);
27     JSONObject currency2Json = (JSONObject) interestRates.
       get(currencies[1]);
28 .
29     final double baseCurrencyBidInterestRate = ((Number) currency1Json.
       get(bid)).doubleValue();
30     final double baseCurrencyAskInterestRate = ((Number) currency1Json.
       get(ask)).doubleValue();
31     final double quoteCurrencyBidInterestRate = ((Number)
       currency2Json.get(bid)).doubleValue();
32     final double quoteCurrencyAskInterestRate = ((Number)
       currency2Json.get(ask)).doubleValue();
33
34     InstrumentPairInterestRate instrumentPairInterestRate = new
       InstrumentPairInterestRate(
35      baseCurrencyBidInterestRate,  baseCurrencyAskInterestRate,
36      quoteCurrencyBidInterestRate,  quoteCurrencyAskInterestRate);
37
38     TradeableInstrument < String > tradeableInstrument = new
       TradeableInstrument < String > (
39      instrument, pip, InstrumentPairInterestRate, null);
40     instrumentsList.add(tradeableInstrument);
41    }
```

```
42      } else {
43        TradingUtils.printErrorMsg(resp);
44      }
45    } catch (Exception e) {
46      LOG.error(e);
47    } finally {
48      TradingUtils.closeSilently(httpClient);
49    }
50    return instrumentsList;
51  }
```

The implementation is pretty straightforward and can be summarized as follows:

- Construct the request URL by calling the getInstrumentUrl() function.

- Fire off the request using an instance of the HttpGet class.

- A successful request will contain an array of instruments.

- For each element in the array, parse the instrument, pip which is readily available in the element. The interestRate must further be treated as an array of two elements, the first one for the base currency and the second for the quoted currency.

- Parse the bid/ask interest rate for each currency and create an instance of the InstrumentPair- InterestRate object.

- We now have all the attributes we need for a given instrument. Store them in the collection that will be returned from this method.

Encapsulating Everything Behind a Generic InstrumentService

This service will provide some useful information regarding tradeable instruments, which we will soon explore. Since the instrument data is fairly immutable, we can safely cache the instrument information internally and then use the cache to service requests for any requested information. Since the cache is immutable and read-only, we do not have to worry about concurrency issues. We begin by discussing the constructor, which just needs an implementation of the InstrumentDataProvider as a dependency.

```
1   private final Map<String, TradeableInstrument<T>> instrumentMap;
2
3   public InstrumentService(InstrumentDataProvider<T>
    instrumentDataProvider) {
4           Preconditions.checkNotNull(instrumentDataProvider);
```

```
5        Collection<TradeableInstrument<T>> instruments =
         instrumentDataProvider.getInstruments();
6        Map<String, TradeableInstrument<T>> tradeableInstrumenMap =
         Maps.newHashMap();
7        for (TradeableInstrument<T> instrument : instruments) {
8                tradeableInstrumenMap.put(instrument.getInstrument(),
                 instrument);
9        }
10       this.instrumentMap = Collections.unmodifiableMap
         (tradeableInstrumenMap);
11   }
```

Within the constructor, we use the InstrumentDataProvider implementation to fetch all instruments at once and then construct our immutable cache instrumentMap. We now turn our attention to discussing the first of our two service methods called getPipForInstrument. This returns the pip for a given instrument. A useful invocation for this method is to say calculate the stop loss or take profit price when placing a limit order for an instrument. Let's say we want to place a limit buy order for EURUSD if the current price drops by 30 pips. Our trigger price would be something like this:

```
1    TradeableInstrument<String> eurusd = new TradeableInstrument<String>
     ("EUR_USD");
2    double triggerPrice = currentPrice - 30 * instrumentService.getPipForIn
     strument(eurusd);
```

Now let's look at the actual code for this useful service method.

```
1    public Double getPipForInstrument(TradeableInstrument < T > instrument)
     {
2      Preconditions.checkNotNull(instrument);
3      TradeableInstrument < T > tradeableInstrument = this.instrumentMap.
       get(instrument.getInstrument());
4      if (tradeableInstrument != null) {
5        return tradeableInstrument.getPip();
6      } else {
7        return 1.0;
8      }
9    }
```

This code is quite straightforward. Using the instrument passed in, fetch the instance of TradeableInstrument that corresponds to the instrument. If it's not found, return 1.0; otherwise, return the pip value for the instrument.

Another useful service method is getAllPairsWithCurrency. This returns a collection of all instruments in which the given currency is either a denominated or quoted currency. For example, to get a collection of all instruments that have CHF as the base or quoted currency, you would invoke it as follows:

```
1  //return instruments such as USDCHF,CHFJPY..
2  Collection<TradeableInstrument<String>> chfpairs = instrumentService.get
   AllPairsWithCurrency("CHF");
```

Now let's look at the actual implementation, which is again quite straightforward:

```
1  public Collection < TradeableInstrument < T >>
   getAllPairsWithCurrency(String currency) {
2   Collection < TradeableInstrument < T >> allPairs = Sets.newHashSet();
3   if (StringUtils.isEmpty(currency)) {
4    return allPairs;
5   }
6   for (Map.Entry < String, TradeableInstrument < T >> entry:
    instrumentMap.entrySet()) {
7    if (entry.getKey().contains(currency)) {
8     allPairs.add(entry.getValue());
9    }
10  }
11  return allPairs;
12 }
```

In this code, we return an empty collection if the passed-in value is null or a blank string. If it's a valid string, we iterate over our cache and use contains to check if the current key contains the passed-in string. If it does, then we just add it to the collection that will be returned from the method. This concludes our discussion of pretty much most of the issues around tradable instruments.

Try It Yourself

In this section we are going to create a demo program that will invoke some of the methods of InstrumentServiceDemo and print output to the console:

```
1  package com.precioustech.fxtrading.instrument;
2
3  import java.util.Collection;
4
5  import org.apache.commons.lang3.StringUtils;
6  import org.apache.log4j.Logger;
7
8  import com.precioustech.fxtrading.oanda.restapi.instrument.
   OandaInstrumentDataProviderService;
9
10 public class InstrumentServiceDemo {
11
```

```
12    private static final Logger LOG = Logger.
      getLogger(InstrumentServiceDemo.class);
13
14    private static void usageAndValidation(String[] args) {
15     if (args.length != 3) {
16      LOG.error("Usage: InstrumentServiceDemo <url> <accountid>
           <accesstoken>");
17      System.exit(1);
18     } else {
19      if (!StringUtils.isNumeric(args[1])) {
20       LOG.error("Argument 2 should be numeric");
21       System.exit(1);
22      }
23     }
24    }
25
26    public static void main(String[] args) {
27     usageAndValidation(args);
28     String url = args[0];
29     Long accountId = Long.parseLong(args[1]);
30     String accessToken = args[2];
31
32     InstrumentDataProvider < String > instrumentDataProvider =
       new OandaInstrumentDataProviderService(url,
33       accountId, accessToken);
34
35     InstrumentService < String > instrumentService = new
       InstrumentService < String > (instrumentDataProvider);
36
37     Collection < TradeableInstrument < String >> gbpInstruments =
38      instrumentService.getAllPairsWithCurrency("GBP");
39
40     LOG.info("+++++++++++++++++++++++++++++++ Dumping Instrument Info +++
        ++++++++++++++++++++++++++");
41     for (TradeableInstrument < String > instrument: gbpInstruments) {
42      LOG.info(instrument);
43     }
44     LOG.info("++++++++++++++++++++++++++Finished Dumping Instrument Info +++
        ++++++++++++++++++++++++++");
45     TradeableInstrument < String > euraud = new TradeableInstrument <
        String > ("EUR_AUD");
46     TradeableInstrument < String > usdjpy = new TradeableInstrument <
        String > ("USD_JPY");
47     TradeableInstrument < String > usdzar = new TradeableInstrument <
        String > ("USD_ZAR");
48
49     Double usdjpyPip = instrumentService.getPipForInstrument(usdjpy);
50     Double euraudPip = instrumentService.getPipForInstrument(euraud);
```

```
51      Double usdzarPip = instrumentService.getPipForInstrument(usdzar);
52
53      LOG.info(String.format("Pip for instrument %s is %1.5f", euraud.
        getInstrument(), euraudPip));
54      LOG.info(String.format("Pip for instrument %s is %1.5f", usdjpy.
        getInstrument(), usdjpyPip));
55      LOG.info(String.format("Pip for instrument %s is %1.5f", usdzar.
        getInstrument(), usdzarPip));
56    }
57
58  }
```

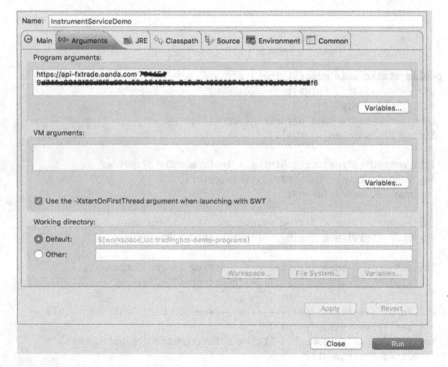

Figure 3-1. *Launch configuration*

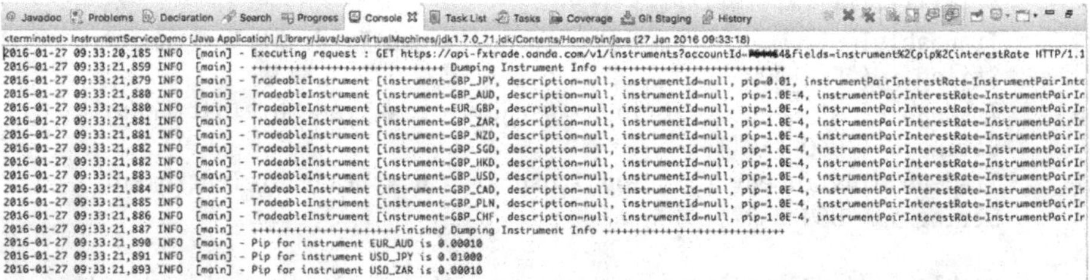

Figure 3-2. *Sample output*

CHAPTER 4

■ ■ ■

Event Streaming: Market Data Events

Now we have reached the point where the true existence of the trading bot will start to become apparent. From here onward, we are going to step into the real aspects of trading, one of which is to handle realtime events and act on them, after meaningfully analyzing them. You could have event streams in the following shape and form:

- Market data events, i.e., changes in the price of an instrument
- Trade/order/account events, i.e., orders filled or stop loss level hit
- Social media events, i.e., tweets from influential people or market movers
- Any other source

As you can see, you can have numerous event streams, bombarding our trading bot with varying degrees of intensity. Handling them and making decisions based on them is the cornerstone of the trading bot design. In this chapter, we exclusively discuss how to handle market data events and how to disseminate them using the Google EventBus.

Streaming Market Data Interface

We begin by defining an interface that stipulates the minimum set of methods required for the market event streaming to work in our bot. On the face of it, it looks there is not much to it, as we just enforce a start and stop requirement on the interface implementer. However, as we will see later, when discussing the implementation, that part of the job of the implementer is to invoke a MarketEventCallback handler that processes the streaming market event received. The assumption is that the startMarketDataStreaming() establishes a continuous connection (event loop) to the event source, i.e. in a separate thread, and this thread receives market data events on that connection. The event is then parsed and passed on to MarketEventCallback to be processed further.

S. Varshney, *Building Trading Bots Using Java*, DOI 10.1007/978-1-4842-2520-2_4

```
1   /**
2    * A service that provides streaming market data. Normally the
3    * implementation would create a dedicated connection to the trading
4    * platform and would receive a stream of prices ideally through a
5    * REST service or a callback from the platform. The implementation
6    * must handle broken connections and attempt to reconnect in a
7    * suitable manner. The service is normally coupled with a heartbeats
8    * from the platform which indicates whether the connection is alive
9    *
10   * or not. Due to the volume of data expected, it is recommended that
11   * the service delegate the handling of market data to another
12   * service in order to avoid building up of queue of events, waiting to
13   * be processed.
14   */
15  public interface MarketDataStreamingService {
16
17   /**
18    * Start the streaming service which would ideally create a
19    * dedicated connection to the platform or a callback listener.
         Ideally
20    * multiple connections requesting the same market data should not
21    * be created. */
22   void startMarketDataStreaming();
23
24   /**
25    * Stop the streaming services and dispose any
26    * resources/connections in a suitable manner such that no
27    * resource leaks are created.
28    */
29   void stopMarketDataStreaming();
30
31  }
```

The MarketEventCallback interface, that is actually responsible for the further dissemination of the market data event synchronously or asynchronously, must be used in tandem.

```
1   /**
2    * A callback handler for a market data event. The separate streaming
3    * event handler upstream, is responsible for handling and parsing the
4    * incoming event from the market data source and invoke the
5    * onMarketEvent of this handler, which in turn can disseminate the
6    * event if required, further downstream. Ideally, the implementer of
7    * this interface, would drop the event on a queue for asynchronous
8    * processing or use an event bus for synchronous processing.
9    * @param <T>
10   *            The type of instrumentId in class TradeableInstrument
```

```
11      * @see TradeableInstrument
12      * @see EventBus
13      */
14     public interface MarketEventCallback < T > {
15      /**
16       * A method, invoked by the upstream handler of streaming market
17       * data events. This invocation of this method is synchronous,
18       * therefore the method should return asap, to make sure that the
19       * upstream events do not queue up.
20       *
21       * @param instrument
22       * @param bid
23       * @param ask
24       * @param eventDate
25       */
26      void onMarketEvent(TradeableInstrument < T > instrument, double bid,
        double ask, DateTime eventDate);
27     }
```

Let's jump straight into the OANDA implementation, as things will become clearer once we look inside the code.

A Concrete Implementation for MarketDataStreamingService

Let's start by looking at the class definition and the constructor for OandaMarketDataStreamingService, which is responsible for reading the market data stream from OANDA and then invoking the onMarketEvent on an instance of MarketEventCallback passed to the constructor.

```
1      public class OandaMarketDataStreamingService extends
       OandaStreamingService implements MarketDataStreamingService {
2
3      private final String url;
4      private final MarketEventCallback < String > marketEventCallback;
5
6      public OandaMarketDataStreamingService(String url, String accessToken,
7       long accountId, Collection < TradeableInstrument < String >>
        instruments,
8       MarketEventCallback < String > marketEventCallback,
9       HeartBeatCallback < DateTime > heartBeatCallback, String
        heartbeatSourceId) {
10
11      super(accessToken, heartBeatCallback, heartbeatSourceId);
```

```
12    this.url = url + OandaConstants.PRICES_RESOURCE + "?accountId=" +
      accountId + "&instruments=" + instrumentsAsCsv(instr\ 13    uments);
14    this.marketEventCallback = marketEventCallback;
15    }
16
17    private String instrumentsAsCsv(Collection < TradeableInstrument <
      String >> instruments) {
18    StringBuilder csvLst = new  StringBuilder();
19    boolean firstTime = true;
20    for (TradeableInstrument < String > instrument: instruments) {
21     if (firstTime) {
22      firstTime = false;
23     } else {
24      csvLst.append(TradingConstants.ENCODED_COMMA);
25     }
26     csvLst.append(instrument.getInstrument());
27    }
28    return csvLst.toString();
29    }
```

The constructor among other params, receives an account ID and a list of instruments for which the ticks are desired. The method instrumentsAsCsv accepts a collection of instruments and returns a flattened string of URL-encoded comma-separated instruments. Assuming the account ID is 123456 and instrument list is ["EUR_USD","GBP_AUD"], the URL computed in the constructor would look like this:

```
1    //given
2    public static final String PRICES_RESOURCE = "/v1/prices";
3    //this.url computed, will look like below
4
5    https://stream-fxtrade.oanda.com/v1/prices?accountId=123456&instruments
     =EUR_USD%2CGBP_AUD
```

OANDA requires us to provide a valid account ID to set up a market data stream, as discussed. The stream URL is also different than the ones we discussed before, for example, the URL to request list of instruments. We will discuss these nuances in detail in a later chapter about configuration and deployment.

This concrete implementation extends the OandaStreamingService class, which is the base class for providing infrastructure methods for all streaming services from OANDA, which includes market data and, as we will discuss in a future chapter, the event streaming. All streams from OANDA comprise a heartbeat payload that indicates the stream is alive, hence the HeartBeatCallback instance. We will discuss heartbeats in a later chapter. For now, it is sufficient to know that heartbeating provides a way to ensure the client (our trading bot), that the persistent connection to the brokerage platform is alive. If the heartbeat payload is not received in a given timeframe in the current stream, then something is not quite in order and we must disconnect and try reconnecting. Let's quickly look at its definition and some important infrastructure methods it provides to its subclasses.

```
1   public abstract class OandaStreamingService implements
    HeartBeatStreamingService {
2     protected volatile boolean serviceUp = true;
3     private final HeartBeatCallback < DateTime > heartBeatCallback;
4     private final String hearbeatSourceId;
5     protected Thread streamThread;
6     private final BasicHeader authHeader;
7
8     protected abstract String getStreamingUrl();
9
10    protected abstract void startStreaming();
11
12    protected abstract void stopStreaming();
13
14    protected OandaStreamingService(String accessToken, HeartBeatCallback
      < DateTime > heartBeatCallback,
15      String heartbeatSourceId) {
16      this.hearbeatSourceId = heartbeatSourceId;
17      this.heartBeatCallback = heartBeatCallback;
18      this.authHeader = OandaUtils.createAuthHeader(accessToken);
19    }
20
21    protected void handleHeartBeat(JSONObject streamEvent) {
22      Long t = Long.parseLong(((JSONObject) streamEvent.get(OandaJsonKeys.
        heartbeat)).get(OandaJsonKeys.time).toString());
23      heartBeatCallback.onHeartBeat(new HeartBeatPayLoad < DateTime > (new
        DateTime(TradingUtils.toMillisFromNanos(t)), hear\
24    beatSourceId));
25    }
26
27    protected BufferedReader setUpStreamIfPossible(CloseableHttpClient
      httpClient) throws Exception {
28      HttpUriRequest httpGet = new HttpGet(getStreamingUrl());
29      httpGet.setHeader(authHeader);
30      httpGet.setHeader(OandaConstants.UNIX_DATETIME_HEADER);
31      LOG.info(TradingUtils.executingRequestMsg(httpGet));
32      HttpResponse resp = httpClient.execute(httpGet);
33      HttpEntity entity = resp.getEntity();
34      if (resp.getStatusLine().getStatusCode() == HttpStatus.SC_OK &&
        entity != null) {
35        InputStream stream = entity.getContent();
36        serviceUp = true;
37        BufferedReader br = new BufferedReader(new
          InputStreamReader(stream));
38        return br;
39      } else {
```

```
40        String responseString = EntityUtils.toString(entity, "UTF-8");
41        LOG.warn(responseString);
42        return null;
43      }
44    }
45
46    protected void handleDisconnect(String line) {
47      serviceUp = false;
48      LOG.warn(
49      String.format("Disconnect message received for stream %s. PayLoad->%s",
50        getHeartBeatSourceId(), line));
51    }
52
53    protected boolean isStreaming() {
54      return serviceUp;
55    }
```

In summary, the base class provides the following infrastructure (or supporting) services to its stream subclasses.

- Set up a persistent stream connection to OANDA using getStreamingUrl() provided by a subclass that implements this abstract method.

- Handle disconnect messages from OANDA, if for some reason OANDA disconnects the current stream.

- Handle heartbeat payload and invoke the downstream HeartBeatCallback handler.

Returning to our concrete implementation, let's look at the most important method of the class, startMarketDataStreaming. It starts the streaming in a separate thread and, once the stream is established, parses the event payload received.

```
1    import static com.precioustech.fxtrading.oanda.restapi.OandaJsonKeys.ask;
2    import static com.precioustech.fxtrading.oanda.restapi.OandaJsonKeys.bid;
3    import static com.precioustech.fxtrading.oanda.restapi.OandaJsonKeys.
     disconnect;
4    import static com.precioustech.fxtrading.oanda.restapi.OandaJsonKeys.
     heartbeat;
5    import static com.precioustech.fxtrading.oanda.restapi.OandaJsonKeys.
     tick;
6    import static com.precioustech.fxtrading.oanda.restapi.OandaJsonKeys.time;
7
8    @Override
9    public void startMarketDataStreaming() {
10     stopMarketDataStreaming();
11     this.streamThread = new Thread(new Runnable() {
12
```

```
13    @Override
14    public void run() {
15     CloseableHttpClient httpClient = getHttpClient();
16     try {
17      BufferedReader br = setUpStreamIfPossible(httpClient);
18      if (br != null) {
19       String line;
20       while ((line = br.readLine()) != null && serviceUp) {
21        Object obj = JSONValue.parse(line);
22        JSONObject instrumentTick = (JSONObject) obj;
23        // unwrap if necessary
24        if (instrumentTick.containsKey(tick)) {
25         instrumentTick = (JSONObject) instrumentTick.get(tick);
26        }
27
28        if (instrumentTick.containsKey(OandaJsonKeys.instrument)) {
29         final String instrument = instrumentTick.get(OandaJsonKeys.
             instrument).toString();
30         final String timeAsString = instrumentTick.get(time).toString();
31         final long eventTime = Long.parseLong(timeAsString);
32         final double bidPrice = ((Number) instrumentTick.get(bid)).
             doubleValue();
33         final double askPrice = ((Number) instrumentTick.get(ask)).
             doubleValue();
34         marketEventCallback.onMarketEvent(
35          new TradeableInstrument < String > (instrument), bidPrice,
             askPrice,
36          new DateTime(TradingUtils.toMillisFromNanos(eventTime)));
37        } else if (instrumentTick.containsKey(heartbeat)) {
38         handleHeartBeat(instrumentTick);
39        } else if (instrumentTick.containsKey(disconnect)) {
40         handleDisconnect(line);
41        }
42       }
43      br.close();
44      }
45     } catch (Exception e) {
46      LOG.error(e);
47     } finally {
48      serviceUp = false;
49      TradingUtils.closeSilently(httpClient);
50     }
51
52    }
53   }, "OandMarketDataStreamingThread");
54   this.streamThread.start();
55
56  }
```

```
57
58   @Override
59   public void stopMarketDataStreaming() {
60     this.serviceUp = false;
61     if (streamThread != null && streamThread.isAlive()) {
62       streamThread.interrupt();
63     }
64   }
```

The startMarketDataStreaming begins by first invoking stopMarketDataStreaming. This is to make sure that we stop existing thread consuming events, if any, and start a new one. The use of this will become clear when you start to recognize the fact that we may have issues with connectivity and occasionally may need to restart the stream.

Assuming that after this, we do not have an existing thread consuming market data events, we can now spawn another thread to start consuming the events. We notice that the run() method only exits if the condition line = br.readLine()) != null && serviceUp evaluates to false. The value of the serviceUp method is set to false when we call the method stopMarketDataStreaming(). If the BufferedReader is set up before for streaming, it stops streaming events and returns a null, which also results in the termination of the while loop, resulting in the termination of the stream thread. Assuming the stream is streaming market data events for the desired instruments, we should see JSON responses such as the following ones in very quick succession.

```
1   {"tick":{"instrument":"EUR_USD","time":"1401919213548144","bid":1.08479
    ,"ask":1.08498}}
2   {"tick":{"instrument":"GBP_AUD","time":"1401919213548822","bid":2.07979
    ,"ask":1.08998}}
3   {"heartbeat":{"time":"1401919213548226"}}
4   {"tick":{"instrument":"EUR_USD","time":"1401919217201682","bid":1.08484
    ,"ask":1.08502}}
```

Basically, if the number of instruments set up is quite large (say > 10), the likelihood is that several ticks may be received per second, especially when London is online.

Looking at the parsing code, we notice that the code handles three types of payload with the following keys:

- Tick

- Heartbeat

- Disconnect

A disconnect payload looks like this:

```
1   {"disconnect":{"code":60,"message":"Access Token connection limit
    exceeded: This connection will now be disconnected","m\
2   oreInfo":"http:\/\/developer.oanda.com\/docs\/v1\/troubleshooting"}}
```

For the `tick` payload, we parse the JSON payload into `bidPrice`, `askPrice`, `instrument`, and `eventTime`, and then delegate to the `marketEventCallback`. `onMarketEvent`, which may process the tick synchronously or asynchronously. In either case, it is supremely important that this invocation is super fast, else the events will start to queue up and we may introduce unwanted lag in the system, which may throw some strategies, consuming these events, off course, as it would not reflect the most recent prices.

The `heartbeat` and the `disconnect` payloads are handled by the super class, as discussed.

```
1   protected void handleHeartBeat(JSONObject streamEvent) {
2     Long t = Long.parseLong(((JSONObject) streamEvent.get(heartbeat)).
      get(time) toString());
3     heartBeatCallback.onHeartBeat(new HeartBeatPayload < DateTime > (new
      DateTime(TradingUtils.toMillisFromNanos(t)), hearb\
4   eatSourceId));
5   }
6
7   protected void handleDisconnect(String line) {
8     serviceUp = false;
9     LOG.warn(
10      String.format("Disconnect message received for stream %s. PayLoad->%s",
11        getHeartBeatSourceId(), line));
12  }
```

That brings us to the end of the discussion of the upstream event handling and parsing. As we will discover in later chapters, heartbeating is central to keeping the stream alive. We must take these heartbeats seriously and act swiftly if these heartbeats cease, in the form of restarting these streams, so that our strategies do not make wrong decisions. In the next section, we discuss how the events might be consumed downstream via the `marketEventCallback.onMarketEvent`.

Downstream Market Data Event Dissemination: MarketEventCallback

In order to understand what exactly happens to our market data event downstream, we need to look into a sample implementation of the `MarketEventCallback` interface.

```
1   public class MarketEventHandlerImpl < T > implements
    MarketEventCallback < T > {
2
3     private final EventBus eventBus;
4
5     public MarketEventHandlerImpl(EventBus eventBus) {
6       this.eventBus = eventBus;
7     }
```

```
8
9    @Override
10   public void onMarketEvent(TradeableInstrument < T > instrument, double
     bid,
11     double ask, DateTime eventDate) {
12     MarketDataPayLoad < T > payload = new  MarketDataPayLoad < T >
       (instrument, bid, ask, eventDate);
13     eventBus.post(payload);
14   }
15
16 }
```

The implementation MarketEventHandlerImpl could not have been simpler.
Basically, it is delegating the event dissemination to the Google EventBus, which
depending on how it is configured (synchronously or asynchronously), will disseminate
this event to any method that has the annotation @Subscribe and has the input
parameter MarketDataPayLoad<T> to a void method. A method signature would look like
this:

```
1   @Subscribe
2   @AllowConcurrentEvents
3   public void handleMarketDataEvent(MarketDataPayLoad<T>
    marketDataPayLoad) {
4   ....
5   ....
6   }
```

That is it!! You can create any number of such subscribers and get a callback from the
event bus with the MarketDataPayLoad payload. You will see in later chapters how you
can plug in subscribers, such as components based on trading strategies, that are heavy
consumers of market data.

Try It Yourself

In this section, we are going to create a demo program that will output market data and
heartbeat events streamed to MarketDataStreamingService by the platform.

```
1   package com.precioustech.fxtrading.oanda.restapi.streaming.marketdata;
2
3   import java.util.Collection;
4
5   import org.apache.commons.lang3.StringUtils;
6   import org.apache.log4j.Logger;
7   import  org.joda.time.DateTime;
8
9   import com.google.common.collect.Lists;
```

```
10  import com.google.common.eventbus.AllowConcurrentEvents;
11  import com.google.common.eventbus.EventBus;
12  import com.google.common.eventbus.Subscribe;
13  import com.precioustech.fxtrading.heartbeats.HeartBeatCallback;
14  import com.precioustech.fxtrading.heartbeats.HeartBeatCallbackImpl;
15  import com.precioustech.fxtrading.heartbeats.HeartBeatPayLoad;
16  import com.precioustech.fxtrading.instrument.TradeableInstrument;
17  import com.precioustech.fxtrading.marketdata.MarketDataPayLoad;
18  import com.precioustech.fxtrading.marketdata.MarketEventCallback;
19  import com.precioustech.fxtrading.marketdata.MarketEventHandlerImpl;
20  import com.precioustech.fxtrading.streaming.marketdata.
    MarketDataStreamingService;
21
22  public class MarketDataStreamingServiceDemo {
23
24   private static final Logger LOG = Logger.getLogger(MarketDataStreaming
     ServiceDemo.class);
25
26   private static void usageAndValidation(String[] args) {
27    if (args.length != 3) {
28     LOG.error("Usage: MarketDataStreamingServiceDemo <url> <accountid>
       <accesstoken>");
29     System.exit(1);
30    } else {
31     if (!StringUtils.isNumeric(args[1])) {
32      LOG.error("Argument 2 should be numeric");
33      System.exit(1);
34     }
35    }
36   }
37
38   private static class DataSubscriber {
39
40    @Subscribe
41    @AllowConcurrentEvents
42    public void handleMarketDataEvent(MarketDataPayLoad < String >
      marketDataPayLoad) {
43     LOG.info(String.format("TickData event: %s @ %s. Bid Price = %3.5f,
       Ask Price = %3.5f",
44      marketDataPayLoad.getInstrument().getInstrument(),
       marketDataPayLoad.getEventDate(),
45      marketDataPayLoad.getBidPrice(), marketDataPayLoad.getAskPrice()));
46    }
47
48    @Subscribe
49    @AllowConcurrentEvents
```

```
50      public void handleHeartBeats(HeartBeatPayLoad < DateTime > payLoad) {
51        LOG.info(String.format("Heartbeat received @ %s from source %s",
          payLoad.getHeartBeatPayLoad(),
52        payLoad.getHeartBeatSource()));
53      }
54
55    }
56
57    public static void main(String[] args) throws Exception {
58
59      usageAndValidation(args);
60      final String url = args[0];
61      final Long accountId = Long.parseLong(args[1]);
62      final String accessToken = args[2];
63      final String heartbeatSourceId="DEMO_MKTDATASTREAM";
64
65      TradeableInstrument < String > eurusd = new TradeableInstrument <
          String > ("EUR_USD");
66      TradeableInstrument < String > gbpnzd = new TradeableInstrument <
          String > ("GBP_NZD");
67
68      Collection < TradeableInstrument < String >> instruments = Lists.
          newArrayList(eurusd, gbpnzd);
69
70      EventBus eventBus = new EventBus();
71      eventBus.register(new DataSubscriber());
72
73      MarketEventCallback < String > mktEventCallback = new
          MarketEventHandlerImpl < String > (eventBus);
74      HeartBeatCallback < DateTime > heartBeatCallback = new
          HeartBeatCallbackImpl < DateTime > (eventBus);
75
76      MarketDataStreamingService mktDataStreaminService = new OandaMarketDa
          taStreamingService(url,
77       accessToken,
78       accountId, instruments, mktEventCallback, heartBeatCallback,
          heartbeatSourceId);
79      LOG.info("+++++++++++++ Starting Market Data Streaming
          +++++++++++++++++++++");
80      mktDataStreaminService.startMarketDataStreaming();
81      Thread.sleep(20000 L);
82      mktDataStreaminService.stopMarketDataStreaming();
83    }
84  }
```

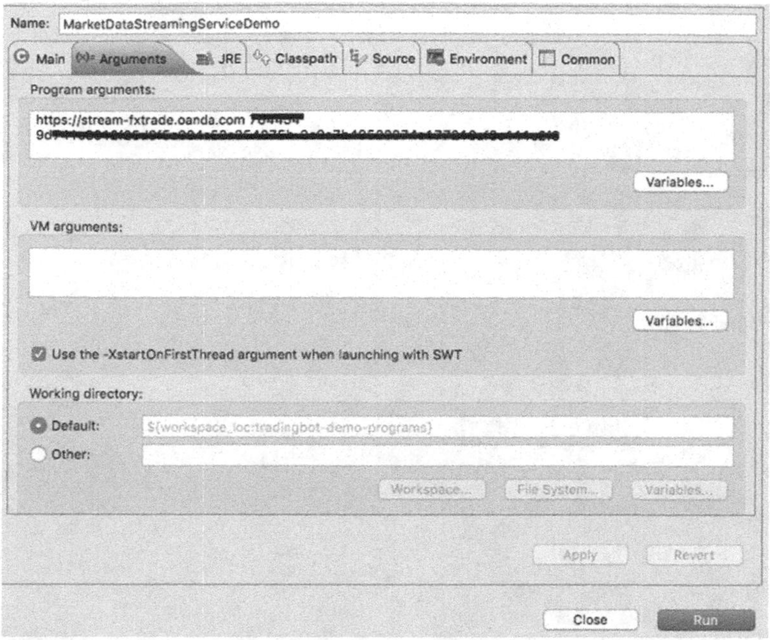

Figure 4-1. *Launch configuration*

Figure 4-2. *Sample output*

■ ■ ■

CHAPTER 5

Historic Instrument Market Data

In this chapter we discuss some of the techniques to build services to query historic market data. This could be of real interest for folks who want to build strategies based on analysis of historic data for given instruments. Traditionally, historical instrument data on charts are represented as candlesticks. Candlestick patterns are a form of technical analysis that can be used over any time frame. They are similar to bar charts and provide opening and closing values, the high and low price for the time frame in question.

How to Read a Candlestick

The length of the candlestick shows the relative change in the open and close prices of the reporting time frame (session). The longer the body, the more the change in the open and close price of the session. This may point to higher volatility in the price. If the close price is higher than the open, the body of the candlestick is white. On the contrary, if the close price is lower than the open, the body is black. The thin lines above and below the body are called *shadows*. The peak of the upper shadow is the high of the session and the bottom of the lower shadow is the low of the session. The length and the color of the candlesticks can point to a bull or a bear market. See Figure 5-1.

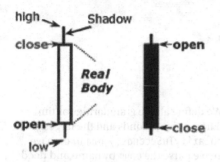

Figure 5-1. Candlestick

© Shekhar Varshney 2016

S. Varshney, *Building Trading Bots Using Java*, DOI 10.1007/978-1-4842-2520-2_5

Enum Defining the Candlestick Granularity

We start our journey of making sense of the market data by first defining an enum that defines various candlesticks' granularity or time frames that we will support. See Listing 5-1.

Listing 5-1. CandleStickGranularity Enum Definition

```
1    public enum CandleStickGranularity {
2
3      S5(5), // 5s
4      S10(10), // 10s
5      S15(15), // 15s
6      S30(30), // 30s
7      M1(60 * 1), // 1min
8      M2(60 * 2), // 2mins
9      M3(60 * 3), // 3mins
10     M5(60 * 5), // 5mins
11     M10(60 * 10), // 10mins
12     M15(60 * 15), // 15mins
13     M30(60 * 30), // 30mins
14     H1(60 * 60), // 1hr
15     H2(60 * 60 * 2), // 2hr
16     H3(60 * 60 * 3), // 3hr
17     H4(60 * 60 * 4), // 4hr
18     H6(60 * 60 * 6), // 6hr
19     H8(60 * 60 * 8), // 8hr
20     H12(60 * 60 * 12), // 12hr
21     D(60 * 60 * 24), // 1day
22     W(60 * 60 * 24 * 7), // 1wk
23     M(60 * 60 * 24 * 30); // 1mth
24
25     private final long granularityInSeconds;
26
27     private CandleStickGranularity(long granularityInSeconds) {
28       this.granularityInSeconds = granularityInSeconds;
29     }
30
31     public long getGranularityInSeconds() {
32       return granularityInSeconds;
33     }
34   }
```

This enum definition is quite straightforward. We define all the granularities or time frames that our API will support. The lowest granularity is five seconds and the largest is one month. We define a constructor to accept granularityInSeconds(), just in case we need to quantify the granularity in a situation where we parse the enum by name and need to get its granularity or session length.

Define POJO to Hold Candlestick Information

We now turn our attention to defining the POJO that will hold all the candlestick information, shown in Listing 5-2.

Listing 5-2. Candlestick POJO

```
1    public class CandleStick < T > {
2      /*All prices are average of bid and ask ,i.e (bid+ask)/2*/
3      private final double openPrice,
4      highPrice,
5      lowPrice,
6      closePrice;
7      private final DateTime eventDate;
8      private final TradeableInstrument < T > instrument;
9      private final CandleStickGranularity candleGranularity;
10     private final String toStr;
11     private final int hash;
12
13     public CandleStick(double openPrice, double highPrice, double
       lowPrice,
14       double closePrice, DateTime eventDate, TradeableInstrument < T >
         instrument,
15       CandleStickGranularity candleGranularity) {
16       super();
17       this.openPrice = openPrice;
18       this.highPrice = highPrice;
19       this.lowPrice = lowPrice;
20       this.closePrice = closePrice;
21       this.eventDate = eventDate;
22       this.instrument = instrument;
23       this.candleGranularity = candleGranularity;
24       this.hash = calcHash();
25       this.toStr = String.format(
26         "Open=%2.5f, high=%2.5f, low=%2.5f,close=%2.5f,date=%s,
           instrument=%s, granularity=%s",
27         openPrice, highPrice, lowPrice, closePrice, eventDate, instrument,
28         candleGranularity.name());
29     }
30
31     private int calcHash() {
32       final int prime = 31;
33       int result = 1;
34       result = prime * result + ((candleGranularity == null) ? -1 :
         candleGranularity.ordinal());
35       result = prime * result + ((eventDate == null) ? 0 : eventDate.
         hashCode());
```

```java
36      result = prime * result + ((instrument == null) ? 0 : instrument.
        hashCode());
37      return result;
38    }
39
40    @Override
41    public int hashCode() {
42      return hash;
43    }
44
45    @Override
46    public boolean equals(Object obj) {
47      if (this == obj)
48        return true;
49      if (obj == null)
50        return false;
51      if (getClass() != obj.getClass())
52        return false;
53      CandleStick other = (CandleStick) obj;
54      if (candleGranularity != other.candleGranularity)
55        return false;
56      if (eventDate == null) {
57        if (other.eventDate != null)
58          return false;
59      } else if (!eventDate.equals(other.eventDate))
60        return false;
61      if (instrument == null) {
62        if (other.instrument != null)
63          return false;
64      } else if (!instrument.equals(other.instrument))
65        return false;
66      return true;
67    }
68
69    @Override
70    public String toString() {
71      return this.toStr;
72    }
73
74    public CandleStickGranularity getCandleGranularity() {
75      return candleGranularity;
76    }
77
78    public TradeableInstrument < T > getInstrument() {
79      return instrument;
80    }
81
```

```
82   public double getOpenPrice() {
83     return openPrice;
84   }
85
86   public double getHighPrice() {
87     return highPrice;
88   }
89
90   public double getLowPrice() {
91     return lowPrice;
92   }
93
94   public double getClosePrice() {
95     return closePrice;
96   }
97
98   public DateTime getEventDate() {
99     return eventDate;
100  }
101 }
```

Except for eventDate, all the attributes are self explanatory following our earlier discussion on "how to read a candlestick". We should have expected a start and end date but we have only a single eventDate attribute. Why is it so? Actually given the granularity of the candlestick and its start time, the end date can be worked out. So eventDate is actually the start of the candlestick period.

Regarding the hashCode() and equals() methods, the following three attributes participate and are deemed to ascertain if a candlestick is unique in a collection or not.

```
1   private final DateTime eventDate;
2   private final TradeableInstrument<T> instrument;
3   private final CandleStickGranularity candleGranularity;
```

All price attributes in the POJO are assumed to be the average of bid and ask prices.

Historical Data Provider Interface

It is now time to define the historical data provider interface that will specify what needs to be implemented in order to retrieve meaningful candlestick data for analysis (see Listing 5-3).

Listing 5-3. HistoricMarketDataProvider Interface

```
1   /**
2    * A provider of candle stick data for a given instrument. The candle
3    * sticks must be in chronological order in order to easily construct
4    * time series information.
5    * @param <T>
```

```
6      *               The type of instrumentId in class TradeableInstrument
7      * @see TradeableInstrument
8      */
9     public interface HistoricMarketDataProvider < T > {
10
11     /**
12      * Construct candle sticks for a given from and to period.
13      *
14      * @param instrument
15      *                , for which the candle stick information is requested
16      * @param granularity
17      *                , the time interval between 2 candle sticks
18      * @param from
19      *                , the start of first candle stick
20      * @param to
21      *                , the end of last candle stick
22      * @return List<CandleStick<T>> chronologically ordered.
23      */
24     List < CandleStick < T >> getCandleSticks(TradeableInstrument < T >
       instrument,
25       CandleStickGranularity granularity, DateTime from, DateTime to);
26
27     /**
28      * Construct last "count" candle sticks. This could be translated to
29      * an invocation of the overloaded method above which requires
30      * "from" and "to" date, if appropriate. The "to" date = now() and
31      * "from" date = now() -granularity *count
32      *
33      * @param instrument
34      *                , for which the candle stick information is requested
35      * @param granularity
36      *                , the time interval between 2 candle sticks
37      * @param count
38      *                ,
39      * @return List<CandleStick<T>> chronologically ordered.
40      */
41     List < CandleStick < T >> getCandleSticks(TradeableInstrument < T >
       instrument,
42       CandleStickGranularity granularity, int count);
43    }
```

As usual, this interface definition looks quite straightforward. The two overloaded methods, one of which accepts a from and to time period, and the other requires the last count of candlesticks, are all that is needed to retrieve the necessary candlesticks. The choice of return type list instead of collection guarantees that there is a certain order to the candlesticks, in this case chronological.

A Concrete Implementation for HistoricMarketDataProvider

We begin our discussion of the OANDA implementation by first taking a quick look at a sample JSON returned when we request candlestick information. Listing 5-4 is for granularity Daily.

Listing 5-4. Sample JSON for Candlesticks

```
1   {
2       "instrument": "GBP_USD",
3       "granularity": "D",
4       "candles": [
5         {
6           "time": "1442098800000000",
7           "openMid": 1.54301,
8           "highMid": 1.544695,
9           "lowMid": 1.54284,
10          "closeMid": 1.544295,
11          "volume": 868,
12          "complete": true
13        },
14        {
15          "time": "1442185200000000",
16          "openMid": 1.544245,
17          "highMid": 1.54594,
18          "lowMid": 1.54376,
19          "closeMid": 1.54406,
20          "volume": 3765,
21          "complete": false
22        }
23      ]
24  }
```

The JSON keys that we need to statically import in our provider class are:

```
1   import static com.precioustech.fxtrading.oanda.restapi.OandaJsonKeys.
    candles;
2   import static com.precioustech.fxtrading.oanda.restapi.OandaJsonKeys.
    closeMid;
3   import static com.precioustech.fxtrading.oanda.restapi.OandaJsonKeys.
    highMid;
4   import static com.precioustech.fxtrading.oanda.restapi.OandaJsonKeys.
    lowMid;
5   import static com.precioustech.fxtrading.oanda.restapi.OandaJsonKeys.
    openMid;
6   import static com.precioustech.fxtrading.oanda.restapi.OandaJsonKeys.time;
```

As usual, replacing T param type in the interface definition with String gives us the following class definition:

```
1  public class OandaHistoricMarketDataProvider implements HistoricMarketDa
   taProvider<String> {
```

For the constructor definition, it is sufficient to provide the OANDA service URL and an access token.

```
1  private final String url;
2  private final BasicHeader authHeader;
3  public OandaHistoricMarketDataProvider(String url, String accessToken) {
4          this.url = url;// OANDA REST service base url
5          this.authHeader = OandaUtils.createAuthHeader(accessToken);
6  }
```

The candlestick resource endpoint is

```
1  public static final String CANDLES_RESOURCE = "/v1/candles";
```

So our functions to compute the URLs to retrieve candlesticks first with the date range and others with the count, respectively, are

```
1   private static final String tzLondon = "Europe%2FLondon";
2
3   String getFromToUrl(TradeableInstrument < String > instrument,
    CandleStickGranularity granularity,
4    DateTime from, DateTime to) {
5    return String.format(
6     "%s%s?instrument=%s&candleFormat=midpoint&granularity=%s&dailyAlignme
     nt=0&alignmentTimezone=%s&start=%d&end=%d",
7            this.url, OandaConstants.CANDLES_RESOURCE, instrument.
            getInstrument(),
8     granularity.name(), tzLondon, TradingUtils.toUnixTime(from),
     TradingUtils.toUnixTime(to));
9   }
10
11  String getCountUrl(TradeableInstrument < String > instrument,
    CandleStickGranularity granularity, int count) {
12
13   return String.format(
14    "%s%s?instrument=%s&candleFormat=midpoint&granularity=%s&dailyAlignme
     nt=0&alignment Timezone=%s&count=%d",
15   this.url, OandaConstants.CANDLES_RESOURCE, instrument.
    getInstrument(), granularity.name(),
16   tzLondon, count);
17  }
18
```

```
19    //Test invocation code
20    TradeableInstrument<String> euraud = new TradeableInstrument<String>("
      EUR_AUD");
21
22    DateTime fromDate=new DateTime(1442098800000L);
23    DateTime toDate = new DateTime(1442185200000L);
24    String fromToUrl = getFromToUrl(euraud, CandleStickGranularity.S5,
      fromDate );
25    System.out.println("FromToUrl:"+fromToUrl);
26    System.out.println("*****");
27    int count=5;
28    String countUrl=getCountUrl(euraud,CandleStickGranularity.S5 ,count);
29    System.out.println("CountUrl:"+countUrl);
```

Output from this test code invocation would look like this:

```
1    FromToUrl:https://api-fxtrade.oanda.com/v1/candles?Instrument=EUR_AUD&ca
     ndleFormat=midpoint&granularity=S5&dailyAlignmen\
2    t=0&alignmentTimezone=Europe%2FLondon&start=1442098800000000&e
     nd=1442185200000000
3    *****
4    CountUrl:https://api-fxtrade.oanda.com/v1/candles?Instrument=EUR_AUD&
     candleFormat=midpoint&granularity=S5&dailyAlignment\
5    =0&alignmentTimezone=Europe%2FLondon&count=5
```

Some key observations from these code snippets are:

- We need to provide an alignment time zone. This is the time zone in which the start timestamp for a candlestick will be reported.

- The from and to timestamps must be provided as a UNIX timestamp, which has nanosecond precision.

- The parameter candleFormat=midpoint is requesting OANDA to provide bid/ask prices as averaged prices instead of providing them separately.

- The dailyAlignment=0 is the hour of day used to align the candlesticks if granularity >= D. The value ranges from 0 to 23. In our case, we are requesting the candlesticks to be aligned at midnight London time.

- More information about candlestick URL params can be found at http://developer.oanda.com/rest- live/rates/#aboutCandle stickRepresentation[1].

We now turn our attention to the discussion of the two overloaded methods that actually delegate the main logic to a private method that retrieves, parses, and returns the list of candlesticks.

---

[1]http://developer.oanda.com/rest-live/rates/#aboutCandlestickRepresentation

```
1    @Override
2    public List < CandleStick < String >> getCandleSticks(TradeableInstrume
     nt < String > instrument,
3     CandleStickGranularity granularity, DateTime from, DateTime to) {
4     return getCandleSticks(instrument,
5       getFromToUrl(instrument, granularity, from, to), granularity);
6    }
7
8    @Override
9    public List < CandleStick < String >> getCandleSticks(TradeableInstrume
     nt < String > instrument,
10    CandleStickGranularity granularity, int count) {
11    return getCandleSticks(instrument,
12      getCountUrl(instrument, granularity, count), granularity);
13   }
14
15   private List < CandleStick < String >> getCandleSticks(TradeableInstrum
     ent < String > instrument,
16    String url, CandleStickGranularity granularity) {
17    List < CandleStick < String >> allCandleSticks = Lists.newArrayList();
18    CloseableHttpClient httpClient = getHttpClient();
19    try {
20     HttpUriRequest httpGet = new HttpGet(url);
21     httpGet.setHeader(authHeader);
22     httpGet.setHeader(OandaConstants.UNIX_DATETIME_HEADER);
23     LOG.info(TradingUtils.executingRequestMsg(httpGet));
24     HttpResponse resp = httpClient.execute(httpGet);
25     String strResp = TradingUtils.responseToString(resp);
26     if (strResp != StringUtils.EMPTY) {
27      Object obj = JSONValue.parse(strResp);
28      JSONObject jsonResp = (JSONObject) obj;
29      JSONArray candlsticks = (JSONArray) jsonResp.get(candles);
30
31       for (Object o: candlsticks) {
32        JSONObject candlestick = (JSONObject) o;
33
34        final double openPrice = ((Number) candlestick.get(openMid)).
             doubleValue();
35        final double highPrice = ((Number) candlestick.get(highMid)).
             doubleValue();
36        final double lowPrice = ((Number) candlestick.get(lowMid)).
             doubleValue();
37        final double closePrice = ((Number) candlestick.get(closeMid)).
             doubleValue();
38        final long timestamp = Long.parseLong(candlestick.get(time).
             toString());
39
```

```
40      CandleStick < String > candle = new  CandleStick < String >
        (openPrice, highPrice,
41       lowPrice, closePrice, new DateTime(TradingUtils.
         toMillisFromNanos(timestamp)),
42       instrument, granularity);
43       allCandleSticks.add(candle);
44      }
45     } else {
46      TradingUtils.printErrorMsg(resp);
47     }
48    } catch (Exception e) {
49     LOG.error(e);
50    } finally {
51     TradingUtils.closeSilently(httpClient);
52    }
53    return  allCandleSticks;
54   }
```

The private method does the bulk of the work. The two public overloaded methods get the URL computed and then delegate the rest to this private method. The following line of code is extremely important since we are passing a UNIX timestamp as a query param (in case of date range) rather than as a formatted date string, which is what OANDA expects if the header is omitted.

```
1   httpGet.setHeader(OandaConstants.UNIX_DATETIME_HEADER);
```

The rest of the code is fairly straightforward. Once a successful response is received, we just have to parse the JSON payload that contains information for all the candlesticks requested.

Discussion: An Alternate Database Implementation

In this section, we briefly touch on an alternate way for retrieving candlestick information. A lot of installations have a tick data warehouse/database and might prefer to tap into these data sources. A tick database table might look like the following (assuming an INSTRUMENT table already exists which defines all tradeable instruments):

```
1  CREATE TABLE TICK_DATA
2  (
3      TICK_ID INTEGER PRIMARY KEY,
4      INSTRUMENT_ID INTEGER NOT NULL REFERENCES INSTRUMENT(INSTRUMENT_ID),
5      TICK_EVENT_TIMESTAMP TIMESTAMP NOT NULL,
6      BID_PRICE DECIMAL NOT NULL,
7      ASK_PRICE DECIMAL NOT NULL
8  )
```

Assuming that there is a market data feed that constantly populates our TICK_DATA table for every tick, we can pretty much provide all the information that OANDA REST API is providing. However, we have some work to do before we can present the data to the client in exactly the way OANDA does. At a high level, the following needs to happen.

Case 1: Retrieve candlesticks given from and to dates and a granularity (G) for a given instrument (I).

- Divide from, to time period into N intervals, each of length G. So interval 1(I1) = [from, from+G], interval 2(I2) = [from+G, from+2G] .. interval N(IN) = [from+(N-1)*G, to].

- Using a SELECT query, retrieve all data for the instrument where TICK_EVENT_TIMES- TAMP is between the from and to dates, ordered by TICK_EVENT_TIMESTAMP.

- For each row R retrieved, assign row to an interval IM such that R[TICK_EVENT_TIMES- TAMP] value >= IM [0] and <= IM [1]. This will yield a collection of rows for each interval.

- We are now in a position to find the open, close, high, and low prices for each interval I_M. Lets say this interval I_M has T rows $R_1..R_T$.

- $Open_M$ = avg(R_1[BID_PRICE], R_1[ASK_PRICE])

- $Close_M$ = avg(R_T [BID_PRICE], R_T [ASK_PRICE])

- $High_M$ = max(avg(R_1[BID_PRICE], R_1[ASK_PRICE]), avg(R_2[BID_PRICE], R_2[ASK_PRICE])..avg(RT [BID PRICE], RT [ASK_PRICE]))

- LowM = min(avg(R_1[BID_PRICE], R_1[ASK_PRICE]), avg(R_2[BID_PRICE], R_2[ASK_PRICE])..avg(R_T [BID_ PRICE], R_T [ASK_PRICE]))

- *EventDateM =IM* [0]

Case 2: Retrieve candlesticks given count N and a granularity (G) for a given instrument (I).

- Calculate date from = now() - N*G to = now()

- Call function that implements Case 1

A skeleton of our database-based provider implementation might look like this:

```
1   import org.apache.commons.lang3.tuple.ImmutablePair;
2   import com.google.common.collect.Maps;
3   ...
4   ...
5   public class DatabaseHistoricMarketDataProvider implements HistoricMark
    etDataProvider<Long> {
6           /*
7       TickDataDao manages the database interaction and retrieves
8       necessary tick data in the form of TickData POJOs. */
9           private final TickDataDao tickDataDao;
```

```
10
11      public DatabaseHistoricMarketDataProvider(TickDataDao tickDataDao)
        {
12              this.tickDataDao = tickDataDao;
13      }
14      private List<ImmutablePair<DateTime,DateTime>>
        getIntervals(DateTime from, DateTime to,
15      CandleStickGranularity granularity) {
16      /*
17      implement the logic to divide from,to into pairs or tuples of date
18      ranges that span granularity */
19      }
20      private Map<ImmutablePair<DateTime,DateTime>, List<TickData>>
21      distributeInTimeBuckets(List<ImmutablePair<DateTime,DateTime>>
        timeBuckets,
22      List<TickData> tickDataList) {
23      Map<ImmutablePair<DateTime,DateTime>, List<TickData>>
        distributionMap = Maps.newLinkedHashMap();
24      /*
25      Implement the logic to assign tick data from the database into
26      various time range buckets. */
27      return distributionMap;
28  }
29      private List<CandleStick<Long>> processTickDataBuckets(Map<Immutabl
        ePair<DateTime,DateTime>,
30          List<TickData>> distributionMap, TradeableInstrument<Long>
            instrument,
31          CandleStickGranularity granularity ) {
32      /*
33      Here each entry of map should generate a CandleStick POJO. Also
34      do the computations such as finding min, max and average of
35      prices as discussed previously. */
36      }
37
38  @Override
39  public List<CandleStick<Long>> getCandleSticks(TradeableInstrument<Lo
    ng> instrument, CandleStickGranularity granularity,\
40   DateTime from, DateTime to) {
41          List<ImmutablePair<DateTime,DateTime>> intervals = getIntervals
            (from,to,granularity);
42          List<TickData> ticks = this.tickDao.getTicks(intrument.getId(),
            from, to);
43      Map<ImmutablePair<DateTime,DateTime>, List<TickData>>
        distributionMap =
44          distributeInTimeBuckets(intervals,  ticks);
45      return processTickDataBuckets(distributionMap,instrument,
        granularity);
46  }
```

```
47
48  private ImmutablePair<DateTime, DateTime> getFromToDates(
    CandleStickGranularity granularity, int count) {
49      DateTime to = DateTime.now();
50      /*
51      Use granularity to go back in time "count" times, to arrive at "to"
        Date
52      */
53  }
54  @Override
55  public List<CandleStick<Long>> getCandleSticks(TradeableInstrument<Long>
    instrument,
56      CandleStickGranularity granularity, int count) {
57          ImmutablePair<DateTime,DateTime> fromToPair = getFromToDates
            (granularity,count);
58      return getCandleSticks(instrument,granularity,fromToPair.
        getLeft(),fromToPair.getRight());
59          }
60  }
```

Candlesticks for Moving Average Calculations

Moving averages are widely used in technical analysis and forecasting methods. All moving averages use candlestick data for computation. The three most widely used moving averages are:

- *SimpleMovingAverage (SMA)*: An SMA, also known as an arithmetic average, is the most common and simplest of the moving averages. It is simply the average of prices of the candlesticks. Each price is equally weighted.

- *WeightedMovingAverage (WMA)*: A WMA assigns a weighting factor to each value in the candlestick list according to its age. The most recent price gets the most weight and the first one gets the least weight. So for example, if there are N candlesticks, the Mth candlestick will have weight $M/(N x (N+1)/2)$. The sum of weights always equates to 1.0.

- *ExponentialMovingAverage (EMA)*: An EMA also assigns a weight to each value, according to its age. And like WMA, the most recent price gets the most weight and the first one in the list gets the least weight. The weight calculation for each candlestick is slightly more involved and is discussed thoroughly at https://en.wikipedia.org/wiki/Moving_average#Exponential_moving_average[2].

---

[2]https://en.wikipedia.org/wiki/Moving_average#Exponential_moving_average

MovingAverageCalculationService

In this section we discuss MovingAverageCalculationService, which computes the averages that can help in technical analysis and forecasting methods. This service will only implement SMA and WMA. Let's start with the constructor definition that only has one dependency, the HistoricMarketDataProvider.

```
1   public class MovingAverageCalculationService < T > {
2
3     private final HistoricMarketDataProvider < T >
      historicMarketDataProvider;
4
5     public MovingAverageCalculationService(HistoricMarketDataProvider < T >
      historicMarketDataProvider) {
6       this.historicMarketDataProvider = historicMarketDataProvider;
7     }
```

The main computations happen in the private methods calculateSMA and calculateWMA:

```
1   /*
2    * Simple average calculation of close price of candle stick
3    */
4   private double calculateSMA(List < CandleStick < T >> candles) {
5     double sumsma = 0;
6     for (CandleStick < T > candle: candles) {
7       sumsma += candle.getClosePrice();
8     }
9     return sumsma / candles.size();
10  }
11
12  /*
13   * If there are N candle sticks then, Mth candle stick will have
         weight
14   * M/(N * (N+1)/2). Therefore the divisor D for each candle is (N *
15   * (N+1)/2) */
16  private double calculateWMA(List < CandleStick < T >> candles) {
17    double divisor = (candles.size() * (candles.size() + 1)) / 2;
18    int count = 0;
19    double  sumwma = 0;
20    for (CandleStick < T > candle: candles) {
21      count++;
22      sumwma += (count * candle.getClosePrice()) / divisor;
23    }
24    return sumwma;
25  }
```

For the calculations, we use the closePrice of the candlestick. The rest of the public methods are very straightforward and, after fetching the candlesticks, they delegate to the private methods for computation and return the results. The service exposes an optimized method calculateSMAand-WMAasPair that can compute the two together and return the results. This is provided so that we do not fetch the same data twice. This can be especially expensive if, for example, we want to get 10 years' worth of data with Daily granularity both from OANDA and from a database query perspective. It might be fine if the data is cached, in which case individual computation methods can be used.

```
1   public double calculateSMA(TradeableInstrument < T > instrument, int
    count,
2    CandleStickGranularity granularity) {
3    List < CandleStick < T >> candles = this.historicMarketDataProvider
4     .getCandleSticks(instrument, granularity, count);
5    return calculateSMA(candles);
6   }
7
8   public double calculateSMA(TradeableInstrument < T > instrument,
    DateTime from, DateTime to,
9     CandleStickGranularity granularity) {
10    List < CandleStick < T >> candles = this.historicMarketDataProvider.
11    getCandleSticks(instrument, granularity, from, to);
12    return calculateSMA(candles);
13   }
14   /*
15    * Optimization to get the two together in one call
16    */
17   public ImmutablePair < Double, Double > calculateSMAandWMAasPair
    (TradeableInstrument < T > instrument,
18    int count, CandleStickGranularity granularity) {
19    List < CandleStick < T >> candles = this.historicMarketDataProvider.
    getCandleSticks(instrument, granularity, count);
20    return new ImmutablePair < Double, Double > (calculateSMA(candles),
    calculateWMA(candles));
21   }
22
23   public ImmutablePair < Double, Double > calculateSMAandWMAasPair(Tradea
    bleInstrument < T > instrument,
24    DateTime from, DateTime to, CandleStickGranularity granularity) {
25    List < CandleStick < T >> candles = this.historicMarketDataProvider.
26    getCandleSticks(instrument, granularity, from, to);
27    return new ImmutablePair < Double, Double > (calculateSMA(candles),
    calculateWMA(candles));
28   }
29
30   public double calculateWMA(TradeableInstrument < T > instrument, int
    count,
```

```
31    CandleStickGranularity granularity) {
32    List < CandleStick < T >> candles = this.historicMarketDataProvider.
33    getCandleSticks(instrument, granularity, count);
34    return calculateWMA(candles);
35    }
36
37    public double calculateWMA(TradeableInstrument < T > instrument,
      DateTime from, DateTime to,
38    CandleStickGranularity granularity) {
39    List < CandleStick < T >> candles = this.historicMarketDataProvider.
40    getCandleSticks(instrument, granularity, from, to);
41    return calculateWMA(candles);
42    }
```

Try It Yourself

In this section we write demo programs to demonstrate the API methods for HistoricMarketDataProvider and MovingAverageCalculationService.

```
1    package com.precioustech.fxtrading.oanda.restapi.marketdata.historic;
2
3    import java.util.List;
4
5    import org.apache.log4j.Logger;
6    import org.joda.time.DateTime;
7
8    import com.precioustech.fxtrading.instrument.TradeableInstrument;
9    import com.precioustech.fxtrading.marketdata.historic.CandleStick;
10   import com.precioustech.fxtrading.marketdata.historic.
     CandleStickGranularity;
11   import com.precioustech.fxtrading.marketdata.historic.
     HistoricMarketDataProvider;
12
13   public class HistoricMarketDataProviderDemo {
14
15    private static final Logger LOG = Logger.getLogger(HistoricMarketDataP
      roviderDemo.class);
16
17    private static void usage(String[] args) {
18     if (args.length != 2) {
19      LOG.error("Usage: HistoricMarketDataProviderDemo <url>
       <accesstoken>");
20      System.exit(1);
21     }
22    }
23
```

```java
24    public static void main(String[] args) {
25    usage(args);
26    final String url = args[0];
27    final String accessToken = args[1];
28    HistoricMarketDataProvider < String > historicMarketDataProvider =
      new
29    OandaHistoricMarketDataProvider(url, accessToken);
30    TradeableInstrument < String > usdchf = new TradeableInstrument <
      String > ("USD_CHF");
31    List < CandleStick < String >> candlesUsdChf =
      historicMarketDataProvider.getCandleSticks(usdchf,
32     CandleStickGranularity.D, 15);
33    LOG.info(String.format("++++++++++++++++++++ Last %d Candle Sticks with
      Daily Granularity for %s +++",
34     candlesUsdChf.size(), usdchf.getInstrument()));
35
36    for (CandleStick < String > candle: candlesUsdChf) {
37     LOG.info(candle);
38    }
39    TradeableInstrument < String > gbpaud = new TradeableInstrument <
      String > ("GBP_AUD");
40    DateTime from = new DateTime(1420070400000 L); // 01 Jan 2015
41    DateTime to = new DateTime(1451606400000 L); // 01 Jan 2016
42    List < CandleStick < String >> candlesGbpAud =
      historicMarketDataProvider.getCandleSticks(gbpaud,
43     CandleStickGranularity.M, from, to);
44
45    LOG.info(String.format("++++++++++++Candle Sticks From %s To %s with
      Monthly Granularity for %s +++",
46     from, to, gbpaud.getInstrument()));
47    for (CandleStick < String > candle: candlesGbpAud) {
48     LOG.info(candle);
49    }
50
51    }
52
53    }
```

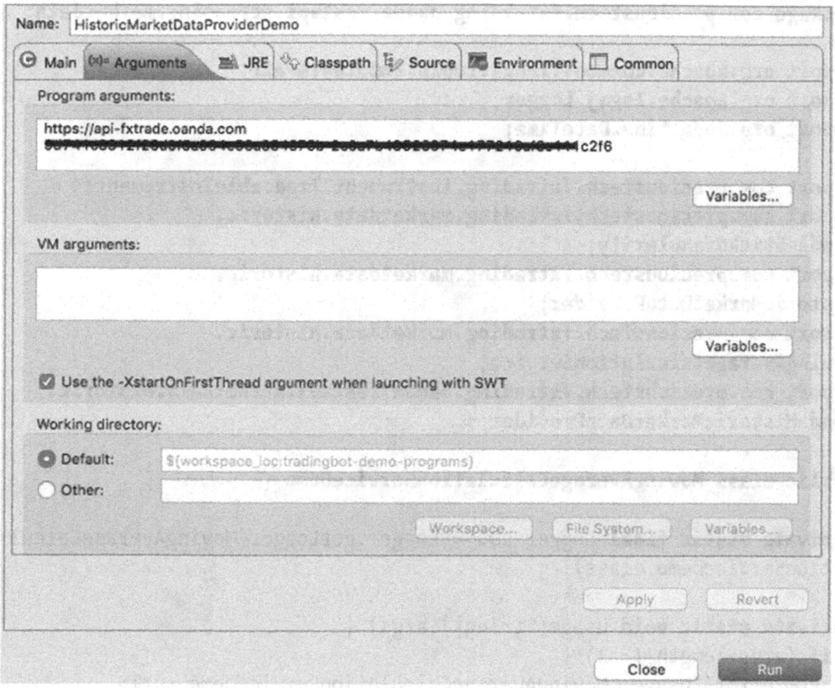

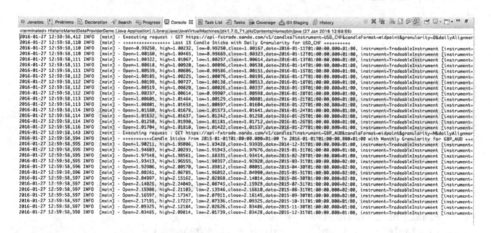

Figure 5-2. *Launch configuration*

Figure 5-3. *Sample output*

```
1   package com.precioustech.fxtrading.oanda.restapi.streaming.marketdata;
2
3   import org.apache.commons.lang3.tuple.ImmutablePair;
4   import org.apache.log4j.Logger;
5   import org.joda.time.DateTime;
6
7   import com.precioustech.fxtrading.instrument.TradeableInstrument;
8   import com.precioustech.fxtrading.marketdata.historic.
    CandleStickGranularity;
9   import com.precioustech.fxtrading.marketdata.historic.
    HistoricMarketDataProvider;
10  import com.precioustech.fxtrading.marketdata.historic.
    MovingAverageCalculationService;
11  import com.precioustech.fxtrading.oanda.restapi.marketdata.historic.
    OandaHistoricMarketDataProvider;
12
13  public class MovingAverageCalculationServiceDemo {
14
15   private static final Logger LOG = Logger.getLogger(MovingAverageCalcul
     ationServiceDemo.class);
16
17   private static void usage(String[] args) {
18    if (args.length != 2) {
19     LOG.error("Usage: MovingAverageCalculationServiceDemo <url>
      <accesstoken>");
20     System.exit(1);
21    }
22   }
23
24   public static void main(String[] args) {
25    usage(args);
26    final String url = args[0];
27    final String accessToken = args[1];
28    HistoricMarketDataProvider < String > historicMarketDataProvider =
29      new OandaHistoricMarketDataProvider(url, accessToken);
30    MovingAverageCalculationService < String > movingAverageCalcService =
31      new MovingAverageCalculationService < String >
        (historicMarketDataProvider);
32    TradeableInstrument < String > eurnzd = new TradeableInstrument <
      String > ("EUR_NZD");
33    final int countIntervals = 30;
34    ImmutablePair < Double, Double > eurnzdSmaAndWma =
      movingAverageCalcService.calculateSMAandWMAasPair(
35     eurnzd, countIntervals, CandleStickGranularity.H1);
36
37    LOG.info(
38     String.format("SMA=%2.5f,WMA=%2.5f for instrument=%s,granularity=%s
       for the last %d intervals",
```

```
39        eurnzdSmaAndWma.left, eurnzdSmaAndWma.right, eurnzd.getInstrument(),
40        CandleStickGranularity.H1, countIntervals));
41    DateTime from = new DateTime(1444003200000 L); // 5 Oct 2015
42    DateTime to = new DateTime(1453075200000 L); // 18 Jan 2016
43
44    TradeableInstrument < String > gbpchf = new TradeableInstrument <
      String > ("GBP_CHF");
45    ImmutablePair < Double, Double > gbpchfSmaAndWma =
46     movingAverageCalcService.calculateSMAandWMAasPair(gbpchf,
47       from, to, CandleStickGranularity.W);
48
49    LOG.info(
50     String.format("SMA=%2.5f,WMA=%2.5f for instrument=%s,granularity=%s
       from %s to %s",
51       gbpchfSmaAndWma.left, gbpchfSmaAndWma.right, gbpchf.getInstrument(),
52       CandleStickGranularity.W, from, to));
53
54    }
55  }
```

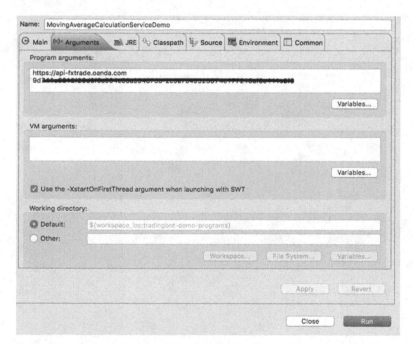

Figure 5-4. *Launch configuration*

```
<terminated> MovingAverageCalculationServiceDemo [Java Application] /Library/Java/JavaVirtualMachines/jdk1.7.0_71.jdk/Contents/Home/bin/java (27 Jan 2016 14:05:32)
2016-01-27 14:05:34,048 INFO  [main] - Executing request : GET https://api-fxtrade.oanda.com/v1/candles?instrument=EUR_NZD&candleFormat=midpoint&granularity=H1&dailyAlignment
2016-01-27 14:05:35,810 INFO  [main] - SMA=1.67333,WMA=1.67341 for instrument=EUR_NZD,granularity=H1 for the last 30 intervals
2016-01-27 14:05:35,852 INFO  [main] - Executing request : GET https://api-fxtrade.oanda.com/v1/candles?instrument=GBP_CHF&candleFormat=midpoint&granularity=W&dailyAlignment
2016-01-27 14:05:36,325 INFO  [main] - SMA=1.49198,WMA=1.48256 for instrument=GBP_CHF,granularity=W from 2015-10-05T02:00:00.000+02:00 to 2016-01-18T01:00:00.000+01:00
```

Figure 5-5. *Sample output*

CHAPTER 6

■ ■ ■

Placing Orders and Trades

In this chapter, we turn our attention to arguably the most interesting part of the whole trading process, placing orders and trades. An *order* is an intention to trade. When you place an order for a security, you intend that your order is filled and hope that the price moves to your advantage. When an order is fully or partly filled, it results in the creation of a trading position. An active trading position creates an unrealized profit or loss situation. When this trading position is closed, the unrealized profit/loss is realized and the trader is left with an increased/decreased total book amount.

Most of the orders can be classified as one of the following:

- *Market*: A market order is an order meant to be fulfilled instantly on the platform at the best available price (spot price), assuming that there is enough liquidity in the market.

- *Limit*: A limit order is where a trader defines the price he wants to buy or sell a security at. In essence, it's an order to either buy below the market price or sell above the market price. For example, EUR_USD is currently trading at 1.06. If we believe that there is very high probability that in the medium term the trajectory is up, but it has still some downside risks, we could place a Limit order to, say, buy EUR_USD when the price hits 1.04, where we believe the bottom is for this pair.

- *Take Profit*: A take-profit order closes an existing trading position that has hit a pre-determined profit level. For example, assuming we put in a market order to sell GBP_USD @ 1.545, we want to close the trading position when the price has moved by at least 200 pips in our favor, i.e., the price reaches 1.525. To automatically realize the profit, we can place a take-profit order.

- *Stop Loss*: A stop-loss order is the opposite of a take-profit order. It is an order to limit losses once the price moves adversely and the open trading position deteriorates in value. Let's say we put a market order to sell EUR_CHF @ 1.07. However, we want to automatically close this position if the price hits 1.085, limiting our losses to 150 pips. This is where a stop-loss order comes in very handy.

© Shekhar Varshney 2016
S. Varshney, *Building Trading Bots Using Java*, DOI 10.1007/978-1-4842-2520-2_6

Take-profit and *stop-loss* orders can be classified as derivatives of a *limit* order. Essentially, to realize our profits or to limit our losses, we are placing an order to be triggered that will automatically close a trading position. These two types orders are defined only if there is an open trading position that risks being closed when these orders are triggered. For that to happen, the trading position must be of the opposite type than that of the order. For example, we must have an open *buy* trade position of a security in order to trigger a *take-profit/stop-loss sell* order for the same security.

Other order types that you might come across are the following:

- Trailing stop

- Immediate or canceled

- Fill or kill

Order POJO Definition

To place an order, we must first define a POJO that will hold all the required order information. Before that, let's take a quick look at the enum that defines the different order types we are going to support and the enum that defines buy/sell sides of an order.

```
1   public enum OrderType {
2     MARKET,
3     LIMIT;
4   }
5
6   public enum TradingSignal {
7     LONG,
8     SHORT,
9     NONE;
10
11  public TradingSignal flip() {
12    switch (this) {
13     case LONG:
14      return SHORT;
15     case SHORT:
16      return LONG;
17     default:
18      return this;
19    }
20   }
21  }
```

The OrderType enum is fairly straightforward. You might question why we do not have the stop-loss or take-profit order types. As discussed earlier, these order types are derivatives of a limit order and do not have to be specified differently. This will become clear when we discuss the mechanics of placing an order. We denote the buy/sell sides of an order using the TradingSignal enum. This enum, as the name suggests, can be returned by a strategy function to indicate that we must buy/sell a security. We will discuss this further when we talk about a few sample-trading strategies.

Listing 6-1. Order POJO Definition

```
1    /**
2     * @param <M>
3     *              The type of instrumentId in class TradeableInstrument
4     * @param <N>
5     *              The type of orderId
6     * @see TradeableInstrument
7     */
8    public class Order < M, N > {
9    private final TradeableInstrument < M > instrument;
10   private final long units;
11   private final TradingSignal side;
12   private final OrderType type;
13   private final double takeProfit;
14   private final double stopLoss;
15   private N orderId;
16   private final double price;
17
18   /*
19    * orderId not included in constructor because normally it is assigned
20    * by the platform only after order is placed successfully.
21    */
22   public Order(TradeableInstrument < M > instrument, long units,
     TradingSignal side, OrderType type,
23    double price) {
24    this(instrument, units, side, type, 0.0, 0.0, price);
25   }
26
27   public Order(TradeableInstrument < M > instrument, long units,
     TradingSignal side, OrderType type) {
28    this(instrument, units, side, type, 0.0, 0.0);
29   }
30
31   public Order(TradeableInstrument < M > instrument, long units,
     TradingSignal side, OrderType type,
32    double takeProfit, double stopLoss) {
33    this(instrument, units, side, type, takeProfit, stopLoss, 0.0);
34   }
35
36   public Order(TradeableInstrument < M > instrument, long units,
     TradingSignal side, OrderType type,
37    double takeProfit, double stopLoss, double price) {
38    this.instrument = instrument;
```

```
39    this.units = units;
40    this.side = side;
41    this.type = type;
42    this.takeProfit = takeProfit;
43    this.stopLoss = stopLoss;
44    this.price = price;
45   }
46
47   public N getOrderId() {
48    return orderId;
49   }
50
51   public void setOrderId(N orderId) {
52    this.orderId = orderId;
53   }
54
55   public double getStopLoss() {
56    return stopLoss;
57   }
58
59   public double getPrice() {
60    return price;
61   }
62
63   public TradeableInstrument < M > getInstrument() {
64    return instrument;
65   }
66
67   public long getUnits() {
68    return units;
69   }
70
71   public TradingSignal getSide() {
72    return side;
73   }
74
75   public OrderType getType() {
76    return type;
77   }
78
79   public double getTakeProfit() {
80    return takeProfit;
81   }
82
83   @Override
84   public String toString() {
85    return "Order [instrument=" + instrument + ", units=" + units + ",
      side=" + side +
```

```
86      ", type=" + type + ", takeProfit=" + takeProfit + ", stopLoss=" +
        stopLoss + ", orderId=" +
87      orderId + ", price=" + price + "]";
88    }
89  }
```

The definition of *Order* POJO is quite straightforward. The thing to point out is the several ways that you can construct the POJO. The simplest is using a constructor with minimal information required, like instrument, units, side, and type. This is a classic case of placing a vanilla market order (without profit target or stop loss) whereby the platform should execute the order straightaway at the best available spot price. On the other hand, you can specify the rest of the attributes—takeProfit, stopLoss, and price— to place a limit order. Another observation you might make is the default value of 0.0 that is assigned to, say, the takeProfit *and* stopLoss attributes while using the simplest constructor discussed before. This is an arguable assignment and may pose a problem on some platforms, as 0.0 may not be an acceptable default value for not setting a stop loss limit. The alternative value preferred could be a *null*. If this is the case, the POJO definition would have to be revised and primitives such as double replaced with Double.

Order Management Provider Interface

We now turn our attention to defining the interface that the provider must implement to provide some useful order management services like placing and querying orders. This is one of the few provider interfaces where we will see all CRUD operations in action. Let's jump straight to the definition of the interface, shown in Listing 6-2.

Listing 6-2. OrderManagementProvider Interface

```
1   /**
2    * A provider of CRUD operations for an instrument Order. An order is
3    * normally placed for a given instrument and/or an accountId. An
         accountId may not be
4    * required if only a single account is allowed by the platform
5    * provider, in which case all orders are created in default account.
6    *
7    * @param <M>
8    *            The type of orderId
9    * @param <N>
10   *            The type of instrumentId in class TradeableInstrument
11   * @param <K>
12   *            The type of accountId
13   * @see TradeableInstrument
14   */
15  public interface OrderManagementProvider < M, N, K > {
16
```

```
17    /**
18     * An order is normally of types market or limit. A market order is
19     * executed straight away by the platform while a limit order is
20     * executed only if the limit price is hit. Therefore for a limit order
21     * this method may not return an orderId.
22     *
23     * @param order
24     * @param accountId
25     * @return a valid orderId if possible.
26     */
27    M placeOrder(Order < N, M > order, K accountId);
28
29    /**
30     * Modify the attributes of a given order. The platform may only
31     * permit to modify attributes like limit price, stop loss, take
           profit,
32     * expiration date, units.
33     *
34     * @param order
35     * @param accountId
36     * @return boolean indicating if the operation was successful.
37     */
38    boolean modifyOrder(Order < N, M > order, K accountId);
39
40    /**
41     * Effectively cancel the order if it is waiting to be executed. A
           valid
42     * orderId and an optional accountId may be required to uniquely
43     * identify an order to close/cancel.
44     *
45     * @param orderId
46     * @param accountId
47     * @return boolean indicating if the operation was successful.
48     */
49    boolean closeOrder(M orderId, K accountId);
50
51    /**
52     *
53     * @return a collection of all pending orders across all accounts
54     */
55    Collection < Order < N,
56    M >> allPendingOrders();
57
58    /**
59     *
60     * @param accountId
61     * @return a collection of all pending orders for a given accountId.
62     */
```

```
63    Collection < Order < N,
64    M >> pendingOrdersForAccount(K accountId);
65
66    /**
67     *
68     * @param orderId
69     * @param accountId
70     * @return Order uniquely identified by orderId and optional
71     * accountId */
72    Order < N,
73    M > pendingOrderForAccount(M orderId, K accountId);
74
75    /**
76     *
77     * @param instrument
78     * @return a collection of all pending orders for a given instrument
79     * for all accounts */
80    Collection < Order < N,
81    M >> pendingOrdersForInstrument(TradeableInstrument < N > instrument);
82    }
```

As you can see, the provider interface provides a rich set of functionality to manage orders. Since interface methods are self-explanatory, let's jump straight into how a concrete implementation would look.

A Concrete Implementation for OrderManagementProvider

Now we come to the fun part where we dive deep into the implementation and discuss how we can implement an OANDA provider. Since we are going implement the full set of CRUD operations, we need to also get acquainted with the REST verbs that are the equivalent of these operations. We already know that HTTP GET equates to R(read). What about the rest—C, U, and D? The following table summarizes the http verb used to accomplish the actions.

Operation	Http Verb
Create new order [C]	POST
Query order details [R]	GET
Update existing order [U]	PATCH
Close pending order [D]	DELETE

With this information at hand, let's first look at the class definition, including the constructor and the JSON keys that are required. We need an `AccountProvider` dependency to be provided, which we will pass in the constructor. The order ID in OANDA is a Long. Therefore, substituting Long for an account ID and STRING for an instrument ID, we get the following definition:

```
1   import static com.precioustech.fxtrading.oanda.restapi.OandaJsonKeys.
    expiry;
2   import static com.precioustech.fxtrading.oanda.restapi.OandaJsonKeys.id;
3   import static com.precioustech.fxtrading.oanda.restapi.OandaJsonKeys.
    instrument;
4   import static com.precioustech.fxtrading.oanda.restapi.OandaJsonKeys.
    orderOpened;
5   import static com.precioustech.fxtrading.oanda.restapi.OandaJsonKeys.
    price;
6   import static com.precioustech.fxtrading.oanda.restapi.OandaJsonKeys.
    side;
7   import static com.precioustech.fxtrading.oanda.restapi.OandaJsonKeys.
    stopLoss;
8   import static com.precioustech.fxtrading.oanda.restapi.OandaJsonKeys.
    takeProfit;
9   import static com.precioustech.fxtrading.oanda.restapi.OandaJsonKeys.
    tradeOpened;
10  import static com.precioustech.fxtrading.oanda.restapi.OandaJsonKeys.
    type;
11  import static com.precioustech.fxtrading.oanda.restapi.OandaJsonKeys.
    units;
12
13  public class OandaOrderManagementProvider implements
    OrderManagementProvider<Long, String, Long> {
14
15          private final String url;
16          private final BasicHeader authHeader;
17          private final AccountDataProvider<Long> accountDataProvider;
18
19          public OandaOrderManagementProvider(String url, String
            accessToken,
20          AccountDataProvider<Long> accountDataProvider) {
21                  this.url = url; // OANDA REST service base url
22                  this.authHeader = OandaUtils.
                    createAuthHeader(accessToken);
23                  this.accountDataProvider = accountDataProvider;
24          }
```

Now let's create the method to place a new order. To place a successful order, we must at least provide the minimum order information (using the minimal constructor in Order POJO) and a valid account ID. Let's first look at the function that creates the `HTTPPost` command, which will be later used in the `placeOrder` function.

```
1   private static final String ordersResource = "/orders";
2
3   HttpPost createPostCommand(Order < String, Long > order, Long
    accountId) throws Exception {
4    HttpPost httpPost = new HttpPost(
5     this.url + OandaConstants.ACCOUNTS_RESOURCE +
6     TradingConstants.FWD_SLASH + accountId + ordersResource);
7    httpPost.setHeader(this.authHeader);
8    List < NameValuePair > params = Lists.newArrayList();
9    // Apply proper rounding to price,stop loss, take profit. Oanda
        rejects 0.960000001
10   params.add(new BasicNameValuePair(instrument, order.getInstrument().
     getInstrument()));
11   params.add(new BasicNameValuePair(side, OandaUtils.toSide(order.
     getSide())));
12   params.add(new BasicNameValuePair(type, OandaUtils.toType(order.
     getType())));
13   params.add(new BasicNameValuePair(units, String.valueOf(order.
     getUnits())));
14   params.add(new BasicNameValuePair(takeProfit, String.valueOf(order.
     getTakeProfit())));
15   params.add(new BasicNameValuePair(stopLoss, String.valueOf(order.
     getStopLoss())));
16   if (order.getType() == OrderType.LIMIT && order.getPrice() != 0.0) {
17    DateTime now = DateTime.now();
18    DateTime nowplus4hrs = now.plusHours(4);
19    String dateStr = nowplus4hrs.toString();
20    params.add(new BasicNameValuePair(price, String.valueOf(order.
     getPrice())));
21    params.add(new BasicNameValuePair(expiry, dateStr));
22   }
23   httpPost.setEntity(new UrlEncodedFormEntity(params));
24   return httpPost;
25  }
```

We first create an instance of the HttpPost object and pass in the URL to the constructor. For example, an url for a valid account ID 123456 would look like this:

```
1   https://api-fxtrade.oanda.com/v1/accounts/123456/orders
```

Now that we have an instance of the HttpPost object, we must create a list of NameValuePair objects. Each NameValuePair defines an attribute of an order such as price. Using the Order POJO, we define all the order attributes. For a LIMIT order we must specify a limit price. If we do not provide this price, our order will be rejected by the platform. Hence we introduce a special check for a LIMIT order and make sure we have a valid price. While defining the price, we also quickly add an expiry of four hours to the order. This means the order will expire automatically on the platform if the limit price is not hit. Once all such order attributes are defined via the list of NameValuePair objects, we wrap these params/attributes inside an UrlEncodedFormEntity and set it on the instance of our HttpPost object. It is always recommended to encode URL parameters. Now we are all set to POST these params to the platform. To do this, we return to the placeOrder method code.

```
1   @Override
2   public Long placeOrder(Order < String, Long > order, Long accountId) {
3    CloseableHttpClient httpClient = getHttpClient();
4    try {
5     HttpPost httpPost = createPostCommand(order, accountId);
6     LOG.info(TradingUtils.executingRequestMsg(httpPost));
7     HttpResponse resp = httpClient.execute(httpPost);
8     if (resp.getStatusLine().getStatusCode() == HttpStatus.SC_OK || resp.
      getStatusLine().getStatusCode() == HttpStatus.SC_\
9   CREATED) {
10     if (resp.getEntity() != null) {
11      String strResp = TradingUtils.responseToString(resp);
12      Object o = JSONValue.parse(strResp);
13      JSONObject orderResponse;
14      if (order.getType() == OrderType.MARKET) {
15       orderResponse = (JSONObject)((JSONObject) o).get(tradeOpened);
16      } else {
17       orderResponse = (JSONObject)((JSONObject) o).get(orderOpened);
18      }
19      Long orderId = (Long) orderResponse.get(OandaJsonKeys.id);
20      LOG.info("Order executed->" + strResp);
21      return orderId;
22     } else {
23      return null;
24      }
25     } else {
26      LOG.info("Order not executed. http code=" +
27       resp.getStatusLine().getStatusCode());
28      return null;
29     }
30    } catch (Exception e) {
31     LOG.warn(e);
32     return null;
33    } finally {
34     TradingUtils.closeSilently(httpClient);
35    }
36  }
```

As described previously, once we have an instance of the `HttpPost` object, with all order attributes set to `NameValuePair` objects, we are ready to post it to the platform. A successful market order post would return a response like the following:

```
1   {
2           "instrument" : "EUR_JPY",
3       "time" : "2015-05-26T16:08:51.000000Z",
4       "price" : 133.819,
5       "tradeOpened" : {
6               "id" : 1856110003,
7           "units" : 3000,
8           "side" : "sell",
9           "takeProfit" : 132.819,
10          "stopLoss" : 134.9,
11          "trailingStop" : 0
12          },
13      "tradesClosed" : [],
14      "tradeReduced" : {}
15  }
```

Whereas a successful limit order would return something like this:

```
1   {
2           "instrument" : "EUR_USD",
3       "time" : "2015-12-02T06:47:51.000000Z",
4       "price" : 1.1,
5       "orderOpened" : {
6               "id" : 12211080075,
7           "units" : 10,
8           "side" : "sell",
9           "takeProfit" : 1.09,
10          "stopLoss" : 1.13,
11          "expiry" : "2015-12-02T11:47:39.000000Z",
12          "upperBound" : 0,
13          "lowerBound" : 0,
14          "trailingStop" : 0
15          }
16  }
```

A characteristic of a market order is that, if fully or partially filled, it results in the creation of an open position or trade. On the contrary, a limit order results in a creation of the order, ready to be triggered if the price level is reached. Therefore we need to interpret the response JSON slightly differently depending on what kind of an order was initially submitted to the platform. For a market order, we parse the `tradeOpened` element for the order ID, whereas for a limit order, we parse the `orderOpened` element. Apart from that, there is nothing else substantial in the method.

Now let's turn our attention to modifyOrder. Now we can only modify an existing limit order since, as per the discussion, only a limit order creates a new pending order. A market order on the other hand, results in a trade straightaway. Before looking at the code, we need to understand that only certain attributes can be modified for a pending order. They are

- units

- takeProfit

- stopLoss

- price

We need a valid order ID that the placeOrder returned and an account ID to actually do the modification. As usual we first focus on the creation of the actual HttpPatch command that would facilitate the modification on the platform.

```
1   String orderForAccountUrl(Long accountId, Long orderId) {
2     return this.url + OandaConstants.ACCOUNTS_RESOURCE + TradingConstants.
      FWD_SLASH + accountId +
3       ordersResource + TradingConstants.FWD_SLASH + orderId;
4   }
5
6   HttpPatch createPatchCommand(Order < String, Long > order, Long
      accountId) throws Exception {
7     HttpPatch httpPatch = new HttpPatch(orderForAccountUrl(accountId,
      order.getOrderId()));
8     httpPatch.setHeader(this.authHeader);
9     List < NameValuePair > params = Lists.newArrayList();
10    params.add(new BasicNameValuePair(takeProfit, String.valueOf(order.
      getTakeProfit())));
11    params.add(new BasicNameValuePair(stopLoss, String.valueOf(order.
      getStopLoss())));
12    params.add(new BasicNameValuePair(units, String.valueOf(order.
      getUnits())));
13    params.add(new BasicNameValuePair(price, String.valueOf(order.
      getPrice())));
14    httpPatch.setEntity(new UrlEncodedFormEntity(params));
15    return httpPatch;
16  }
```

The creation of the patch command is very similar to the creation of the post command that we saw earlier. We create a list of NameValuePair objects and set the name/value pairs from the JSON keys/Order POJO, but only those that we are allowed to change for a pending order. We also bring into the mix a function to compute the URL to modify the order and other order-related services, which we will soon see and use in other places. For account ID 123456 and order 234567, the function would compute as follows:

```
1  https://api-fxtrade.oanda.com/v1/accounts/123456/orders/234567
```

Now turning our attention back to modifyOrder, it looks like this:

```
1   @Override
2   public boolean modifyOrder(Order < String, Long > order, Long
    accountId) {
3     CloseableHttpClient httpClient = getHttpClient();
4     try {
5       HttpPatch httpPatch = createPatchCommand(order, accountId);
6       LOG.info(TradingUtils.executingRequestMsg(httpPatch));
7       HttpResponse resp = httpClient.execute(httpPatch);
8       if (resp.getStatusLine().getStatusCode() == HttpStatus.SC_OK &&
9         resp.getEntity() != null) {
10        LOG.info("Order Modified->" + TradingUtils.responseToString(resp));
11        return true;
12      }
13      LOG.warn(String.format("order %s could not be modified.",
14        order.toString()));
15    } catch (Exception e) {
16      LOG.error(e);
17    } finally {
18      TradingUtils.closeSilently(httpClient);
19    }
20    return false;
21  }
```

The code looks quite straightforward. Once we have an instance of HttpPatch successfully set with all the values, we just post it to the platform. If the order is successfully modified, it returns HTTP code 200 in the header and the state of the modified order in the response. On receipt of code 200, we return true to indicate successful modification; otherwise, we return false.

```
1  ##header
2  HTTP/1.1 200 OK
3  Server: nginx/1.2.9
4  Content-Type: application/json
5  Content-Length: 284
```

```
1  ##response body
2  {
3      "id": 1001,
4      "instrument": "USD_JPY",
5      "units": 125,
```

```
 6        "side": "sell",
 7        "type": "limit",
 8        "time": "2015-09-22T00:00:00Z",
 9        "price": 122.15,
10        "takeProfit": 119.25,
11        "stopLoss": 125.00,
12        "expiry": "2015-09-25T00:00:00Z",
13        "upperBound": 0,
14        "lowerBound": 0,
15        "trailingStop": 0
16    }
```

The next one to elaborate on is closeOrder. For deleting or closing an order, it is sufficient to send an HttpDelete command to the URL returned by the orderForAccountUrl function. The code to do that is as follows:

```
 1    @Override
 2    public boolean closeOrder(Long orderId, Long accountId) {
 3    CloseableHttpClient httpClient = getHttpClient();
 4    try {
 5    HttpDelete httpDelete = new HttpDelete(orderForAccountUrl(accountId,
      orderId));
 6    httpDelete.setHeader(authHeader);
 7    LOG.info(TradingUtils.executingRequestMsg(httpDelete));
 8    HttpResponse resp = httpClient.execute(httpDelete);
 9    if (resp.getStatusLine().getStatusCode() == HttpStatus.SC_OK) {
10     LOG.info(String.format("Order %d successfully deleted for account
       %d", orderId, accountId));
11     return true;
12    } else {
13     LOG.warn(String.format(
14      "Order %d could not be deleted. Recd error code %d", orderId, resp
15      .getStatusLine().getStatusCode()));
16    }
17    } catch (Exception e) {
18    LOG.warn("error deleting order id:" + orderId, e);
19    } finally {
20    TradingUtils.closeSilently(httpClient);
21    }
22    return false;
23    }
```

If the order ID and and the account to which it belongs to are both valid, we should see an HTTP 200 returned in the header after a successful deletion of the order.

```
 1    HTTP/1.1 200 OK
 2    Content-Type: application/json
 3    Content-Length: 127
```

Now we turn our attention to implementation of rest of the methods, which are all order query methods, and use the old fashioned HttpGet to fetch order related information. Let's jump straight into the first one, pendingOrdersForAccount. This method returns a collection of orders that are pending and ready to be filled when the price is hit.

```
1   @Override
2   public Collection < Order < String, Long >>
    pendingOrdersForAccount(Long accountId) {
3    return this.pendingOrdersForAccount(accountId, null);
4   }
5
6   private Collection < Order < String, Long >>
    pendingOrdersForAccount(Long accountId,
7    TradeableInstrument < String > instrument) {
8    Collection < Order < String, Long >> pendingOrders = Lists.
    newArrayList();
9    CloseableHttpClient httpClient = getHttpClient();
10   try {
11    HttpUriRequest httpGet = new  HttpGet(this.url +
12     OandaConstants.ACCOUNTS_RESOURCE + TradingConstants.FWD_SLASH +
      accountId + ordersResource + (instrument != null ? "?\
13   instrument=" + instrument.getInstrument() :
14      StringUtils.EMPTY));
15    httpGet.setHeader(this.authHeader);
16    httpGet.setHeader(OandaConstants.UNIX_DATETIME_HEADER);
17    LOG.info(TradingUtils.executingRequestMsg(httpGet));
18    HttpResponse resp = httpClient.execute(httpGet);
19    String strResp = TradingUtils.responseToString(resp);
20    if (strResp != StringUtils.EMPTY) {
21     Object obj = JSONValue.parse(strResp);
22     JSONObject jsonResp = (JSONObject) obj;
23     JSONArray accountOrders = (JSONArray) jsonResp.get(orders);
24
25     for (Object o: accountOrders) {
26      JSONObject order = (JSONObject) o;
27      Order < String, Long > pendingOrder = parseOrder(order);
28      pendingOrders.add(pendingOrder);
29     }
30    } else {
31     TradingUtils.printErrorMsg(resp);
32    }
33   } catch (Exception e) {
34    LOG.error(e);
35   } finally {
36    TradingUtils.closeSilently(httpClient);
37   }
38   return pendingOrders;
39  }
```

The public method delegates to an internal private method that retrieves pending orders for an account and optionally filters for an instrument if provided. Since we want all orders irrespective of instrument, we pass a null for an instrument to this method. Let's take a closer look at the code that generates this URL with or without an instrument value passed in.

```
1  this.url + OandaConstants.ACCOUNTS_RESOURCE + TradingConstants.FWD_SLASH
   + accountId
2  + ordersResource + (instrument != null ? "?instrument="
3  + instrument.getInstrument() : StringUtils.EMPTY
```

If instrument is null then the output for account ID 123456 would be:

```
1  https://api-fxtrade.oanda.com/v1/accounts/123456/orders
```

But if an instrument EUR_USD is passed in, we get this result:

```
1  https://api-fxtrade.oanda.com/v1/accounts/123456/orders?instrument=EUR_
   USD
```

A sample JSON that would be returned when we ask for all orders looks like this:

```
1  {
2    "orders": [
3      {
4        "id": 1001,
5        "instrument": "USD_CAD",
6        "units": 100,
7        "side": "buy",
8        "type": "marketIfTouched",
9        "time": "1444116207000000",
10       "price": 1.3,
11       "takeProfit": 1.31,
12       "stopLoss": 1.2,
13       "expiry": "1444721003000000",
14       "upperBound": 0,
15       "lowerBound": 0,
16       "trailingStop": 0
17     },
18     {
19       "id": 1002,
20       "instrument": "EUR_USD",
21       "units": 150,
22       "side": "buy",
23       "type": "marketIfTouched",
24       "time": "1444108460000000",
25       "price": 1.115,
26       "takeProfit": 0,
```

```
27        "stopLoss": 0,
28        "expiry": "1444713259000000",
29        "upperBound": 0,
30        "lowerBound": 0,
31        "trailingStop": 0
32      }
33    ]
34  }
```

Now what remains is to parse this response into a collection of orders, which this method is contracted to return. The parseOrder private method does that for us for each order element in the JSON orders array.

```
1   private Order < String, Long > parseOrder(JSONObject order) {
2     final String orderInstrument = (String) order.get(instrument);
3     final Long orderUnits = (Long) order.get(units);
4     final TradingSignal orderSide = OandaUtils.toTradingSignal((String)
      order.get(side));
5     final OrderType orderType = OandaUtils.toOrderType((String) order.
      get(type));
6     final double orderTakeProfit = ((Number) order.get(takeProfit)).
      doubleValue();
7     final double orderStopLoss = ((Number) order.get(stopLoss)).
      doubleValue();
8     final double orderPrice = ((Number) order.get(price)).doubleValue();
9     final Long orderId = (Long) order.get(id);
10    Order < String, Long > pendingOrder = new Order < String, Long > (
11      new TradeableInstrument < String > (orderInstrument), orderUnits,
        orderSide, orderType,
12      orderTakeProfit, orderStopLoss, orderPrice);
13    pendingOrder.setOrderId(orderId);
14    return pendingOrder;
15  }
```

The next one we turn our attention to is the pendingOrdersForInstrument method. The mandate for this method is to find all orders across all accounts for a given instrument. We already have seen that we have a private method, which can return all orders for a given account and an instrument if provided. Therefore, what we need to do is get a list of all accounts that the trading account has and loop for each account and call this internal method to retrieve all orders. This is pretty much what this code does:

```
1   @Override
2   public Collection < Order < String, Long >> pendingOrdersForInstrument
    (TradeableInstrument < String > instrument) {
3     Collection < Account < Long >> accounts = this.accountDataProvider.
      getLatestAccountInfo();
4     Collection < Order < String, Long >> allOrders = Lists.newArrayList();
```

```
5    for (Account < Long > account: accounts) {
6      allOrders.addAll(this.pendingOrdersForAccount(account.getAccountId(),
       instrument));
7    }
8    return allOrders;
9    }
```

The implementation of this code paves the way for a very straightforward implementation of the allPendingOrders method:

```
1    @Override
2    public Collection<Order<String, Long>> allPendingOrders() {
3            return pendingOrdersForInstrument(null);
4    }
```

The last one left on our plate to describe is the pendingOrderForAccount method. This method retrieves a single order for a given account if we provide the precise order ID. This method calls the orderForAccountUrl to return the URL to request the information from. This method was called previously when we tried to modify an existing order using HttpPatch. This time we just need to use a different HTTP verb, HttpGet, to retrieve the order information from the same URL. A sample JSON response looks like this:

```
1    {
2        "id": 1001,
3        "instrument": "USD_JPY",
4        "units": 125,
5        "side": "sell",
6        "type": "marketIfTouched",
7        "time": "1444116207000000",
8        "price": 122.15,
9        "takeProfit": 119.25,
10       "stopLoss": 125.00,
11       "expiry": "1444721003000000",
12       "upperBound": 0,
13       "lowerBound": 0,
14       "trailingStop": 0
15   }
```

The code that initiates this kind of response is as follows:

```
1    @Override
2    public Order < String, Long > pendingOrderForAccount(Long orderId, Long
     accountId) {
3      CloseableHttpClient httpClient = getHttpClient();
4      try {
5        HttpUriRequest httpGet = new HttpGet(orderForAccountUrl(accountId,
         orderId));
6        httpGet.setHeader(this.authHeader);
```

```
7     httpGet.setHeader(OandaConstants.UNIX_DATETIME_HEADER);
8     LOG.info(TradingUtils.executingRequestMsg(httpGet));
9     HttpResponse resp = httpClient.execute(httpGet);
10    String strResp = TradingUtils.responseToString(resp);
11    if (strResp != StringUtils.EMPTY) {
12      JSONObject order = (JSONObject) JSONValue.parse(strResp);
13      return parseOrder(order);
14    } else {
15      TradingUtils.printErrorMsg(resp);
16    }
17    } catch (Exception e) {
18      LOG.error(e);
19    } finally {
20      TradingUtils.closeSilently(httpClient);
21    }
22    return null;
23  }
```

With this, we conclude our discussion of all the methods that OandaOrderManagement-Provider provides for order management services.

A Simple OrderInfoService

In keeping with the theme of encapsulating our provider methods behind a service, we need to code an OrderInfoService that encapsulates all the read-only methods of the OrderManagementProvider. It is fairly straightforward and reads as follows:

```
1   public class OrderInfoService < M, N, K > {
2
3     private final OrderManagementProvider < M,
4     N,
5     K > orderManagementProvider;
6
7     public OrderInfoService(OrderManagementProvider < M, N, K >
    orderManagementProvider) {
8       this.orderManagementProvider = orderManagementProvider;
9     }
10
11    public Collection < Order < N,
12    M >> allPendingOrders() {
13      return this.orderManagementProvider.allPendingOrders();
14    }
15
16    public Collection < Order < N,
17    M >> pendingOrdersForAccount(K accountId) {
18      return this.orderManagementProvider.pendingOrdersForAccount(accountId);
19    }
```

```
20
21    public Collection < Order < N,
22    M >>
23    pendingOrdersForInstrument(TradeableInstrument < N > instrument) {
24     return this.orderManagementProvider.pendingOrdersForInstrument
       (instrument);
25    }
26
27    public Order < N,
28    M > pendingOrderForAccount(M orderId, K accountId) {
29     return this.orderManagementProvider.pendingOrderForAccount(orderId,
       accountId);
30    }
31
32    public int findNetPositionCountForCurrency(String currency) {
33     Collection < Order < N, M >> allOrders = allPendingOrders();
34     int positionCount = 0;
35     for (Order < N, M > order: allOrders) {
36      positionCount +=
37        TradingUtils.getSign(order.getInstrument().getInstrument(),
38          order.getSide(), currency);
39     }
40     return positionCount;
41    }
42   }
```

All the methods except findNetPositionCountForCurrency delegate to the underlying Order-ManagementProvider to fulfill the requested information. Therefore, what remains to be discussed is the findNetPositionCountForCurrency method. Taking a closer look at the method code; it requests for all the pending orders across all accounts and calculates the net position for a currency by looking at the sign (-1 or +1) returned from the TradingUtils.getSign method. Recall that this method returns a -1 if we are selling the given currency or +1 if we are buying it. For example, if we sell the pair EUR_CHF by placing a limit order, passing the currency EUR would yield -1 and CHF +1.

Using the findNetPositionCountForCurrency method is not immediately apparent. However, it is quite useful from a risk-management perspective, which we discuss in later chapters, in order to know how much long or short we are on a given currency.

Validating Orders Before Execution: PreOrderValidationService

Before we turn our attention to discussing the service that encapsulates the order execution, modification, and deletion part, we discuss an important service that does some preorder execution checks, and only if those checks succeed, that an order is executed. This again is purely in place from a risk-management perspective and can be bypassed if needed. We will discuss in later chapters why it is important to have risk-management controls in place, especially on highly leveraged accounts. However, for our discussion, I came up with some rules or checks that must be done in order to give a green light to the order execution. These set of checks might not be sufficient for all cases, but the point is that we must do some due diligence upfront, before placing an order. The rules I came up with are as follows:

- Be overweight or underweight by a currency only up to a given level. This is to say that, you must have both long and short positions for, say, AUD, and if you do have net long or short positions, they must not exceed a given configurable number, say 4. So, if you already have four open trades like long AUD_USD, long AUD_CHF, short GBP_AUD, and short EUR_AUD, that means we are quite heavyweight with AUD, so any further long AUD positions must be rejected. For example, if a strategy recommends placing a market order for long AUD_JPY, this order must be rejected, as the mandate is not to exceed a long or short position if it is already at max level, four in this case.

- Do not trade a currency pair if its 10-year weighted moving average (WMA) is within x% of its historical high or low. This needs a bit of explanation. Let's say the 10-year WMA of EUR_USD is 1.3 and the current spot price is 1.08. You should be extremely reluctant to place a short EUR_USD order at this level. This is because, according to the rule, you can only go short, up to 10% (assuming x=10) of the 10-year WMA. So subtracting 10% of 1.3 from 1.3 gives 1.17. So if the price dips below that, the check will not allow to place a short EUR_USD order. Similarly, you could not go long EUR_USD if the current price is 1.45 (it is greater than 1.3+10% of 1.3 = 1.43).

- Don't place an order if an existing trade with the pair is already active. This is to ensure that you do not accidentally close/reduce an existing trading position by placing an order in the opposite direction or add to an existing position and double up on a trade.

These rules of course may not make complete sense and may go against the advice of your winning strategy, but the point is to have some sort of pre-validation rules that do not unnecessarily increase the risk in your portfolio. Of course, you are welcome to completely trash these rules and write your own. As long as you have some meaningful set of rules/checks, they always help you in the long run.

Now let's jump straight into the code, which attempts to program these rules in the service. We begin first by defining the constructor that accepts all the dependencies of this service.

```
1   public class PreOrderValidationService < M, N, K > {
2     private final TradeInfoService < M,
3     N,
4     K > tradeInfoService;
5     private final MovingAverageCalculationService < N >
6     movingAverageCalculationService;
```

```
7    private final BaseTradingConfig baseTradingConfig;
8    private final OrderInfoService < M,
9    N,
10   K > orderInfoService;
11   static final int TEN_YRS_IN_MTHS = 120;
12
13   public PreOrderValidationService(TradeInfoService < M, N, K >
     tradeInfoService,
14    MovingAverageCalculationService < N >
      movingAverageCalculationService,
15    BaseTradingConfig baseTradingConfig,
16    OrderInfoService < M, N, K > orderInfoService) {
17    this.tradeInfoService = tradeInfoService;
18    this.movingAverageCalculationService =
      movingAverageCalculationService;
19    this.baseTradingConfig = baseTradingConfig;
20    this.orderInfoService = orderInfoService;
21  }
```

The TradeInfoService is something we will cover later in this chapter. The methods
invoked to obtain various trade-related information are pretty self-explanatory in the
current context but will be elaborated on later. The rest, I believe, follow naturally from
our discussion of the validation rules. MovingAverageCalculationService is required
for computation of the WMA, the BaseTradingConfig is for various configuration
parameters, like maximum allowed net positions for a currency, and OrderInfoService
is for information regarding pending orders.

Let's now look at the service method that codes the first validation check in our list.

```
1    public boolean checkLimitsForCcy(TradeableInstrument < N > instrument,
     TradingSignal signal) {
2     String currencies[] = TradingUtils.splitInstrumentPair(instrument.
      getInstrument());
3     for (String currency: currencies) {
4      int positionCount =
5       this.tradeInfoService.findNetPositionCountForCurrency(currency) +
6       this.orderInfoService.findNetPositionCountForCurrency(currency);
7      int sign = TradingUtils.getSign(instrument.getInstrument(), signal,
8       currency);
9      int newPositionCount = positionCount + sign;
10     if (Math.abs(newPositionCount) >
11      this.baseTradingConfig.getMaxAllowedNetContracts() && Integer.
       signum(sign) == Integer.signum(positionCount)) {
12      LOG.warn(String.format(
13       "Cannot place trade %s because max limit exceeded. max allowed=%d
        and " + "current net positions=%d for currency %s"\
14    , instrument,
15      this.baseTradingConfig.getMaxAllowedNetContracts(),
```

```
16        newPositionCount, currency));
17     return false;
18   }
19 }
20 return true;
21 }
```

This method returns a false if the check fails; otherwise, it returns true. The method begins by first splitting the currency pair into individual currencies and, for each currency, getting the current state of affairs, i.e., the sum of all open trading positions and pending orders. This we call the current position count. So if we have four sell CHF trading positions and one pending order to buy CHF, our net position count would be -3. (Remember that negative numbers denote a sell position.) Therefore, if we want to place a new market order to buy USD_CHF, the TradingUtils.getSign would return -1 for CHF. This would increase our short CHF positions to 4 if we were to go ahead with this order. Now the evaluation of the check happens in this part of the code.

```
1 if (Math.abs(newPositionCount) >
2                         this.baseTradingConfig.
                          getMaxAllowedNetContracts() &&
3 Integer.signum(sign) == Integer.signum(positionCount)) {
```

If the maximum allowed net contracts for each currency is configured as 4, we are still in a position to place this market order, as the new position count will then take it to the maximum allowed level. Since we are actually comparing the absolute value as part of the if statement, we must also add the sign check to make sure that the future position count has the same sign as the sign returned by TradingUtils.getSign.

Now let's look at the service method code for our second validation check.

```
1  public boolean isInSafeZone(TradingSignal signal, double price,
   TradeableInstrument < N > instrument) {
2   double wma10yr = this.movingAverageCalculationService.calculateWMA(
3    instrument, TEN_YRS_IN_MTHS,
4    CandleStickGranularity.M);
5   final double max10yrWmaOffset = baseTradingConfig.
   getMax10yrWmaOffset();
6   double minPrice = (1.0 - max10yrWmaOffset) * wma10yr;
7   double maxPrice = (1.0 + max10yrWmaOffset) * wma10yr;
8   if ((signal == TradingSignal.SHORT && price > minPrice) || (signal ==
   TradingSignal.LONG && price <
9    maxPrice)) {
10    return true;
11   } else {
12   LOG.info(String.format(
13    "Rejecting %s %s because price %2.5f is 10pct on either side of wma
       10yr
```

```
14      price of % 2.5 f ",
15      signal, instrument, price, wma10yr));
16    return false;
17  }
18  }
```

We begin by calculating the 10-year WMA for this instrument by
passing monthly granularity as an input parameter. The value returned by
movingAverageCalculationService.calculateWMA is the basis for our safe zone
calculation. Assuming the value of getMax10yrWmaOffset is configured as 0.1 (10%), our
safe zone then becomes 10% on either side of this value. What that means is that we are
willing to place a short order only if the price fall from this value is less than or equal to
10%. Similarly, we are willing to place a long order only if the price increase is less than or
equal to 10%. Since this value is configurable, we can always broaden our safe zone.

Now for the last validation check from our discussion, the method code is as follows:

```
1   public boolean checkInstrumentNotAlreadyTraded(TradeableInstrument < N
    > instrument) {
2    Collection < K > accIds = this.tradeInfoService.findAllAccountsWithIns
     trumentTrades(instrument);
3    if (accIds.size() > 0) {
4     LOG.warn(String.format("Trade with instrument %s as one already
      exists", instrument));
5     return false;
6    } else {
7     Collection < Order < N, M >> pendingOrders = this.orderInfoService.
8     pendingOrdersForInstrument(instrument);
9     if (!pendingOrders.isEmpty()) {
10     LOG.warn(String.format("Pending order with instrument %s already
       exists", instrument));
11     return false;
12    }
13    return true;
14   }
15  }
```

Our method begins by calling on TradeInfoService to check if there are any
accounts that have an open trade position for the given instrument. If we do have any,
then we straightaway exit the method returning false. However, if no such accounts
exist, we check if there are any pending orders for the given instrument. If we do find
any pending orders, we again return false from the method or we return true. With this
we conclude our discussion of the service to pre-validate orders. The next logical step
is to move on TO the actual service, which places these orders after all the checks pass.
Remember that although some of these validation checks do not arguably fit in the grand
scheme of things, at least we all agree that we need to have a set of checks before we are
absolutely sure that an order needs to be placed.

Putting It All Together in an OrderExecutionService

We conclude our discussion of order-management services by diving deep into the OrderExecutionService. The design of this service is based on a queue, where orders are picked up. After all the checks pass, an order is sent to the platform. The idea is that, from our various strategies and maybe from other services, we can simply drop the order in a queue and rest is taken care of by this service, which is listening on this queue for new orders. By doing this, we have decoupled the act of arriving at a decision to place an order (based on a trading signal that our strategy has advised) for a given instrument and the mechanics of placing the order. Let's begin by looking at the constructor and the dependencies that it expects.

```
1   public class OrderExecutionService < M, N, K > implements Runnable {
2
3     private static final Logger LOG = Logger.
      getLogger(OrderExecutionService.class);
4
5     private final BlockingQueue < TradingDecision < N >> orderQueue;
6     private final AccountInfoService < K, N > accountInfoService;
7     private final OrderManagementProvider < M, N, K >
      orderManagementProvider;
8     private final BaseTradingConfig baseTradingConfig;
9     private final PreOrderValidationService < M, N, K >
      preOrderValidationService;
10    private final CurrentPriceInfoProvider < N >
      currentPriceInfoProvider;
11    private volatile boolean serviceUp = true;
12    Thread orderExecThread;
13
14    public OrderExecutionService(BlockingQueue < TradingDecision < N >>
      orderQueue,
15      AccountInfoService < K, N > accountInfoService,
16      OrderManagementProvider < M, N, K >
17      orderManagementProvider, BaseTradingConfig baseTradingConfig,
18      PreOrderValidationService < M, N, K > preOrderValidationService,
19      CurrentPriceInfoProvider < N > currentPriceInfoProvider) {
20      this.orderQueue = orderQueue;
21      this.accountInfoService = accountInfoService;
22      this.orderManagementProvider = orderManagementProvider;
23      this.baseTradingConfig = baseTradingConfig;
24      this.preOrderValidationService = preOrderValidationService;
25      this.currentPriceInfoProvider = currentPriceInfoProvider;
26    }
```

```
27    @PostConstruct
28    public void init() {
29     orderExecThread = new Thread(this, this.getClass().getSimpleName());
30     orderExecThread.start();
31    }
```

The first thing we notice is that our service implements the Runnable interface, which suggests that this service is going to spawn a thread to continuously monitor the order queue. The thread is initialized in the init method, which is automatically invoked by a DI framework like Spring once the application context is initialized (due to the @ PostConstruct annotation), or needs to be explicitly called if we are not using one. In our thread, we continuously monitor the order queue for a new order. Once an order is received from the queue, we bring these dependencies into play (the use of each will become evident soon). Let's look at the run method where all the action seems to happen.

```
1    @Override
2    public void run() {
3      while (serviceUp) {
4        try {
5          TradingDecision < N > decision = this.orderQueue.take();
6          if (!preValidate(decision)) {
7           continue;
8          }
9          Collection < K > accountIds = this.accountInfoService.
           findAccountsToTrade();
10         if (accountIds.isEmpty()) {
11          LOG.info("Not a single eligible account found as the reserve may
12           have been exhausted.
13           ");
14          continue;
15         }
16         Order < N, M > order = null;
17         if (decision.getLimitPrice() == 0.0) { // market order
18           order = new  Order < N, M > (decision.getInstrument(),
19            this.baseTradingConfig.getMaxAllowedQuantity(), decision.
             getSignal(),
20            OrderType.MARKET,  decision.getTakeProfitPrice(),
21            decision.getStopLossPrice());
22         } else {
23          order = new Order < N, M > (decision.getInstrument(),
24            this.baseTradingConfig.getMaxAllowedQuantity(), decision.
             getSignal(),
25            OrderType.LIMIT,
26            decision.getTakeProfitPrice(),  decision.getStopLossPrice(),
27            decision.getLimitPrice());
28         }
```

```
29        for (K accountId: accountIds) {
30          M orderId = this.orderManagementProvider.placeOrder(order,
            accountId);
31          if (orderId != null) {
32            order.setOrderId(orderId);
33          }
34          break;
35        }
36      } catch (Exception e) {
37        LOG.error(e);
38      }
39    }
40
41  }
42
43  private boolean preValidate(TradingDecision < N > decision) {
44    if (TradingSignal.NONE != decision.getSignal() &&
45    this.preOrderValidationService.checkInstrumentNotAlreadyTraded(
46      decision.getInstrument()) &&
47    this.preOrderValidationService.checkLimitsForCcy(
48      decision.getInstrument(), decision.getSignal())) {
49    Collection < TradeableInstrument < N >> instruments = Lists.
      newArrayList();
50    instruments.add(decision.getInstrument());
51    Map < TradeableInstrument < N > , Price < N >> priceMap =
52      this.currentPriceInfoProvider.getCurrentPricesForInstruments(instru
      ments);
53    if (priceMap.containsKey(decision.getInstrument())) {
54      Price < N > currentPrice = priceMap.get(decision.getInstrument());
55      return this.preOrderValidationService.isInSafeZone(decision.
        getSignal(),
56        decision.getSignal() ==
57        TradingSignal.LONG ? currentPrice.getAskPrice() : currentPrice.
          getBidPrice(),
58        decision.getInstrument());
59      }
60    }
61    return false;
62  }
```

Our run method will forever loop until the value of the volatile variable serviceUp is set to false.

We will come back to how to set this to false shortly to terminate the loop, and as a consequence the method that results in the termination of the thread. The this. orderQueue.take() statement blocks until an order is available in the queue to be processed. Assuming an order is available and taken off the queue, the first thing we do is make sure that it passes our series of validation checks in the preValidate method. This method just applies all the three validation checks we discussed in the previous section, but if we look carefully, it actually does an optimization. Since doing the safe zone checks requires a fetch of the last 10 years' worth of candlesticks data, this is only done if the other two checks pass.

Assuming our checks succeed, we now need to find accounts with which we can trade. Now if you recall the discussion about selecting accounts eligible for trade, there were also a set of checks that need to pass before an account is deemed eligible to trade, for instance, the amount available must be at least x% of the total amount. Again, you can call it a second level of checks, based on the account level. If no accounts are available, we leave the rest of the processing and go back to the start of the while loop. However, if we do find at least one account, we are now ready to place the order. To do so, we must first prepare an *Order* POJO from the TradingSignal instance that we picked up from the queue.

The first thing to decide is whether it's a market or a limit order. Reminding ourselves that a limit order must have a trigger price set, we check if the trading decision has a trigger price set. If it is set, then we prepare the Order POJO as type LIMIT; otherwise, it's a MARKET order. Now that we have a fully primed Order POJO to be sent across to place the order, we loop over all the eligible accounts that we have. As soon as we find the first one with which we are successful at placing the order (a valid orderId is returned when an order is placed successfully), we break out of the loop and then go back again to the beginning of the loop.

Coming back to the point, which was how the variable serviceUp can be set to false so that the thread can stop. For this we create a shutdown hook in the service, which again is invoked automatically by a DI framework when the application is being shut down. The magic happens due to the annotation @PreDestroy, which these frameworks deem as methods to be called before destroying the bean. Again if we are not using a DI framework, then one has to manually call the shutdown() method externally to terminate the thread.

```
1  @PreDestroy
2  public void shutDown() {
3    this.serviceUp = false;
4  }
```

With this we conclude our discussion about most of the stuff that you need to know about orders. Now it's time to turn our attention to what happens when these orders are executed and result in the creation of a trading position. A trading position equates to risk in your portfolio, and you must be ready to manage this position in order to minimize losses and maximize profits. We begin our detailed discussion by defining the Trade POJO.

Trade POJO Definition

The Trade POJO, like Order POJO, holds all the necessary information to manage trades and describe open trading positions in the system. As we will see, the two POJOs have lots of attributes in common, simply because an order, when executed, translates into an open position. Like an order, a trade must have an underlying instrument, stop-loss price, take-profit price, buy/sell side, etc. Let's discover the Trade POJO in more detail by looking at this code:

```
1    /**
2     *
3     * @param <M> The type of tradeId
4     * @param <N> The type of instrumentId in class TradeableInstrument
5     * @param <K> The type of accountId
6     * @see TradeableInstrument
7     */
8    public class Trade < M, N, K > {
9      private final M tradeId;
10     private final long units;
11     private final TradingSignal side;
12     private final TradeableInstrument < N > instrument;
13     private final DateTime tradeDate;
14     private final double takeProfitPrice,
15     executionPrice,
16     stopLoss;
17     private final K accountId;
18     private final String toStr;
19
20     public Trade(M tradeId, long units, TradingSignal side,
21       TradeableInstrument < N > instrument, DateTime tradeDate, double
       takeProfitPrice,
22       double executionPrice, double stopLoss, K accountId) {
23       this.tradeId = tradeId;
24       this.units = units;
25       this.side = side;
26       this.instrument = instrument;
27       this.tradeDate = tradeDate;
28       this.takeProfitPrice = takeProfitPrice;
29       this.executionPrice = executionPrice;
30       this.stopLoss = stopLoss;
31       this.accountId = accountId;
32       this.toStr = String.format(
33         "Trade Id=%d, Units=%d, Side=%s, Instrument=%s, TradeDate=%s,
         TP=%3.5f,
34         Price = % 3.5 f, SL = % 3.5 f ",
35         tradeId, units, side, instrument, tradeDate.toString(),
         takeProfitPrice,
36         executionPrice, stopLoss);
37     }
38
39     @Override
40     public int hashCode() {
41       final int prime = 31;
```

```
42    int result = 1;
43    result = prime * result + ((accountId == null) ? 0 : accountId.
      hashCode());
44    result = prime * result + ((tradeId == null) ? 0 : tradeId.
      hashCode());
45    return result;
46   }
47
48   @Override
49   public boolean equals(Object obj) {
50    if (this == obj)
51     return true;
52    if (obj == null)
53     return false;
54    if (getClass() != obj.getClass())
55     return false;
56    @SuppressWarnings("unchecked")
57    Trade < M, N, K > other = (Trade < M, N, K > ) obj;
58    if (accountId == null) {
59     if (other.accountId != null)
60      return false;
61    } else if (!accountId.equals(other.accountId))
62     return false;
63     if (tradeId == null) {
64      if (other.tradeId != null)
65       return false;
66     } else if (!tradeId.equals(other.tradeId))
67      return false;
68     return true;
69    }
70
71   public double getStopLoss() {
72    return stopLoss;
73   }
74
75   public K getAccountId() {
76    return accountId;
77   }
78
79   @Override
80   public String toString() {
81    return toStr;
82   }
83
84   public double getExecutionPrice() {
85    return  executionPrice;
86   }
87
```

```
88    public M getTradeId() {
89      return tradeId;
90    }
91
92    public long getUnits() {
93      return units;
94    }
95
96    public TradingSignal getSide() {
97      return side;
98    }
99
100   public TradeableInstrument < N > getInstrument() {
101     return instrument;
102   }
103
104   public DateTime getTradeDate() {
105     return tradeDate;
106   }
107
108   public double getTakeProfitPrice() {
109     return  takeProfitPrice;
110   }
111   }
```

Looking at this code, note that it bears quite a bit of resemblance to the Order POJO in terms of the attributes. Apart from that, the POJO looks fairly simply. Hence, we can move on to the discussion of the trade management provider interface definition.

Trade Management Provider Interface

Just like its cousin, OrderManagementProvider, TradeManagementProvider has very similar actions except one notable one. From the CRUD set of operations, the provider provides all except the C. This is because only an order placed and filled can create a trade and you can only then modify, close, or retrieve information regarding the trade. Let's move straight to its definition:

```
1    /**
2     * A provider of RUD operations on a single Trade. Normally Trades
3     * are grouped under an account, so in order to perform these
4     * operations, a valid accountId is normally required. Some providers
5     * may just have the concept of a single account, so any operation on
6     * the Trade may always default to that single account, in which case
7     * the accountId may be null.
8     * A bulk operation to closeAll trades is deliberately left out to avoid
9     * potential misuse.
10    *
```

```
11    * @param <M> The type of tradeId
12    * @param <N> The type of instrumentId in class TradeableInstrument
13    * @param <K> The type of accountId
14    * @see TradeableInstrument
15    */
16   public interface TradeManagementProvider < M, N, K > {
17    /**
18     * Modify an existing trade by providing accountId and tradeId to
19     * identify the trade. In some cases the tradeId may be sufficient to
20     * identify the trade and therefore accountId may be null. Only
21     * stopLoss and takeProfit parameters for the trade can be modified
22     * through this operation.
23     * @param accountId
24     * @param tradeId
25     * @param stopLoss
26     * @param takeProfit
27     * @return boolean to indicate whether the modification was
28     * successful or not.
29     */
30    boolean modifyTrade(K accountId, M tradeId, double stopLoss, double
      takeProfit);
31
32    /**
33     * Close an existing trade by providing accountId and tradeId to
34     * identify a given trade. Again, the accountId may be optional to
35     * close the trade
36     * @param tradeId
37     * @param accountId
38     * @return boolean to indicate when the trade was successfully
39     *  closed or not.
40     */
41    boolean closeTrade(M tradeId, K accountId);
42
43    /**
44     * Retrieve trade for the given tradeId and/or accountId
45     *
46     * @param tradeId
47     * @param accountId
48     * @return a Trade or null if not found.
49     */
50    Trade < M,
51    N,
52    K > getTradeForAccount(M tradeId, K accountId);
53
54    /**
55     * All Trades for a given account or an empty collection if none
56     * found. The ordering of trades such as by instruments or in
57     * chronological order is not guaranteed.
```

```
58    *
59    * @param accountId
60    * @return a Collection of trades for the given account Id.
61    */
62    Collection < Trade < M,
63    N,
64    K >> getTradesForAccount(K accountId);
65  }
```

This looks remarkably similar, right? Except of course a missing placeTrade method, the reason for which we discussed earlier.

A Concrete Implementation for TradeManagementProvider

The OANDA API implementation OandaTradeManagementProvider has lots of things in common with its Order implementation counterpart, as you might expect. Since a lot of the discussion around the Order implementation applies to the Trade implementation, we will just jump straight into the code and point out any differences if applicable. Apart from that, most of the principles applicable to the Order implementation are applicable here. We begin as usual by defining the provider class, its constructor, and the JSON keys used:

```
1   import static com.precioustech.fxtrading.oanda.restapi.OandaJsonKeys.id;
2   import static com.precioustech.fxtrading.oanda.restapi.OandaJsonKeys.
    instrument;
3   import static com.precioustech.fxtrading.oanda.restapi.OandaJsonKeys.
    price;
4   import static com.precioustech.fxtrading.oanda.restapi.OandaJsonKeys.
    side;
5   import static com.precioustech.fxtrading.oanda.restapi.OandaJsonKeys.
    stopLoss;
6   import static com.precioustech.fxtrading.oanda.restapi.OandaJsonKeys.
    takeProfit;
7   import static com.precioustech.fxtrading.oanda.restapi.OandaJsonKeys.
    time;
8   import static com.precioustech.fxtrading.oanda.restapi.OandaJsonKeys.
    trades;
9   import static com.precioustech.fxtrading.oanda.restapi.OandaJsonKeys.
    units;
10
11  public class OandaTradeManagementProvider implements
    TradeManagementProvider < Long, String, Long > {
12    private final String url;
13    private final BasicHeader authHeader;
14
```

```
15    public OandaTradeManagementProvider(String url, String accessToken) {
16      this.url = url;
17      this.authHeader = OandaUtils.createAuthHeader(accessToken);
18    }
```

As seen from this listing, the constructor has one less dependency of
AccountDataProvider compared to the Order counterpart. We can appreciate this
difference, as a trading position is already attached to an account, while for an Order, we
can choose which account we want to use. To fetch the list of available accounts, we need
the services of AccountDataProvider. The rest of the stuff is fairly straightforward and we
can progress to the definition of modifyTrade. Remember that you can only modify the
following attributes of a trade:

- takeProfit
- stopLoss

```
1   private static final String tradesResource = "/trades";
2
3   String getTradeForAccountUrl(Long tradeId, Long accountId) {
4     return this.url + OandaConstants.ACCOUNTS_RESOURCE +
5       TradingConstants.FWD_SLASH + accountId + tradesResource +
      TradingConstants.FWD_SLASH + tradeId;
6   }
7
8   HttpPatch createPatchCommand(Long accountId, Long tradeId, double
    stopLoss, double takeProfit)
9   throws Exception {
10    HttpPatch httpPatch = new HttpPatch(getTradeForAccountUrl(tradeId,
      accountId));
11    httpPatch.setHeader(this.authHeader);
12    List < NameValuePair > params = Lists.newArrayList();
13    params.add(new BasicNameValuePair(OandaJsonKeys.takeProfit,  String.
      valueOf(takeProfit)));
14    params.add(new BasicNameValuePair(OandaJsonKeys.stopLoss,  String.
      valueOf(stopLoss)));
15    httpPatch.setEntity(new       UrlEncodedFormEntity(params));
16    return httpPatch;
17    }
18
19    @Override
20    public boolean modifyTrade(Long accountId, Long tradeId, double
    stopLoss, double takeProfit) {
21    CloseableHttpClient httpClient = getHttpClient();
22    try {
23      HttpPatch httpPatch = createPatchCommand(accountId, tradeId,
      stopLoss,
24       takeProfit);
```

```
25      LOG.info(TradingUtils.executingRequestMsg(httpPatch));
26      HttpResponse resp = httpClient.execute(httpPatch);
27      if (resp.getStatusLine().getStatusCode() == HttpStatus.SC_OK) {
28       if (resp.getEntity() != null) {
29        LOG.info("Trade Modified->" + TradingUtils.
           responseToString(resp));
30       } else {
31        LOG.warn(String.format(
32         "trade %d could not be modified with stop loss %3.5f and take
           profit % 3.5 f.httpcode = % d ",
33         tradeId, stopLoss, takeProfit, resp.getStatusLine().
           getStatusCode()));
34       }
35       return true;
36      } else {
37       LOG.warn(String.format("trade %d could not be modified with stop
          loss %3.5f. http code=%d",
38        tradeId, stopLoss, resp.getStatusLine().getStatusCode()));
39      }
40     } catch (Exception e) {
41      LOG.error(e);
42     } finally {
43      TradingUtils.closeSilently(httpClient);
44     }
45     return false;
46    }
```

We begin our discussion by looking at the getTradeForAccountUrl function that
computes the REST resource URL that we need to send our patch request to, in order
to modify the trade. For account ID 123456 and trade ID 234567, the function would
compute as follows:

```
1    https://api-fxtrade.oanda.com/v1/accounts/123456/trades/234567
```

Once the URL is computed, we can create an instance of the HttpPatch object to
prepare our patch command. This time for the list of NameValuePair objects we just have
to create two of them for take-profit and stop-loss. The list can then be URL-encoded
and set on the instance of the HttpPatch object. At this point we are ready to fire off the
modification request to the platform. A successful modification would return an HTTP
header like this:

```
1    HTTP/1.1 200 OK
2    Content-Type: application/json
3    Content-Length: 179
```

Once we receive an HTTP status code 200, we can return true from the method.
Otherwise, we return a false in case of another code or error. This is it; that's all there is
to the modifyTrade method.

The next one on our list is the closeTrade method. It is pretty much identical to the closeOrder method and the discussion of the order counterpart applies here. Therefore, listing the code should suffice:

```
1   @Override
2   public boolean closeTrade(Long tradeId, Long accountId) {
3    CloseableHttpClient httpClient = getHttpClient();
4    try {
5     HttpDelete httpDelete = new HttpDelete(getTradeForAccountUrl(tradeId,
6      accountId));
7     httpDelete.setHeader(authHeader);
8     LOG.info(TradingUtils.executingRequestMsg(httpDelete));
9     HttpResponse resp = httpClient.execute(httpDelete);
10    if (resp.getStatusLine().getStatusCode() == HttpStatus.SC_OK) {
11     LOG.info(String.format("Trade %d successfully closed for account %d",
12      tradeId, accountId));
13     return true;
14    } else {
15     LOG.warn(String.format("Trade %d could not be closed. Recd error
        code %d",
16      tradeId,  resp.getStatusLine().getStatusCode()));
17    }
18   } catch (Exception e) {
19    LOG.warn("error deleting trade id:" + tradeId, e);
20   } finally  {
21    TradingUtils.closeSilently(httpClient);
22   }
23   return false;
24  }
```

Turning our attention to the R operation for trades, we will observe that there is a remarkable resemblance to the Order counterpart. Let's first look at the method to fetch all trades for an account:

```
1   String getTradesInfoUrl(Long accountId) {
2    return this.url + OandaConstants.ACCOUNTS_RESOURCE + TradingConstants.
     FWD_SLASH + accountId + tradesResource;
3   }
4   @Override
5   public Collection < Trade < Long, String, Long >>
     getTradesForAccount(Long accountId) {
6    Collection < Trade < Long, String, Long >> allTrades = Lists.
     newArrayList();
7    CloseableHttpClient httpClient = getHttpClient();
8    try {
9     HttpUriRequest httpGet = new HttpGet(getTradesInfoUrl(accountId));
10    httpGet.setHeader(this.authHeader);
11    httpGet.setHeader(OandaConstants.UNIX_DATETIME_HEADER);
```

```
12      LOG.info(TradingUtils.executingRequestMsg(httpGet));
13      HttpResponse resp = httpClient.execute(httpGet);
14      String strResp = TradingUtils.responseToString(resp);
15      if (strResp != StringUtils.EMPTY) {
16       Object obj = JSONValue.parse(strResp);
17       JSONObject jsonResp = (JSONObject) obj;
18       JSONArray accountTrades = (JSONArray) jsonResp.get(trades);
19       for (Object accountTrade: accountTrades) {
20        JSONObject trade = (JSONObject) accountTrade;
21        Trade < Long, String, Long > tradeInfo = parseTrade(trade,
             accountId);
22        allTrades.add(tradeInfo);
23       }
24      } else {
25       TradingUtils.printErrorMsg(resp);
26      }
27     } catch (Exception ex) {
28      LOG.error(ex);
29     } finally {
30      TradingUtils.closeSilently(httpClient);
31     }
32     return allTrades;
33    }
```

We begin by calling getTradesInfoUrl to compute the URL that can be fired off to the platform to retrieve all the orders for an account. For an account 123456, the method would return the value:

```
1    https://api-fxtrade.oanda.com/v1/accounts/123456/trades
```

A successful call would result in a JSON payload like the following being returned from the platform:

```
1    {
2       "trades": [
3         {
4           "id": 1800805337,
5           "units": 3000,
6           "side": "sell",
7           "instrument": "CHF_JPY",
8           "time": "1426660416000000",
9           "price": 120.521,
10          "takeProfit": 105.521,
11          "stopLoss": 121.521,
12          "trailingStop": 0,
13          "trailingAmount": 0
14        },
```

```
15        {
16            "id": 1800511850,
17            "units": 3000,
18            "side": "buy",
19            "instrument": "USD_CHF",
20            "time": "1426260592000000",
21            "price": 1.0098,
22            "takeProfit": 1.15979,
23            "stopLoss": 0.9854,
24            "trailingStop": 0,
25            "trailingAmount": 0
26        },
27    ]
28  }
```

Now what remains is to parse such a payload to create our collection of trades to be returned. Since it's a JSONArray of *trades*, we need to write a for loop to process each element and delegate the attributes parsing to the parseTrade method, as shown here, to create and return the Trade POJO.

```
1    private Trade < Long, String, Long > parseTrade(JSONObject trade, Long
     accountId) {
2     final Long tradeTime = Long.parseLong(trade.get(time).toString());
3     final Long tradeId = (Long) trade.get(id);
4     final Long tradeUnits = (Long) trade.get(units);
5     final TradingSignal tradeSignal = OandaUtils.toTradingSignal((String)
       trade.get(side));
6     final TradeableInstrument < String > tradeInstrument = new
      TradeableInstrument < String > ((String) trade
7      .get(instrument));
8     final double tradeTakeProfit = ((Number) trade.get(takeProfit)).
       doubleValue();
9     final double tradeExecutionPrice = ((Number) trade.get(price)).
       doubleValue();
10    final double tradeStopLoss = ((Number) trade.get(stopLoss)).
       doubleValue();
11
12    return new Trade < Long, String, Long > (tradeId, tradeUnits,
      tradeSignal, tradeInstrument, new DateTime(
13      TradingUtils.toMillisFromNanos(tradeTime)), tradeTakeProfit,
        tradeExecutionPrice, tradeStopLoss,
14    accountId);
15
16  }
```

The parsing logic is self-explanatory. The last one to discuss is retrieving a trade with a given trade ID and a given account ID.

```
1    @Override
2    public Trade < Long, String, Long > getTradeForAccount(Long tradeId,
     Long accountId) {
3      CloseableHttpClient httpClient = getHttpClient();
4      try {
5      HttpUriRequest httpGet = new HttpGet(getTradeForAccountUrl(tradeId,
       accountId));
6      httpGet.setHeader(this.authHeader);
7      httpGet.setHeader(OandaConstants.UNIX_DATETIME_HEADER);
8      LOG.info(TradingUtils.executingRequestMsg(httpGet));
9      HttpResponse resp = httpClient.execute(httpGet);
10     String strResp = TradingUtils.responseToString(resp);
11     if (strResp != StringUtils.EMPTY) {
12       JSONObject trade = (JSONObject) JSONValue.parse(strResp);
13       return parseTrade(trade, accountId);
14     } else {
15       TradingUtils.printErrorMsg(resp);
16     }
17     } catch (Exception ex) {
18     LOG.error(ex);
19     } finally {
20     TradingUtils.closeSilently(httpClient);
21     }
22     return null;
23   }
```

The method begins by calling the getTradeForAccountUrl function to compute the
URL for a given account and trade ID that should be fired to retrieve the JSON response.
If the trade ID is not found, we should technically receive an HTTP 404 response, in
which case we return a null. If we do get a valid JSON payload back, it should look like the
following:

```
1    {
2      "id": 1800805337,
3      "units": 3000,
4      "side": "sell",
5      "instrument": "CHF_JPY",
6      "time": "1426660416000000",
7      "price": 120.521,
8      "takeProfit": 105.521,
9      "stopLoss": 121.521,
10     "trailingStop": 0,
11     "trailingAmount": 0
12   }
```

The rest of the code involves invoking the parseTrade method to parse this JSON
payload and return the Trade POJO.

Encapsulating Read Operations Behind TradeInfoService

This service is arguably a really nice and simple but yet powerful example of why we should embrace the concept of services. It demonstrates how a service could, for example, introduce an internal cache as an optimization step to avoid going to the data provider for the same data again and again, be it a REST service or a database fetch via DAO. If we were directly going to the provider for data, even though it does not change very often, we would just be introducing unwanted latency and re-computations in the request operation even though the results are exactly the same as the last one. By using a service, we can introduce an internal cache to manage data provided from the data provider (database or an external source like REST) and store computed results that may consume CPU cycles or are resource intensive. Let's start by looking at the definition and constructor for this service:

```
1   /**
2    * A service that provides information regarding a Trade. It maintains
3    * an internal cache of all trades grouped per account in order to
4    * minimize latency.
5    *
6    * <p>
7    * It is strongly recommended to use this service as a singleton and
8    * not create multiple instances in order to minimize the memory
9    * footprint incurred by the cache and the latency induced during the
10   * cache construction. This class exposes a method to refresh the
11   * cache if required in a ThreadSafe manner and it is imperative that
12   * it be called for events which close, create or modify a trade in
13   * order to keep the cache in sync with the trades on the trading
14   * platform. If such event callback is not supported by the trading
15   * platform, then a timer based approach can be implemented externally
         that periodically refreshes the cache.
16   * </p>
17   * <p>
18   * The accountId is the key of the internal cache. If accountId is a
19   * user defined object, rather than the commonly used ones such as
20   * Integer, Long, or String, make sure hashCode() and equals() methods
         are implemented.
21   * </p>
22   *
23   * @param <M>
24   *            The type of tradeId
25   * @param <N>
26   *            The type of instrumentId in class TradeableInstrument
27   * @param <K>
28   *            The type of accountId
29   * @see TradeableInstrument
```

```
30    * @see refreshTradesForAccount
31    */
32   public class TradeInfoService < M, N, K > {
33
34    private final TradeManagementProvider < M,
35    N,
36    K > tradeManagementProvider;
37    private final AccountInfoService < K,
38    N > accountInfoService;
39
40    public TradeInfoService(TradeManagementProvider < M, N, K >
      tradeManagementProvider,
41     AccountInfoService < K, N > accountInfoService) {
42     this.tradeManagementProvider = tradeManagementProvider;
43     this.accountInfoService = accountInfoService;
44   }
```

We have two dependencies that are provided to the constructor, namely the
TradeManagementProvider and AccountInfoService. We will see soon that as part of the
initialization process, the first thing the service does is create an internal cache of trades
per instrument and per account.

```
1    //K -> account id type
2    private final ConcurrentMap < K, Map < TradeableInstrument < N > ,
3    Collection < Trade < M, N, K >>> > tradesCache = Maps
4    .newConcurrentMap();
5    private final ReadWriteLock lock = new ReentrantReadWriteLock();
6    /**
7     * A method that initializes the service and primarily the cache of
8     * trades per account for the service. This method is automatically
9     * invoked by Spring Framework(if used) once the ApplicationContext
10    * is initialized. If not using Spring, the consumer of this service
11    * must call this method first in order to construct the cache.
12    *
13    * @see TradeManagementProvider
14    */
15   @PostConstruct
16   public void init() {
17    reconstructCache();
18   }
19
20   private void reconstructCache() {
21    lock.writeLock().lock();
22    try {
23     tradesCache.clear();
24     Collection < Account < K >> accounts - this.accountInfoService.
       getAllAccounts();
```

```
25      for (Account < K > account: accounts) {
26       Map < TradeableInstrument < N > , Collection < Trade < M, N, K >>>
         tradeMap =
27        getTradesPerInstrumentForAccount(account.getAccountId());
28       tradesCache.put(account.getAccountId(),  tradeMap);
29      }
30     } finally {
31      lock.writeLock().unlock();
32     }
33    }
34    private Map < TradeableInstrument < N > , Collection < Trade < M, N, K
      >>>
35     getTradesPerInstrumentForAccount(K accountId) {
36      Collection < Trade < M, N, K >> trades =
37       this.tradeManagementProvider.getTradesForAccount(accountId);
38      Map < TradeableInstrument < N > , Collection < Trade < M, N, K >>>
        tradeMap =
39      Maps.newHashMap();
40      for (Trade < M, N, K > ti: trades) {
41       Collection < Trade < M, N, K >> tradeLst = null;
42       if (tradeMap.containsKey(ti.getInstrument())) {
43        tradeLst = tradeMap.get(ti.getInstrument());
44       } else {
45        tradeLst = Lists.newArrayList();
46        tradeMap.put(ti.getInstrument(),  tradeLst);
47       }
48       tradeLst.add(ti);
49      }
50      return tradeMap;
51    }
```

As you can see, the init() method, which automatically gets invoked by DI frameworks like Spring, invokes the internal method reconstructCache(). This method begins by first seeking an exclusive write lock that makes sure no other thread is either reading or writing from the internal tradesCache. Recall that a ReadWriteLock allows access to multiple readers but only to a single writer. Therefore, rightly so, in order to preserve the consistency of the cache and what other threads view as the state of the cache, we seek the writeLock before updating the cache, putting other threads in the wait state should they try to read or write from the cache.

Once the write lock is granted, we have the permission to start re-populating the cache. Since we have to organize all trades per instrument first and then the resulting map of instrument-trade list per account ID, we begin by obtaining a list of all accounts using accountInfoService.getAllAccounts(). For each of the accounts in the collection of accounts in a loop, we compute the map of collection of trades per instrument by invoking the internal method getTradesPerInstrumentForAccount. This method in turn uses tradeManagementProvider.getTradesForAccount to get all trades for the given account ID. Once we have all the trades, we can loop over them to put them in a map keyed by the instrument that they represent the open position for. This is what needs to happen to create this internal cache.

We should now be able to service lots of queries around trades without having to go to the underlying provider. We discuss later how and when this cache gets refreshed. First let's start looking at all the services this service offers and how these services use the cache to service the request. We begin with a very simple one—isTradeExistsForInstru ment, which will be used by other service methods as well.

```
1   /**
2    *
3    * @param instrument
4    * @return boolean to indicate whether a trade with given instrument
5    exists. */
6   public boolean isTradeExistsForInstrument(TradeableInstrument < N >
    instrument) {
7     lock.readLock().lock();
8     try {
9       for (K accountId: this.tradesCache.keySet()) {
10        if (isTradeExistsForInstrument(instrument, accountId)) {
11          return true;
12        }
13      }
14    } finally {
15      lock.readLock().unlock();
16    }
17    return false;
18  }
19  private boolean isTradeExistsForInstrument(TradeableInstrument < N >
    instrument, K accountId) {
20    Map < TradeableInstrument < N > , Collection < Trade < M, N, K >>>
      tradesForAccount =
21      this.tradesCache.get(accountId);
22    synchronized(tradesForAccount) {
23      if (TradingUtils.isEmpty(tradesForAccount)) {
24        return false;
25      }
26      return tradesForAccount.containsKey(instrument);
27    }
28
29  }
```

The method begins by seeking a ReadLock to read data from the cache. This involves looping over all available account ID keys of the cache and trying to ascertain if an instrument key exists in the underlying map. This is encapsulated in the private overloaded method with the same name. You might ask why are we synchronizing on the underlying map, which is the value in the cache that's keyed by account ID? The answer lies in the method refreshTradesForAccount:

```
1   /**
2    * A convenient method to refresh the internal cache of trades for an
3    * account in a ThreadSafe manner. Ideally this method should be
4    * invoked when the Trading platform notifies of a Trading event such
5    * as a creation of Trade when an Order is filled or the Trade is
         settled
6    * when a stopLoss or a takeProfit level is hit.
7    *
8    * @param accountId
9    */
10  public void refreshTradesForAccount(K accountId) {
11    Map < TradeableInstrument < N > , Collection < Trade < M, N, K >>>
      tradeMap =
12    getTradesPerInstrumentForAccount(accountId);
13    Map < TradeableInstrument < N > , Collection < Trade < M, N, K >>>
      oldTradeMap = tradesCache.get(accountId);
14    synchronized(oldTradeMap) {
15      oldTradeMap.clear();
16      oldTradeMap.putAll(tradeMap);
17    }
18
19  }
```

In summary, this method gives external clients of this service the ability to refresh the cache based on an event that they deem might require the cache to be refreshed for a given account ID. As we will discuss in later chapters, we can register handlers for various platform events like OrderFilled, for which we receive a callback when, for example, a pending order is filled. This event results in the creation of a new trade on the platform, which means our cache needs updating and brought in sync with the platform. When the underlying value map for the given account ID needs to be refreshed, we must make sure that the refresh code is *synchronized* on the underlying value map. This is why we see these *synchronized* blocks of code in the methods, which guarantees that if the map is being refreshed as a result of event, another reader waits and, vice versa, the refresh process waits until the read is finished.

The next service method we discuss is getTradesForAccountAndInstrument, which as the name says, retrieves a list of trades for a given account ID and instrument.

```
1   /**
2    * @param accountId
3    * @param instrument
4    * @return a Collection of Trades for a given instrument and for a given
```

```
5    * account.An empty Collection is returned if none found.
6    */
7    public Collection < Trade < M, N, K >> getTradesForAccountAndInstrume
     nt(K accountId,
8     TradeableInstrument < N > instrument) {
9     Map < TradeableInstrument < N > , Collection < Trade < M, N, K >>>
      tradesForAccount =
10      this.tradesCache.get(accountId);
11    synchronized(tradesForAccount) {
12     if (!TradingUtils.isEmpty(tradesForAccount) &&
13      tradesForAccount.containsKey(instrument))  {
14      return Lists.newArrayList(tradesForAccount.get(instrument));
15     }
16    }
17    return Collections.emptyList();
18   }
```

This service method code is fairly straightforward. The only thing worth mentioning again is the use of synchronized block to access the value map for the given account ID. The rest of the code is self-explanatory. The next one and again a very simple one is getTradesForAccount. This method returns all trades for a given account ID.

```
1    /**
2     *
3     * @param accountId
4     * @return a Collection of all Trades for a given accountId. An empty
5     * Collection is returned if none found.
6     */
7    public Collection < Trade < M, N, K >> getTradesForAccount(K accountId)
     {
8     Map < TradeableInstrument < N > , Collection < Trade < M, N, K >>>
      tradesForAccount =
9      this.tradesCache.get(accountId);
10    Collection < Trade < M, N, K >> trades = Lists.newArrayList();
11    synchronized(tradesForAccount) {
12     if (TradingUtils.isEmpty(tradesForAccount)) {
13      return trades;
14     }
15     for (Collection < Trade < M, N, K >> tradeLst: tradesForAccount.
       values()) {
16       trades.addAll(tradeLst);
17     }
18    }
19    return trades;
20   }
```

The same principle applies as usual to this code. We get the map of trades keyed by instrument for a given account ID. We loop for all entries in the map in a *synchronized* block and add the values of the map entry in a collection and return it.

The next method we discuss, getAllTrades, returns a collection of all trades for each account. The code involves looping through all account IDs, i.e., the keys of our cache, and for each key, it calls the method getTradesForAccount and adds the collection of trades to an existing collection, which contains all trades fetched for previous keys (account IDs).

```
1   /**
2    * @return a Collection of all trades that belong to all accounts for the
3    user */
4   public Collection < Trade < M, N, K >> getAllTrades() {
5    lock.readLock().lock();
6    try {
7     Collection < Trade < M, N, K >> trades = Lists.newArrayList();
8     for (K accId: this.tradesCache.keySet()) {
9      trades.addAll(getTradesForAccount(accId));
10    }
11    return trades;
12   } finally {
13    lock.readLock().unlock();
14   }
15  }
```

We can use this internal cache and derive some other useful information such as:

- What is the net count of positions for a given currency?

- Find all accounts that have trades for a given instrument.

- What is the value of total open positions?

We are going to code the first two questions to demonstrate how quickly we can get answers to various questions using this cache. The first one is called findNetPositionCountForCurrency, and it returns the net count of open positions for the given currency.

```
1   /**
2    *
3    * @param currency
4    * @return the net position for a given currency considering all Trades
5    *  for all Accounts. A negative value suggests that the system has net
6    *       short position for the given currency, while a positive
               value
7    *       suggests a net long position.
8    * @see TradingUtils#getSign(String,
9    *     com.precioustech.fxtrading.TradingSignal,  String)
10   */
```

```
11  public int findNetPositionCountForCurrency(String currency) {
12    int posCt = 0;
13    lock.readLock().lock();
14    try {
15      for (K accountId: this.tradesCache.keySet()) {
16        posCt += findNetPositionCountForCurrency(currency, accountId);
17      }
18    } finally {
19      lock.readLock().unlock();
20    }
21    return posCt;
22  }
23
24  private int findNetPositionCountForCurrency(String currency, K
    accountId) {
25    Map < TradeableInstrument < N > , Collection < Trade < M, N, K >>>
      tradeMap = this.tradesCache.get(accountId);
26    synchronized(tradeMap) {
27      if (TradingUtils.isEmpty(tradeMap)) {
28        return 0;
29      } else {
30        int positionCtr = 0;
31        for (Collection < Trade < M, N, K >> trades: tradeMap.values()) {
32          for (Trade < M, N, K > tradeInfo: trades) {
33            positionCtr += TradingUtils.getSign(tradeInfo.getInstrument().
            getInstrument(),
34              tradeInfo.getSide(), currency);
35          }
36        }
37        return positionCtr;
38      }
39    }
40  }
```

From this code, you can see that most of the work is done in the internal overloaded method with the same name. The public API method just loops through the account ID keys in the cache and delegates to the private method. The private method, as we will soon see, returns a net count of positions for the given currency and account. This result is added to a running count of positions, which, after the loop terminates, is returned from the method as the final answer.

Now, returning to the internal private method findNetPositionCountForCurrency, the code is extremely straightforward. For each instance of the account ID key, we get the map of trades keyed by the instrument. For each of the trades in the list of trades for the given instrument, we just delegate to our versatile function TradingUtils.getSign, which does all the computation. Notice that we just pass the instrument pair for the trade and the currency in question directly to the function, without even checking if the currency in question is part of the pair. This is taken care of by the function, as it returns 0 for such cases.

Now we come to the last service method left to discuss, called findAllAccountsWithInstrumentTrades, which, as the name suggests, returns a list of all account IDs that have an open position for the given instrument. The following code, which is extremely straightforward, does not require much explanation. The method delegates to isTradeExistsForInstrument, which ascertains if we should add the current account ID in the loop to the collection to be returned.

```
1   /**
2    * @param instrument
3    * @return a Collection of accountIds that have at least 1 trade for the
4    *  given instrument. An empty Collection is returned if none
5    *  satisfy this condition.
6    */
7   public Collection < K > findAllAccountsWithInstrumentTrades(TradeableInstrument < N > instrument) {
8     Collection < K > accountIds = Sets.newHashSet();
9     lock.readLock().lock();
10    try {
11      for (K accountId: this.tradesCache.keySet()) {
12        if (isTradeExistsForInstrument(instrument, accountId)) {
13          accountIds.add(accountId);
14        }
15      }
16    } finally {
17      lock.readLock().unlock();
18    }
19    return accountIds;
20  }
```

Try It Yourself

In this section we write demo programs for all trade and order services that we have discussed in this chapter. First we write a demo program to place a limit order using OrderExecutionService:

```
1   package com.precioustech.fxtrading.order;
2
3   import java.util.concurrent.BlockingQueue;
4   import java.util.concurrent.LinkedBlockingQueue;
5
6   import org.apache.log4j.Logger;
7
8   import com.precioustech.fxtrading.BaseTradingConfig;
9   import com.precioustech.fxtrading.TradingDecision;
10  import com.precioustech.fxtrading.TradingSignal;
11  import com.precioustech.fxtrading.account.AccountDataProvider;
```

```
12  import com.precioustech.fxtrading.account.AccountInfoService;
13  import com.precioustech.fxtrading.account.AccountInfoServiceDemo;
14  import com.precioustech.fxtrading.helper.ProviderHelper;
15  import com.precioustech.fxtrading.instrument.TradeableInstrument;
16  import com.precioustech.fxtrading.marketdata.CurrentPriceInfoProvider;
17  import com.precioustech.fxtrading.marketdata.historic.
    HistoricMarketDataProvider;
18  import com.precioustech.fxtrading.marketdata.historic.
    MovingAverageCalculationService;
19  import com.precioustech.fxtrading.oanda.restapi.account.
    OandaAccountDataProviderService;
20  import com.precioustech.fxtrading.oanda.restapi.helper.
    OandaProviderHelper;
21  import com.precioustech.fxtrading.oanda.restapi.marketdata.
    OandaCurrentPriceInfoProvider;
22  import com.precioustech.fxtrading.oanda.restapi.marketdata.historic.
    OandaHistoricMarketDataProvider;
23  import com.precioustech.fxtrading.oanda.restapi.order.
    OandaOrderManagementProvider;
24  import com.precioustech.fxtrading.oanda.restapi.trade.
    OandaTradeManagementProvider;
25  import com.precioustech.fxtrading.trade.TradeInfoService;
26  import com.precioustech.fxtrading.trade.TradeManagementProvider;
27
28  public class OrderExecutionServiceDemo {
29
30    private static final Logger LOG = Logger.getLogger(AccountInfoService
      Demo.class);
31
32    private static void usage(String[] args) {
33     if (args.length != 3) {
34      LOG.error("Usage: OrderExecutionServiceDemo <url> <username>
          <accesstoken>");
35      System.exit(1);
36     }
37    }
38
39    public static void main(String[] args) throws Exception {
40
41     usage(args);
42     String url = args[0];
43     String userName = args[1];
44     String accessToken = args[2];
45
46     BlockingQueue < TradingDecision < String >> orderQueue =
47      new LinkedBlockingQueue < TradingDecision < String >> ();
48
```

```
49    AccountDataProvider < Long > accountDataProvider =
50     new OandaAccountDataProviderService(url, userName, accessToken);
51    CurrentPriceInfoProvider < String > currentPriceInfoProvider =
52     new OandaCurrentPriceInfoProvider(url, accessToken);
53    BaseTradingConfig tradingConfig = new BaseTradingConfig();
54    tradingConfig.setMinReserveRatio(0.05);
55    tradingConfig.setMinAmountRequired(100.00);
56    tradingConfig.setMaxAllowedQuantity(10);
57    ProviderHelper < String > providerHelper = new
      OandaProviderHelper();
58    AccountInfoService < Long, String > accountInfoService =
59     new AccountInfoService < Long, String > (accountDataProvider,
60      currentPriceInfoProvider, tradingConfig, providerHelper);
61
62    OrderManagementProvider < Long, String, Long >
      orderManagementProvider =
63     new OandaOrderManagementProvider(url, accessToken,
       accountDataProvider);
64
65    TradeManagementProvider < Long, String, Long >
      tradeManagementProvider =
66     new OandaTradeManagementProvider(url, accessToken);
67
68    OrderInfoService < Long, String, Long > orderInfoService =
69     new OrderInfoService < Long, String, Long >
       (orderManagementProvider);
70
71    TradeInfoService < Long, String, Long > tradeInfoService =
72     new TradeInfoService < Long, String, Long >
       (tradeManagementProvider,
73      accountInfoService);
74
75    HistoricMarketDataProvider < String > historicMarketDataProvider =
76     new OandaHistoricMarketDataProvider(url, accessToken);
77
78    MovingAverageCalculationService < String >
      movingAverageCalculationService =
79     new MovingAverageCalculationService < String >
       (historicMarketDataProvider);
80
81    PreOrderValidationService < Long, String, Long >
      preOrderValidationService =
82     new PreOrderValidationService < Long, String, Long > (
83      tradeInfoService, movingAverageCalculationService, tradingConfig,
       orderInfoService);
84
```

```
85    OrderExecutionService < Long, String, Long > orderExecService =
86     new OrderExecutionService < Long, String, Long > (
87      orderQueue, accountInfoService, orderManagementProvider,
88      tradingConfig, preOrderValidationService,
89      currentPriceInfoProvider);
90    orderExecService.init();
91
92    TradingDecision < String > decision =
93     new TradingDecision < String > (new TradeableInstrument < String >
       ("GBP_USD"),
94      TradingSignal.LONG, 1.44, 1.35, 1.4);
95    orderQueue.offer(decision);
96    Thread.sleep(10000); // enough time to place an order
97    orderExecService.shutDown();
98
99    }
100  }
```

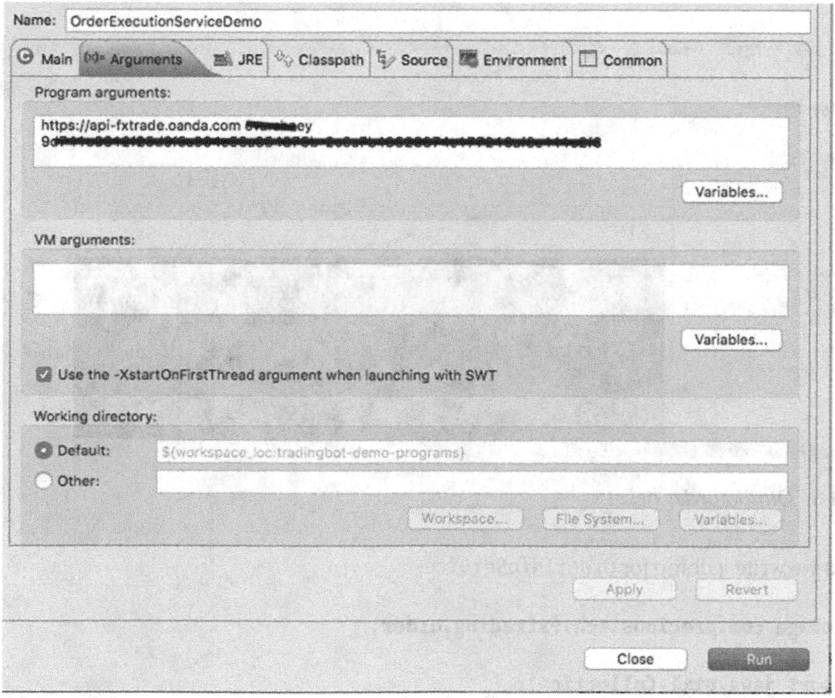

Figure 6-1. Launch configuration

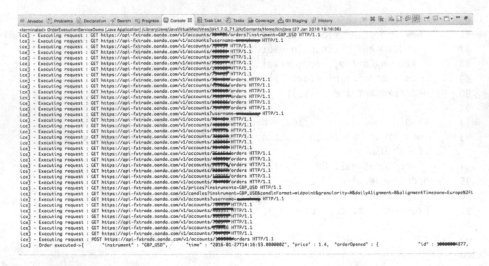

Figure 6-2. *Sample output*

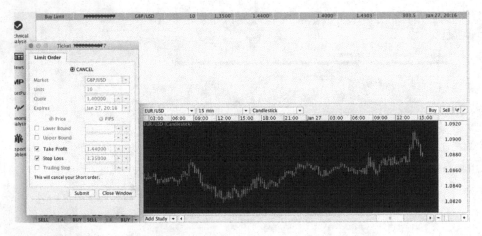

Figure 6-3. *Oanda order ticket*

Next we write a demo for `OrderInfoService`:

```
1    package com.precioustech.fxtrading.order;
2
3    import java.util.Collection;
4
5    import org.apache.log4j.Logger;
6
```

```
7   import com.precioustech.fxtrading.account.AccountDataProvider;
8   import com.precioustech.fxtrading.instrument.TradeableInstrument;
9   import com.precioustech.fxtrading.oanda.restapi.account.
    OandaAccountDataProviderService;
10  import com.precioustech.fxtrading.oanda.restapi.order.
    OandaOrderManagementProvider;
11
12  public class OrderInfoServiceDemo {
13
14    private static final Logger LOG = Logger.
      getLogger(OrderInfoServiceDemo.class);
15
16    private static void usage(String[] args) {
17     if (args.length != 3) {
18      LOG.error("Usage: OrderExecutionServiceDemo <url> <username>
         <accesstoken>");
19     System.exit(1);
20     }
21    }
22
23    public static void main(String[] args) {
24
25     usage(args);
26     String url = args[0];
27     String userName = args[1];
28     String accessToken = args[2];
29
30     AccountDataProvider < Long > accountDataProvider =
31      new OandaAccountDataProviderService(url, userName, accessToken);
32
33     OrderManagementProvider < Long, String, Long > orderManagementProvider =
34      new OandaOrderManagementProvider(url, accessToken,
         accountDataProvider);
35
36     OrderInfoService < Long, String, Long > orderInfoService =
37      new OrderInfoService < Long, String, Long >
         (orderManagementProvider);
38
39     TradeableInstrument < String > gbpusd = new  TradeableInstrument <
       String > ("GBP_USD");
40
41     orderInfoService.allPendingOrders();
42     Collection < Order < String, Long >> pendingOrdersGbpUsd =
43      orderInfoService.pendingOrdersForInstrument(gbpusd);
44
```

```
45    LOG.info(
46    String.format("+++++++++++++++++++++ Dumping all pending orders for %s
      +++",
47     gbpusd.getInstrument()));
48    for (Order < String, Long > order: pendingOrdersGbpUsd) {
49    LOG.info(
50     String.format("units=%d,   takeprofit=%2.5f,stoploss=%2.5f,limitpri
      ce=%2.5f,side=%s",
51      order.getUnits(), order.getTakeProfit(), order.getStopLoss(),
52      order.getPrice(),  order.getSide()));
53    }
54
55    int usdPosCt = orderInfoService.findNetPositionCountForCurrency
      ("USD");
56    int gbpPosCt = orderInfoService.findNetPositionCountForCurrency
      ("GBP");
57    LOG.info("Net Position count for USD = " + usdPosCt);
58    LOG.info("Net Position count for GBP = " + gbpPosCt);
59    Collection < Order < String, Long >> pendingOrders =
      orderInfoService.allPendingOrders();
60    LOG.info("+++++++++++++++++++ Dumping all pending orders ++++++++");
61    for (Order < String, Long > order: pendingOrders) {
62     LOG.info(
63      String.format("instrument=%s,units=%d, takeprofit=%2.5f,stoploss=%2
      .5f,limitprice=%2.5f,side=%s",
64       order.getInstrument().getInstrument(),  order.getUnits(),  order.
      getTakeProfit(),
65       order.getStopLoss(), order.getPrice(), order.getSide()));
66     }
67    }
68  }
```

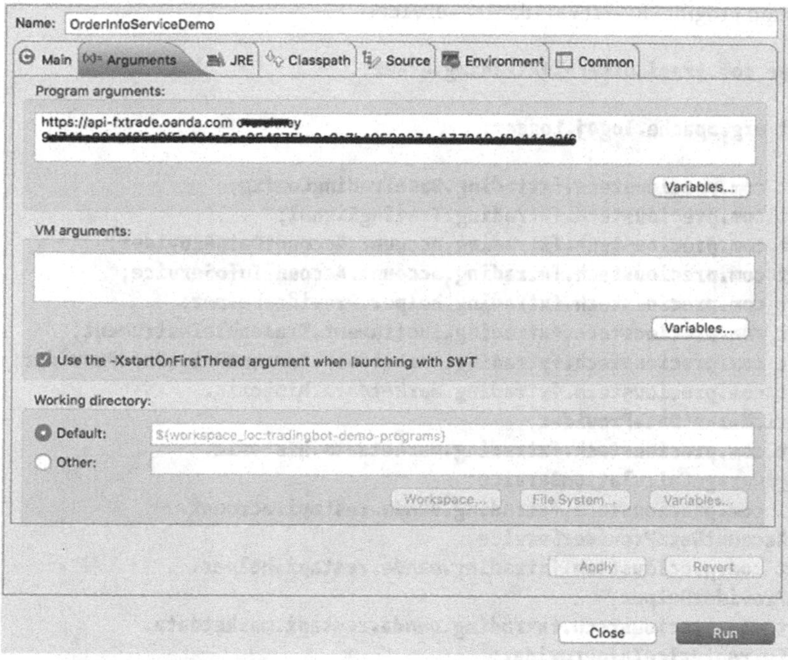

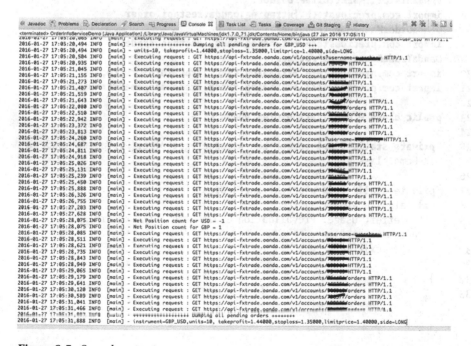

Figure 6-4. Launch configuration

Figure 6-5. Sample output

Now a demo program for PreValidationService:

```
1   package com.precioustech.fxtrading.order;
2
3   import org.apache.log4j.Logger;
4
5   import com.precioustech.fxtrading.BaseTradingConfig;
6   import com.precioustech.fxtrading.TradingSignal;
7   import com.precioustech.fxtrading.account.AccountDataProvider;
8   import com.precioustech.fxtrading.account.AccountInfoService;
9   import com.precioustech.fxtrading.helper.ProviderHelper;
10  import com.precioustech.fxtrading.instrument.TradeableInstrument;
11  import com.precioustech.fxtrading.marketdata.CurrentPriceInfoProvider;
12  import com.precioustech.fxtrading.marketdata.historic.
    HistoricMarketDataProvider;
13  import com.precioustech.fxtrading.marketdata.historic.
    MovingAverageCalculationService;
14  import com.precioustech.fxtrading.oanda.restapi.account.
    OandaAccountDataProviderService;
15  import com.precioustech.fxtrading.oanda.restapi.helper.
    OandaProviderHelper;
16  import com.precioustech.fxtrading.oanda.restapi.marketdata.
    OandaCurrentPriceInfoProvider;
17  import com.precioustech.fxtrading.oanda.restapi.marketdata.historic.
    OandaHistoricMarketDataProvider;
18  import com.precioustech.fxtrading.oanda.restapi.order.
    OandaOrderManagementProvider;
19  import com.precioustech.fxtrading.oanda.restapi.trade.
    OandaTradeManagementProvider;
20  import com.precioustech.fxtrading.trade.TradeInfoService;
21  import com.precioustech.fxtrading.trade.TradeManagementProvider;
22
23  public class PreValidationServiceDemo {
24
25    private static final Logger LOG = Logger.getLogger(PreValidationServ
      iceDemo.class);
26
27    private static void usage(String[] args) {
28    if (args.length != 3) {
29      LOG.error("Usage: PreValidationServiceDemo <url> <username>
        <accesstoken>");
30      System.exit(1);
31    }
32  }
33
```

```java
34    public static void main(String[] args) {
35    usage(args);
36    String url = args[0];
37    String userName = args[1];
38    String accessToken = args[2];
39
40    AccountDataProvider < Long > accountDataProvider =
41     new OandaAccountDataProviderService(url, userName, accessToken);
42
43    OrderManagementProvider < Long, String, Long >
      orderManagementProvider =
44     new OandaOrderManagementProvider(url, accessToken,
       accountDataProvider);
45
46    TradeManagementProvider < Long, String, Long >
      tradeManagementProvider =
47     new OandaTradeManagementProvider(url, accessToken);
48    CurrentPriceInfoProvider < String > currentPriceInfoProvider =
49     new OandaCurrentPriceInfoProvider(url, accessToken);
50    BaseTradingConfig tradingConfig = new BaseTradingConfig();
51    tradingConfig.setMinReserveRatio(0.05);
52    tradingConfig.setMinAmountRequired(100.00);
53    tradingConfig.setMaxAllowedQuantity(10);
54    tradingConfig.setMaxAllowedNetContracts(3);
55    ProviderHelper < String > providerHelper = new
      OandaProviderHelper();
56
57    AccountInfoService < Long, String > accountInfoService =
58     new AccountInfoService < Long, String > (accountDataProvider,
59      currentPriceInfoProvider, tradingConfig, providerHelper);
60
61    TradeInfoService < Long, String, Long > tradeInfoService =
62     new TradeInfoService < Long, String, Long > (
63      tradeManagementProvider,  accountInfoService);
64
65    tradeInfoService.init();
66
67    HistoricMarketDataProvider < String > historicMarketDataProvider =
68     new OandaHistoricMarketDataProvider(url, accessToken);
69
70    MovingAverageCalculationService < String >
      movingAverageCalculationService =
71     new MovingAverageCalculationService < String >
      (historicMarketDataProvider);
72
```

```
73   OrderInfoService < Long, String, Long > orderInfoService =
74    new OrderInfoService < Long, String, Long >
     (orderManagementProvider);

75
76   PreOrderValidationService < Long, String, Long >
     preOrderValidationService =
77    new PreOrderValidationService < Long, String, Long >
     (tradeInfoService,
78     movingAverageCalculationService, tradingConfig, orderInfoService);
79
80   TradeableInstrument < String > eurusd = new TradeableInstrument <
     String > ("EUR_USD");
81   TradeableInstrument < String > usdjpy = new TradeableInstrument <
     String > ("USD_JPY");
82   boolean isEurUsdTraded = preOrderValidationService.checkInstrumentNo
     tAlreadyTraded(eurusd);
83   boolean isUsdJpyTraded = preOrderValidationService.checkInstrumentNo
     tAlreadyTraded(usdjpy);
84   LOG.info(eurusd.getInstrument() + " trade present? " +
     !isEurUsdTraded);
85   LOG.info(usdjpy.getInstrument() + " trade present? " +
     !isUsdJpyTraded);
86
87   TradeableInstrument < String > usdzar = new TradeableInstrument <
     String > ("USD_ZAR");
88
89   boolean isUsdZarTradeInSafeZone = preOrderValidationService.
90   isInSafeZone(TradingSignal.LONG, 17.9, usdzar);
91   LOG.info(usdzar.getInstrument() + " in safe zone? " +
     isUsdZarTradeInSafeZone);
92   boolean isEurUsdTradeInSafeZone = preOrderValidationService.
93   isInSafeZone(TradingSignal.LONG, 1.2, eurusd);
94   LOG.info(eurusd.getInstrument() + " in safe zone? " +
     isEurUsdTradeInSafeZone);
95
96   TradeableInstrument < String > nzdchf = new TradeableInstrument <
     String > ("NZD_CHF");
97
98   preOrderValidationService.checkLimitsForCcy(nzdchf, TradingSignal.
     LONG);
99   }
100
101  }
```

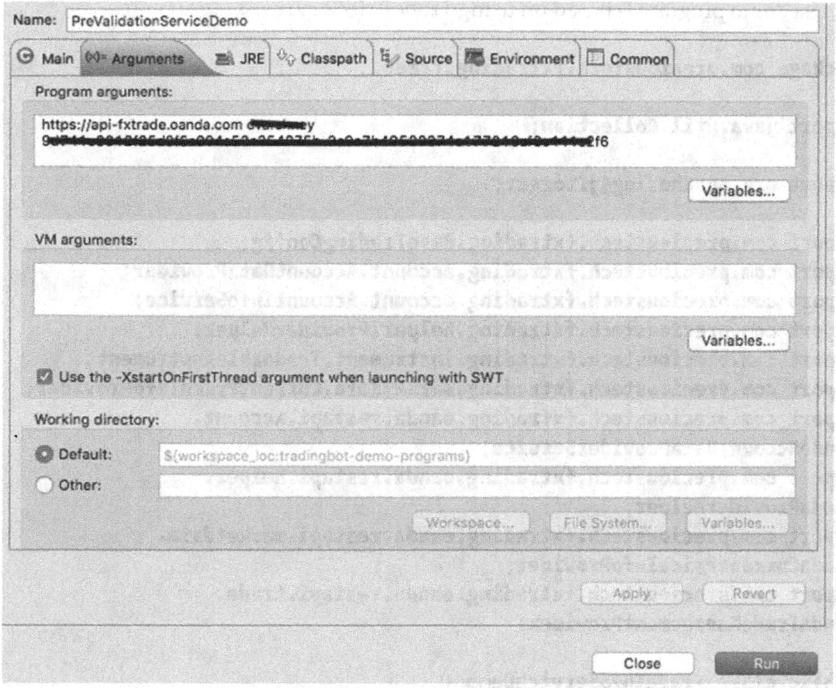

Figure 6-6. *Launch configuration*

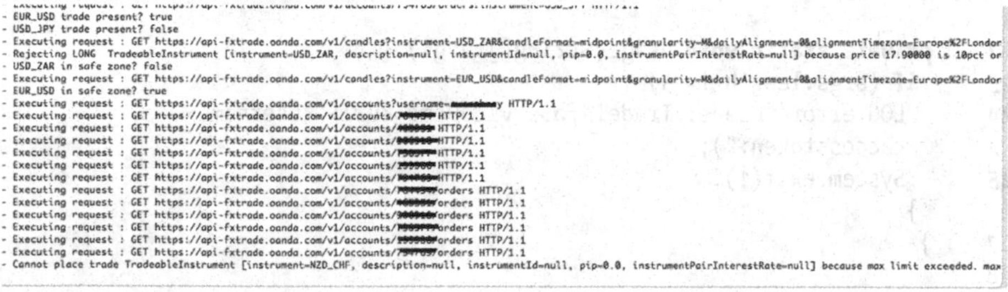

Figure 6-7. *Sample output*

The last demo program is based on using TradeInfoService:

```
1    package com.precioustech.fxtrading.trade;
2
3    import java.util.Collection;
4
5    import org.apache.log4j.Logger;
6
7    import com.precioustech.fxtrading.BaseTradingConfig;
8    import com.precioustech.fxtrading.account.AccountDataProvider;
9    import com.precioustech.fxtrading.account.AccountInfoService;
10   import com.precioustech.fxtrading.helper.ProviderHelper;
11   import com.precioustech.fxtrading.instrument.TradeableInstrument;
12   import com.precioustech.fxtrading.marketdata.CurrentPriceInfoProvider;
13   import com.precioustech.fxtrading.oanda.restapi.account.
     OandaAccountDataProviderService;
14   import com.precioustech.fxtrading.oanda.restapi.helper.
     OandaProviderHelper;
15   import com.precioustech.fxtrading.oanda.restapi.marketdata.
     OandaCurrentPriceInfoProvider;
16   import com.precioustech.fxtrading.oanda.restapi.trade.
     OandaTradeManagementProvider;
17
18   public class TradeInfoServiceDemo {
19
20     private static final Logger LOG = Logger.
       getLogger(TradeInfoServiceDemo.class);
21
22     private static void usage(String[] args) {
23      if (args.length != 3) {
24       LOG.error("Usage: TradeInfoServiceDemo <url> <username>
        <accesstoken>");
25       System.exit(1);
26      }
27     }
28
29     public static void main(String[] args) {
30      usage(args);
31      String url = args[0];
32      String userName = args[1];
33      String accessToken = args[2];
34      AccountDataProvider < Long > accountDataProvider =
35       new OandaAccountDataProviderService(url, userName, accessToken);
36      CurrentPriceInfoProvider < String > currentPriceInfoProvider =
37       new OandaCurrentPriceInfoProvider(url, accessToken);
38      BaseTradingConfig tradingConfig = new BaseTradingConfig();
39      tradingConfig.setMinReserveRatio(0.05);
40      tradingConfig.setMinAmountRequired(100.00);
```

```
41      tradingConfig.setMaxAllowedQuantity(10);
42      ProviderHelper < String > providerHelper = new OandaProviderHelper();
43      AccountInfoService < Long, String > accountInfoService =
44       new AccountInfoService < Long, String > (accountDataProvider,
45        currentPriceInfoProvider, tradingConfig, providerHelper);
46      TradeManagementProvider < Long, String, Long >
        tradeManagementProvider =
47       new OandaTradeManagementProvider(url,
48        accessToken);
49
50      TradeInfoService < Long, String, Long > tradeInfoService =
51       new TradeInfoService < Long, String, Long > (
52        tradeManagementProvider,  accountInfoService);
53
54      tradeInfoService.init();
55      Collection < Trade < Long, String, Long >> allTrades =
        tradeInfoService.getAllTrades();
56      LOG.info("################ Dumping All Trades ################");
57      for (Trade < Long, String, Long > trade: allTrades) {
58       LOG.info(
59        String.format("Units=%d,Side=%s,Instrument=%s,Price=%2.5f",
         trade.getUnits(),
60         trade.getSide(),  trade.getInstrument().getInstrument(),
61         trade.getExecutionPrice()));
62      }
63      int chfTrades = tradeInfoService.findNetPositionCountForCurrency
        ("CHF");
64      int cadTrades = tradeInfoService.findNetPositionCountForCurrency
        ("CAD");
65      LOG.info("Net Position for CHF = " + chfTrades);
66      LOG.info("Net Position for CAD = " + cadTrades);
67      TradeableInstrument < String > cadchf = new  TradeableInstrument <
        String > ("CAD_CHF");
68      TradeableInstrument < String > usdcad = new  TradeableInstrument <
        String > ("USD_CAD");
69      boolean isCadChdTradeExists = tradeInfoService.isTradeExistsForInstr
        ument(cadchf);
70      boolean isUsdCadTradeExists = tradeInfoService.isTradeExistsForInstr
        ument(usdcad);
71      LOG.info(cadchf.getInstrument() + " exists?" + isCadChdTradeExists);
72      LOG.info(usdcad.getInstrument() + " exists?" + isUsdCadTradeExists);
73
74      }
75
76  }
```

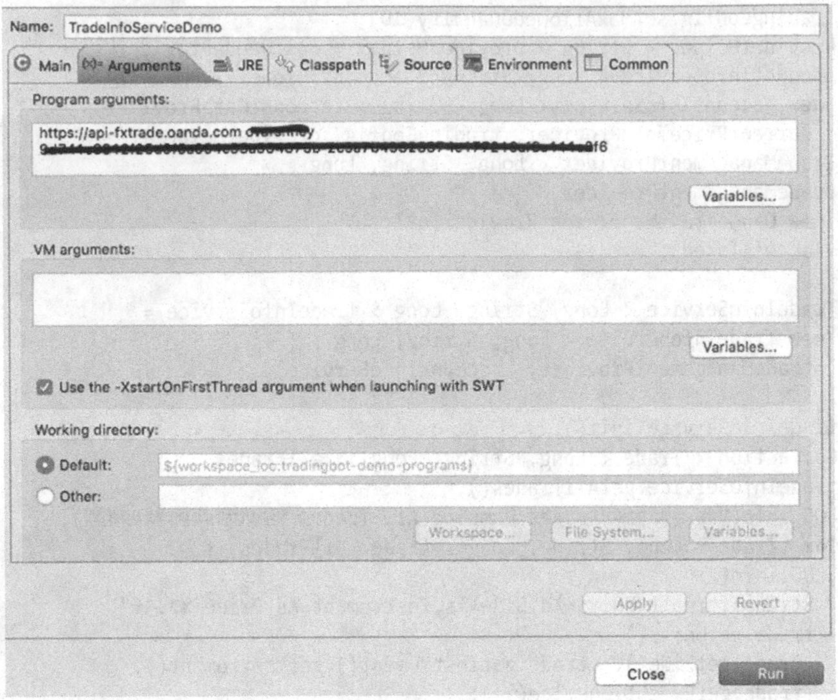

Figure 6-8. *Launch configuration*

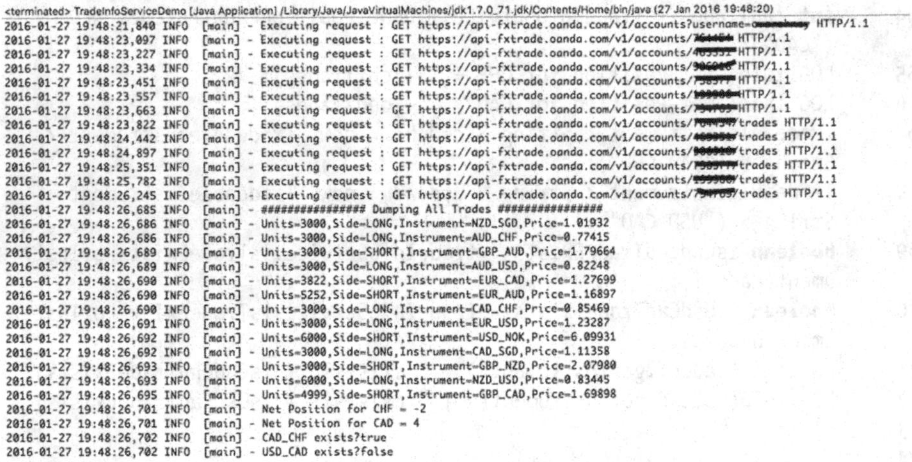

Figure 6-9. *Sample output*

■ ■ ■

CHAPTER 7

Event Streaming: Trade/ Order/Account Events

Events are generated on a trading platform when a state of an order/trade/account or any other entity changes on the platform. Here are some examples that could trigger an event:

- Limit order filled

- Trade stopped out

- Margin closeout of account

We will discuss many such state-changing events later in the chapter and how we handle them but will focus on events that affect only trades/orders and accounts.

As discussed in the introduction of the book, we need to create an infinite event loop in order to receive the state changes that happen on the platform. The platform, via the event stream, just like market data stream, pushes these events and we need to adopt the same paradigm to process these events. However, there is one stark difference. The market data stream (excluding heartbeats) only has tick events that conform to a standard payload. However, with the event stream, we could have differing payloads depending on what state change happened on what entity. For example, when a limit order is filled on the OANDA platform[1], a response like this one is normally sent down the event stream:

```
1   {
2       "transaction": {
3           "id": 10002,
4           "accountId": 123456,
5           "time": "1443968041000000",
6           "type": "ORDER_FILLED",
7           "instrument": "EUR_USD",
8           "units": 10,
9           "side": "sell",
10          "price": 1,
11          "pl": 1.234,
```

---

[1]http://developer.oanda.com/rest-live/streaming/#eventsStreaming

© Shekhar Varshney 2016
S. Varshney, *Building Trading Bots Using Java*, DOI 10.1007/978-1-4842-2520-2_7

```
12        "interest": 0.034,
13        "accountBalance": 10000,
14        "orderId": 0,
15        "tradeReduced": {
16          "id": 54321,
17          "units": 10,
18          "pl": 1.234,
19          "interest": 0.034
20        }
21     }
22   }
```

On the other hand, when a trade is stopped out, we could see the following response:

```
1    {
2        "transaction": {
3          "id": 10004,
4          "accountId": 234567,
5          "time": "1443968081000000",
6          "type": "STOP_LOSS_FILLED",
7          "tradeId": 1782812741,
8          "instrument": "USD_SGD",
9          "units": 3000,
10         "side": "sell",
11         "price": 1.39101,
12         "pl": 3.3039,
13         "interest": -0.0123,
14         "accountBalance": 5915.8745
15     }
16   }
```

Looking at these varied responses, we need to create event handlers for each of the event types that we are interested in handling. This is where we get the chance to exploit the polymorphic behavior of Google EventBus, which would try to deliver the message to an exact type if found and then proceed to its supertypes.

Let's summarize the different important events that we might see being callbacked for. This is by no means a full list, but are the ones that we see often on various platforms and will discuss in greater detail later:

1. Order

   - Create New Market Order

   - Create New Limit Order

   - Order Update

   - Order Cancelled

   - Order Filled

2. Trade

- Take Profit Filled

- Stop Loss Filled

- Trade Update

- Trade Closed

3. Account

- Margin Closeout

- Financing (Interest Paid or Received)

Streaming Event Interface

The first step is to define an interface that establishes the event loop with the platform. This is exactly similar in concept to a market data streaming interface. After establishing the event loop, all the events are delegated to the appropriate event handlers via the EventCallback that we shall discuss soon. First let's quickly look at this interface:

```
1   /**
2    * A service that provides trade/order/account related events
3    * streaming. Normally the implementation would create a dedicated
4    * connection to the platform or register callback listener(s) to
         receive
5    * events. It is recommended that the service delegate the handling of
6    * events to specific handlers which can parse and make sense of the
7    * different plethora of events received.
8    *
9    *
10   */
11  public interface {
12
13      /**
14       * Start the streaming service which would ideally create a
15       * dedicated connection to the platform or callback listener(s).
16       * Ideally multiple connections requesting the same event types
17       * should not be created. */
18      void startEventsStreaming();
19
20      /**
21       * Stop the events streaming services and dispose any
22       * resources/connections in a suitable manner such that no resource
23       * leaks are created.*/
24      void stopEventsStreaming();
25  }
```

The definition of EventCallback that must be used in tandem to disseminate the events is:

```
1   public interface EventCallback<T> {
2
3     void onEvent(EventPayLoad<T> eventPayLoad);
4   }
```

These two interfaces have similar design objectives as that of the market data ones. The real differences emerge in the downstream dissemination of these different payloads, which we will soon discover when the EventBus enters the scene. But before that, let's quickly look at the OANDA implementation for EventsStreamingService.

A Concrete Implementation for EventsStreamingService

Let's kick start the discussion of this implementation by looking at the class definition and its constructor:

```
1   public class OandaEventsStreamingService extends OandaStreamingService
2     implements EventsStreamingService {
3
4     private static final Logger LOG =
5       Logger.getLogger(OandaEventsStreamingService.class);
6     private final String url;
7     private final AccountDataProvider < Long > accountDataProvider;
8     private final EventCallback < JSONObject > eventCallback;
9
10    public OandaEventsStreamingService(final String url, final String
      accessToken,
11      AccountDataProvider < Long > accountDataProvider, EventCallback <
        JSONObject >
12      eventCallback,
13      HeartBeatCallback < DateTime > heartBeatCallback, String
        heartBeatSourceId) {
14      super(accessToken, heartBeatCallback, heartBeatSourceId);
15      this.url = url;
16      this.accountDataProvider = accountDataProvider;
17      this.eventCallback = eventCallback;
18    }
```

Similar to OandaMarketDataStreamingService, this class extends from the OandaStreamingService, which provides the infrastructure methods for all OANDA streaming services, as discussed. Apart from the usual params, url and accessToken passed in, the params HeartBeatCallBack and heartBeatSourceId are required for the super class, we also need the AccountDataProvider service that provides the list of accounts we want event callbacks for. These accounts must be passed as parameters in the streaming URL as shown:

```
1   @Override
2   protected String getStreamingUrl() {
3    Collection < Account < Long >> accounts =
4     accountDataProvider.getLatestAccountInfo();
5    return this.url + OandaConstants.EVENTS_RESOURCE + "?accountIds=" +
6     accountsAsCsvString(accounts);
7   }
8
9   private String accountsAsCsvString(Collection < Account < Long >>
    accounts) {
10   StringBuilder accountsAsCsv = new StringBuilder();
11   boolean firstTime = true;
12   for (Account < Long > account: accounts) {
13    if (firstTime) {
14     firstTime = false;
15    } else {
16     accountsAsCsv.append(TradingConstants.ENCODED_COMMA);
17    }
18    accountsAsCsv.append(account.getAccountId());
19   }
20   return accountsAsCsv.toString();
21  }
```

The accountDataProvider.getLatestAccountInfo() returns a collection of all accounts that belong to the user. This collection is then passed to accountsAsCsvString, which returns a CSV (URL encoded)-separated list of accounts. Assuming the user has accounts 123456 and 2345678, the function getStreamingUrl should compute the following:

```
1   //given
2   public static final String EVENTS_RESOURCE = "/v1/events";
3   //the url computed will look like
4   https://stream-fxtrade.oanda.com/v1/events?accountIds=123456%2C2345678
```

With the streaming URL now computed, we are ready to start streaming in an infinite loop in a separate thread, which is the same paradigm we used for the market data event stream.

```
1   @Override
2   public void startEventsStreaming() {
3    stopEventsStreaming();
4    streamThread = new Thread(new Runnable() {
5
```

```
6    @Override
7    public void run() {
8     CloseableHttpClient httpClient = getHttpClient();
9     try {
10     BufferedReader br = setUpStreamIfPossible(httpClient);
11     if (br != null) {
12      String line;
13      while ((line = br.readLine()) != null && serviceUp) {
14       Object obj = JSONValue.parse(line);
15       JSONObject jsonPayLoad = (JSONObject) obj;
16       if (jsonPayLoad.containsKey(heartbeat)) {
17        handleHeartBeat(jsonPayLoad);
18       } else if (jsonPayLoad.containsKey(transaction)) {
19        JSONObject transactionObject = (JSONObject)
20        jsonPayLoad.get(transaction);
21        String transactionType = transactionObject.get(type).toString();
22        /*convert here so that event bus can post to an appropriate
23         * handler event though this does not belong here*/
24        EventPayLoad < JSONObject > payLoad = OandaUtils
25         .toOandaEventPayLoad(transactionType,  transactionObject);
26        if (payLoad != null) {
27         eventCallback.onEvent(payLoad);
28        }
29       } else if (jsonPayLoad.containsKey(OandaJsonKeys.disconnect)) {
30        handleDisconnect(line);
31       }
32      }
33      br.close();
34     }
35
36    } catch (Exception e) {
37     LOG.error(e);
38    } finally {
39     serviceUp = false;
40     TradingUtils.closeSilently(httpClient);
41    }
42   }
43  }, "OandEventStreamingThread");
44  streamThread.start();
45 }
```

The code looks very similar to the market data example, except for these lines where
something different is happening:

```
1  if (jsonPayLoad.containsKey(transaction)) {
2  JSONObject transactionObject = (JSONObject) jsonPayLoad.
   get(transaction);
3  String transactionType = transactionObject.get(type).toString();
```

```
4     /*convert here so that event bus can post to an appropriate handler,
5      * event though this does not belong here*/
6     EventPayLoad < JSONObject > payLoad = OandaUtils.toOandaEventPayLoad
      (transactionType,
7       transactionObject);
8     if (payLoad != null) {
9       eventCallback.onEvent(payLoad);
10    }
```

This snippet of code is where most of the magic seems to happen. All the JSON payloads for an event have the key transaction. Therefore if our payload has this key, we know it's a platform event that we need to handle. Here we bring in the concept of fine-grained event handling by the EventBus. Remember from our introduction of the EventBus, it is up to the developer to decide how fine- or coarse-grained you want the subscribers or handlers to be. We really want to exploit this feature to our advantage by going as fine-grained as possible. Therefore we create payloads that derive from the EventPayLoad class and then create handlers with methods that handle specific subclasses of EventPayLoad. Let's first define this parent class of all events:

```
1     /**
2      * Interface to be implemented by platform events. The implementers
3      * of this interface would be enums which already have the method
4      * name() implemented. The reason for its existence is to have a base
5      * implementation of all platform events.
6      *
7      */
8     public interface Event {
9       String name();
10    }
```

```
1     public class EventPayLoad < T > {
2
3       private final Event event;
4       private final T payLoad;
5
6       public EventPayLoad(Event event, T payLoad) {
7         this.event = event;
8         this.payLoad = payLoad;
9       }
10
11      public Event getEvent() {
12        return this.event;
13      }
14
15      public T getPayLoad() {
16        return this.payLoad;
17      }
18    }
```

This base class for all event payloads stipulates that we must define a constructor that accepts the enum of type Event and payload T.

From our discussion, it is evident we need a subclass implementation for each of the types of expected payloads, i.e., Account, Trade, and Order.

- Account

```
1  public enum AccountEvents implements Event {
2          MARGIN_CALL_ENTER,
3    MARGIN_CALL_EXIT,
4    MARGIN_CLOSEOUT,
5    SET_MARGIN_RATE,
6    TRANSFER_FUNDS,
7    DAILY_INTEREST, FEE;
8  }
```

```
1  public class AccountEventPayLoad extends EventPayLoad < JSONObject > {
2
3    public AccountEventPayLoad(AccountEvents event, JSONObject payLoad) {
4      super(event, payLoad);
5    }
6  }
```

- Trade

```
1  public enum TradeEvents implements Event {
2          TRADE_UPDATE,
3          TRADE_CLOSE,
4          MIGRATE_TRADE_OPEN,
5          MIGRATE_TRADE_CLOSE,
6          STOP_LOSS_FILLED,
7          TAKE_PROFIT_FILLED,
8          TRAILING_STOP_FILLED;
9  }
```

```
1  public class TradeEventPayLoad extends EventPayLoad < JSONObject > {
2
3    public TradeEventPayLoad(TradeEvents event, JSONObject payLoad) {
4      super(event, payLoad);
5    }
6
7  }
```

- Order

```
1  public enum OrderEvents implements Event {
2          MARKET_ORDER_CREATE,
3          STOP_ORDER_CREATE,
```

```
4              LIMIT_ORDER_CREATE,
5              MARKET_IF_TOUCHED_ORDER_CREATE,
6              ORDER_UPDATE,
7              ORDER_CANCEL,
8              ORDER_FILLED;
9     }
```

```
1     public class OrderEventPayLoad extends EventPayLoad < JSONObject > {
2
3       private final OrderEvents orderEvent;
4
5       public OrderEventPayLoad(OrderEvents event, JSONObject payLoad) {
6         super(event, payLoad);
7         this.orderEvent = event;
8       }
9
10      @Override
11      public OrderEvents getEvent() {
12        return this.orderEvent;
13      }
14
15    }
```

Now what remains is to convert the JSON payload into an instance of EventPayLoad, which is accomplished by OandaUtils.toOandaEventPayLoad(). This method requires a type, which is passed in the event JSON payload and helps determine which business entity this event relates to, i.e., Trade, Order, or Account. The type actually is the name of an event in one of our three enums.

```
1     public static EventPayLoad < JSONObject > toOandaEventPayLoad(String
      transactionType, JSONObject payLoad) {
2       Preconditions.checkNotNull(transactionType);
3       Event evt = findAppropriateType(AccountEvents.values(),
        transactionType);
4       if (evt == null) {
5         evt = findAppropriateType(OrderEvents.values(), transactionType);
6         if (evt == null) {
7           evt = findAppropriateType(TradeEvents.values(), transactionType);
8           if (evt == null) {
9             return null;
10          } else {
11            return new TradeEventPayLoad((TradeEvents) evt, payLoad);
12          }
13        } else {
14          return new OrderEventPayLoad((OrderEvents) evt, payLoad);
15        }
```

```
16    } else {
17      return new AccountEventPayLoad((AccountEvents) evt, payLoad);
18    }
19
20  }
21
22  private static final Event findAppropriateType(Event[] events, String
      transactionType) {
23    for (Event evt: events) {
24    if (evt.name().equals(transactionType)) {
25      return evt;
26    }
27    }
28    return null;
29  }
```

This utility method does a brute force comparison of all three event types we have and returns as soon as it finds the first match. If no match is found (it is possible if a new event is introduced by the platform), it returns null. If we do have a non-null instance of the EventPayLoad, we are now ready to dispatch it to an instance of EventCallback, which inevitably must use the EventBus to dispatch to the interested subscribers.

```
1   public class EventCallbackImpl < T > implements EventCallback < T > {
2
3     private final EventBus eventBus;
4
5     public EventCallbackImpl(final EventBus eventBus) {
6       this.eventBus = eventBus;
7     }
8
9     @Override
10    public void onEvent(EventPayLoad < T > eventPayLoad) {
11      this.eventBus.post(eventPayLoad);
12    }
13
14  }
```

At the time onEvent method is invoked, it already has an appropriate subtype of the EventPayLoad, ready to be dispatched.

Since we want to exploit the fine-grained dispatching of the subtypes of EventPayLoad by the EventBus, we need to create payload handlers that can polymorphically handle these specific payloads. To achieve that, we need to first define an EventHandler interface that has a method to do exactly that.

```
1   public interface EventHandler<K, T extends EventPayLoad<K>> {
2
3     void handleEvent(T payload);
4   }
```

In this definition, we are stipulating that the handleEvent will handle events that are subtypes of EventPayLoad.

For the set of events relating to the Trade business entity, an implementation of the TradeEventHandler would look like this:

```
1   public class TradeEventHandler implements EventHandler < JSONObject,
2     TradeEventPayLoad > {
3
4     private final Set < TradeEvents > tradeEventsSupported =
5     Sets.newHashSet(TradeEvents.STOP_LOSS_FILLED,
6       TradeEvents.TRADE_CLOSE,  TradeEvents.TAKE_PROFIT_FILLED);
7     private final TradeInfoService < Long,
8     String,
9     Long > tradeInfoService;
10
11    public TradeEventHandler(TradeInfoService < Long, String, Long >
12      tradeInfoService) {
13      this.tradeInfoService = tradeInfoService;
14    }
15
16    @Override
17    @Subscribe
18    @AllowConcurrentEvents
19    public void handleEvent(TradeEventPayLoad payLoad) {
20      Preconditions.checkNotNull(payLoad);
21      if (!tradeEventsSupported.contains(payLoad.getEvent())) {
22        return;
23      }
24      JSONObject jsonPayLoad = payLoad.getPayLoad();
25      long accountId = (Long) jsonPayLoad.get(OandaJsonKeys.accountId);
26      tradeInfoService.refreshTradesForAccount(accountId);
27    }
28  }
```

The TradeEventHandler handles the TradeEventPayLoad payload as per its definition. There are couple of things worth noting about this simple handler. First it stipulates through the tradeEventsSupported set which subset of all trade events it wants to consume. Hence one of the first things it does is perform the check

```
1   if (!tradeEventsSupported.contains(payLoad.getEvent())) {
2     return;
3   }
```

and promptly return if the type is not in [STOP_LOSS_FILLED,TRADE_CLOSE, TAKE_ PROFIT_FILLED]. If it is, then it does a very interesting action of refreshing the *trades cache*. Remember, from our discussion from previous chapter, that TradeInfoService has an internal cache of trades, in order to avoid making frequent calls to fetch trades, which is quite expensive. Now, here it is where this cache gets refreshed. We only refresh the trades cache for the given account and resist refreshing everything, as it is not required here.

An equivalent handler for orders is the OrderFilledEventHandler whose definition is:

```
1   public class OrderFilledEventHandler implements EventHandler <
    JSONObject,
2    OrderEventPayLoad > , EmailContentGenerator < JSONObject > {
3    private final Set < OrderEvents > orderEventsSupported =
4    Sets.newHashSet(OrderEvents.ORDER_FILLED);
5    private final TradeInfoService < Long,
6    String,
7    Long > tradeInfoService;
8
9    public OrderFilledEventHandler(
10    TradeInfoService < Long, String, Long > tradeInfoService) {
11    this.tradeInfoService = tradeInfoService;
12    }
13
14    @Override
15    @Subscribe
16    @AllowConcurrentEvents
17    public void handleEvent(OrderEventPayLoad payLoad) {
18    Preconditions.checkNotNull(payLoad);
19    if (!orderEventsSupported.contains(payLoad.getEvent())) {
20     return;
21    }
22    JSONObject jsonPayLoad = payLoad.getPayLoad();
23
24    long accountId = (Long) jsonPayLoad.get(OandaJsonKeys.accountId);
25    tradeInfoService.refreshTradesForAccount(accountId);
26    }
27  }
```

As the name of this handler suggests, we are only interested in the ORDER_FILLED event. When an order is filled, a trade is created as a result. Therefore, we refresh the trades cache again by invoking tradeInfoService.refreshTradesForAccount.

Coming back to the dissemination by the EventBus, since we are creating payloads of the types TradeEventPayLoad, OrderEventPayLoad, and AccountEventPayLoad and have methods with @Subscribe that match the types, the EventBus should deliver to the relevant handleEvent method and not to all three.

This concludes our discussion of the events related to Trade, Order, and Accounts. There are several other things that you might choose to do when such events happen, for example, send an e-mail or an SMS notification. It is up to developers to decide what to write in the handleEvent method.

Try It Yourself

In this section we are going to create a demo program that will output events from the platform. To see this in action and see the LIMIT_ORDER_CREATE event outputted, run the OrderExecutionServiceDemo program. It will create a new order, which will generate a platform event. The demo program will process and output it.

```
1  package com.precioustech.fxtrading.oanda.restapi.streaming.events;
2
3  import static com.precioustech.fxtrading.oanda.restapi.OandaJsonKeys.
   type;
4
5  import org.apache.log4j.Logger;
6  import org.joda.time.DateTime;
7  import org.json.simple.JSONObject;
8
9  import com.google.common.eventbus.AllowConcurrentEvents;
10 import com.google.common.eventbus.EventBus;
11 import com.google.common.eventbus.Subscribe;
12 import com.precioustech.fxtrading.account.AccountDataProvider;
13 import com.precioustech.fxtrading.events.EventCallback;
14 import com.precioustech.fxtrading.events.EventCallbackImpl;
15 import com.precioustech.fxtrading.events.EventPayLoad;
16 import com.precioustech.fxtrading.heartbeats.HeartBeatCallback;
17 import com.precioustech.fxtrading.heartbeats.HeartBeatCallbackImpl;
18 import com.precioustech.fxtrading.oanda.restapi.account.
   OandaAccountDataProviderService;
19 import com.precioustech.fxtrading.streaming.events.
   EventsStreamingService;
20
21 public class EventsStreamingServiceDemo {
22
23   private static final Logger LOG = Logger.getLogger(EventsStreamingSer
     viceDemo.class);
24
25   private static void usage(String[] args) {
26    if (args.length != 4) {
27     LOG.error("Usage: EventsStreamingServiceDemo <url> <url2> <username>
        <accesstoken>");
28     System.exit(1);
29    }
30   }
31
```

```java
32    private static class EventSubscriber {
33
34      @Subscribe
35      @AllowConcurrentEvents
36      public void handleEvent(EventPayLoad < JSONObject > payLoad) {
37        String transactionType = payLoad.getPayLoad().get(type).toString();
38        LOG.info(String.format("Type:%s, payload=%s", transactionType,
          payLoad.getPayLoad()));
39      }
40    }
41
42    public static void main(String[] args) throws Exception {
43      usage(args);
44      String url = args[0];
45      String url2 = args[1];
46      String userName = args[2];
47      String accessToken = args[3];
48      final String heartBeatSourceId="DEMO_EVTDATASTREAM";
49
50      EventBus eventBus = new EventBus();
51      eventBus.register(new EventSubscriber());
52      HeartBeatCallback < DateTime > heartBeatCallback = new
        HeartBeatCallbackImpl < DateTime > (eventBus);
53      AccountDataProvider < Long > accountDataProvider =
54       new OandaAccountDataProviderService(url2, userName, accessToken);
55      EventCallback < JSONObject > eventCallback = new EventCallbackImpl <
        JSONObject > (eventBus);
56
57      EventsStreamingService evtStreamingService =
58       new OandaEventsStreamingService(url, accessToken,
59        accountDataProvider, eventCallback, heartBeatCallback,
          heartBeatSourceId);
60      evtStreamingService.startEventsStreaming();
61      //Run OrderExecutionServiceDemo in the next 60s
62      Thread.sleep(60000 L);
63      evtStreamingService.stopEventsStreaming();
64    }
65  }
```

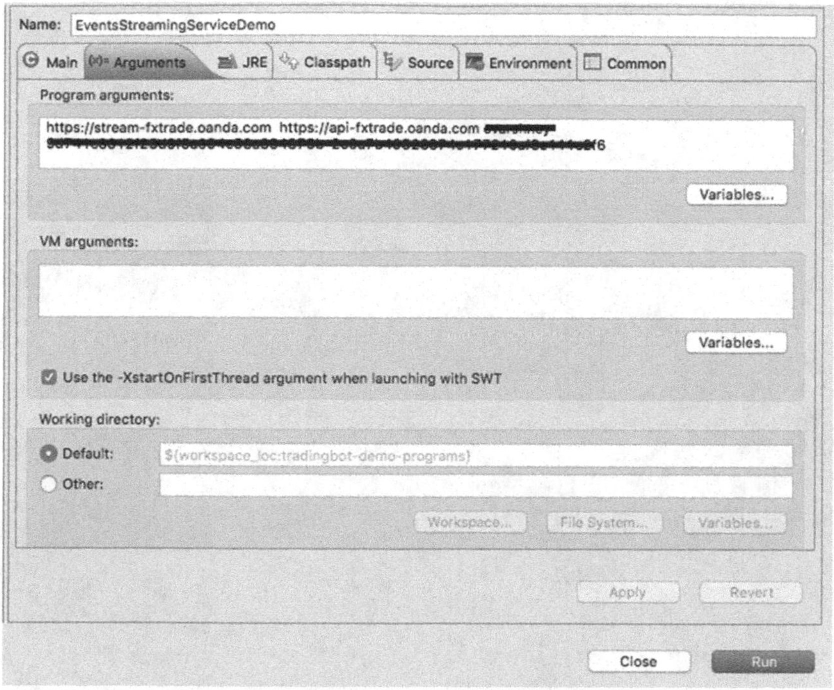

Figure 7-1. Launch configuration

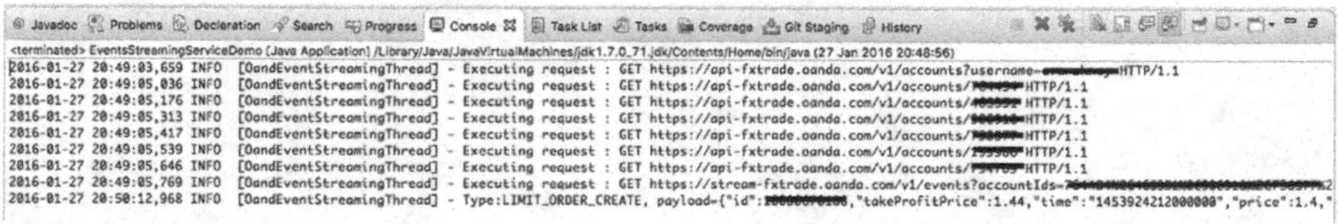

Figure 7-2. Sample output

■ ■ ■

CHAPTER 8

Integration with Twitter

We have now reached probably the most exciting part of our journey in building the trading bot. Interacting with social media is probably one of the most important things a bot should be able to do. It probably wasn't important a few years ago but now it is extremely so because most news, events, and leaks seem to appear on social media first, which affect the markets. The ability to subscribe to these feeds in realtime, make sense of them and make a decision, adds a layer of sophistication to any bot. Ours is no exception, except that we will not attempt to consume thousands of tweets per second but learn the basics of integrating with Twitter. We aim to achieve the following by the end of this chapter:

- Connect to a Twitter account

- Search for tweets

- Parse tweets and make sense of them

In particular, we will focus on FX tweets from users whose tweets have a well defined structure and have information about orders and trades. The idea is that by doing so, we can build a strategy to copy what others are doing and maybe either do what they are doing or do the opposite. This will be discussed in detail in the next chapter, as part of a strategy that involves this concept.

Creating a Twitter Application

Before we can automate the process of tweeting and reading tweets automatically via a user account, we need to associate a Twitter app to the user account. The tokens generated for this app will be used to log in to Twitter and perform the required operations via the bot. Let's follow the step-by-step procedure to get to a state where we have the necessary tokens to connect via a Java application.

1. Go to `https://apps.twitter.com/app/new`[1], where you will see the screen shown in Figure 8-1.

---

[1]`https://apps.twitter.com/app/new`

© Shekhar Varshney 2016

S. Varshney, *Building Trading Bots Using Java*, DOI 10.1007/978-1-4842-2520-2_8

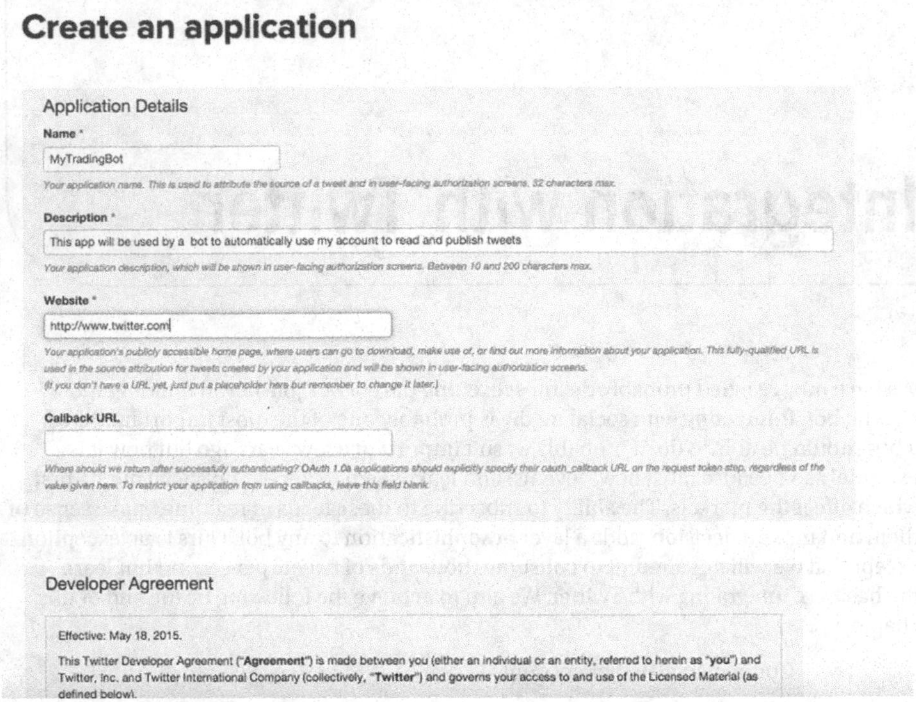

Create an application

Application Details

Name *

MyTradingBot

Your application name. This is used to attribute the source of a tweet and in user-facing authorization screens. 32 characters max.

Description *

This app will be used by a bot to automatically use my account to read and publish tweets

Your application description, which will be shown in user-facing authorization screens. Between 10 and 200 characters max.

Website *

http://www.twitter.com

Your application's publicly accessible home page, where users can go to download, make use of, or find out more information about your application. This fully-qualified URL is used in the source attribution for tweets created by your application and will be shown in user-facing authorization screens.

(If you don't have a URL yet, just put a placeholder here but remember to change it later.)

Callback URL

Where should we return after successfully authenticating? OAuth 1.0a applications should explicitly specify their oauth_callback URL on the request token step, regardless of the value given here. To restrict your application from using callbacks, leave this field blank.

Developer Agreement

Effective: May 18, 2015.

This Twitter Developer Agreement ("**Agreement**") is made between you (either an individual or an entity, referred to herein as "**you**") and Twitter, Inc. and Twitter International Company (collectively, "**Twitter**") and governs your access to and use of the Licensed Material (as defined below).

Figure 8-1. *Creating an app for bot*

2. After accepting the agreement and submitting the form, you should see the confirmation screen shown in Figure 8-2.

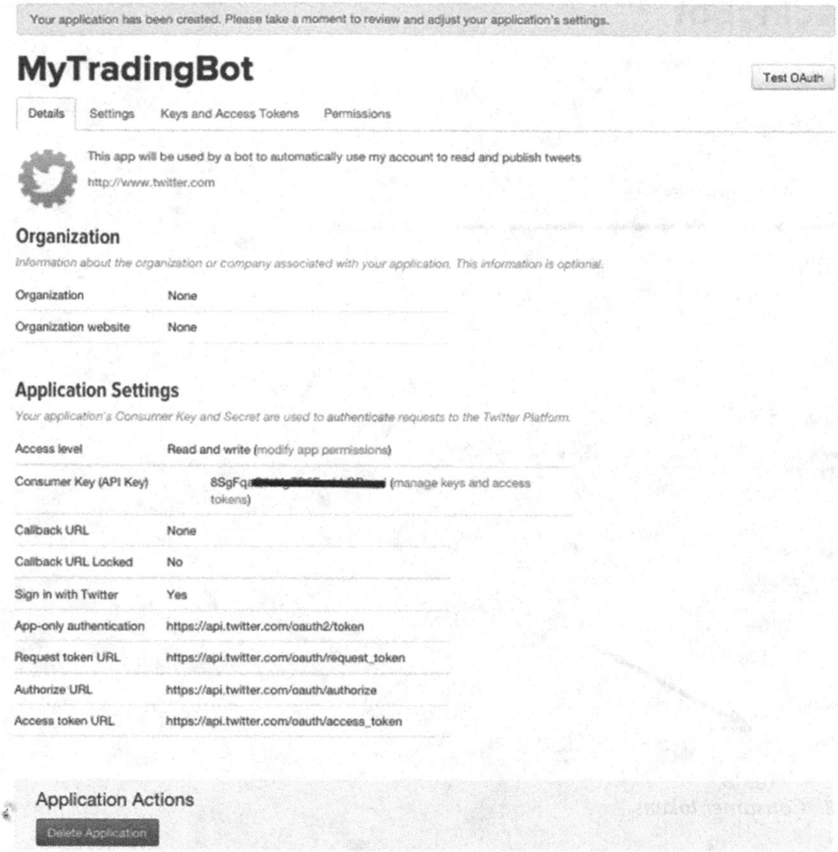

Your application has been created. Please take a moment to review and adjust your application's settings.

MyTradingBot

Test OAuth

Details | Settings | Keys and Access Tokens | Permissions

This app will be used by a bot to automatically use my account to read and publish tweets

http://www.twitter.com

Organization

Information about the organization or company associated with your application. This information is optional.

Organization   None

Organization website   None

Application Settings

Your application's Consumer Key and Secret are used to authenticate requests to the Twitter Platform.

Access level   Read and write (modify app permissions)

Consumer Key (API Key)   8SgFqa▆▆▆▆▆▆▆▆▆▆▆▆ (manage keys and access tokens)

Callback URL   None

Callback URL Locked   No

Sign in with Twitter   Yes

App-only authentication   https://api.twitter.com/oauth2/token

Request token URL   https://api.twitter.com/oauth/request_token

Authorize URL   https://api.twitter.com/oauth/authorize

Access token URL   https://api.twitter.com/oauth/access_token

Application Actions

Delete Application

Figure 8-2. Twitter app created successfully

3. While on the confirmation screen, you must now click on the Keys and Access Tokens tab, where you should see the Consumer Key Token and Consumer Key Secret display (see Figure 8-3). Make a note of these tokens, as you will need them later.

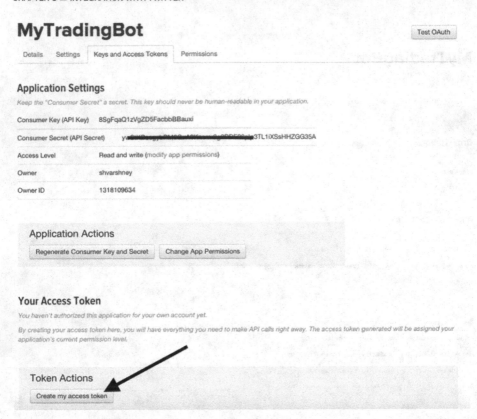

Figure 8-3. *Consumer tokens*

4. You can now create the other access tokens. Click on the button below Token Actions to generate the tokens. You should see the screen shown in Figure 8-4.

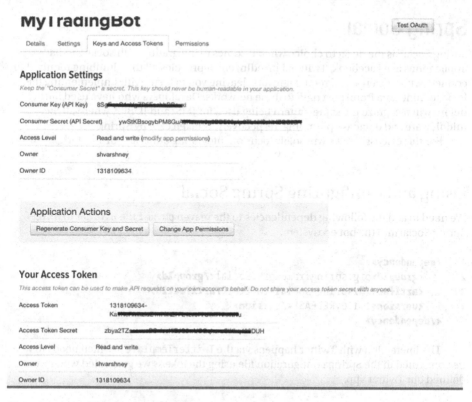

Figure 8-4. *Authorization tokens*

You should now have the following four tokens, which are required for the trading bot app to log in using your account.

- Consumer key
- Consumer secret
- Access key token
- Access key secret

Spring Social

Spring Social[2] is the de facto choice when it comes to integrating with social media applications like Facebook, Twitter, LinkedIn, etc. It provides all the plumbing required to connect with a given social media network, leaving you to focus with implementing the logic to mine data from/post data to these networks. Developers who have used Spring before will recognize the same pattern being used for JMS[3] and JDBC[4], where all the middleware and database plumbing, respectively, is taken care by Spring.

For this discussion, we will solely focus on integrating our bot with Twitter[5].

Using and Configuring Spring Social

We need to add the following dependencies to the maven pm.xml file in order to bring Spring Social into the bot ecosystem.

```
1    <dependency>
2        <groupId>org.springframework.social</groupId>
3        <artifactId>spring-social-twitter</artifactId>
4        <version>1.1.0.RELEASE</version>
5    </dependency>
```

The interaction with Twitter happens via the TwitterTemplate,[6] which needs to be configured in the Spring configuration file using the tokens we generated when we defined our Twitter app.

```
1    <bean id="twitter" class="org.springframework.social.twitter.api.impl.
     TwitterTemplate">
2                    <constructor-arg index="0" value="${twitter.
                    consumerKey}"/>
3                    <constructor-arg index="1" value="${twitter.
                    consumerSecret}"/>
4                    <constructor-arg index="2" value="${twitter.
                    accessToken}"/>
5                    <constructor-arg index="3" value="${twitter.
                    accessTokenSecret}"/>
6    </bean>
```

With this code, TwitterTemplate is ready to be injected in any services.

---

[2]http://docs.spring.io/spring-social/docs/1.0.x/reference/html/overview.html
[3]http://docs.spring.io/spring/docs/current/javadoc-api/org/springframework/jms/core/JmsTemplate.html
[4]http://docs.spring.io/spring/docs/current/javadoc-api/org/springframework/jdbc/core/JdbcTemplate.html
[5]https://dev.twitter.com/overview/documentation
[6]http://docs.spring.io/spring-social-twitter/docs/1.0.5.RELEASE/api/org/springframework/social/twitter/api/impl/TwitterTemplate.html

Harvesting FX Tweets

Now we come to the meat of the chapter, where we discuss how to harvest (search) well structured trade/order tweets. Our aim is to find well structured tweets that can be parsed to create the following POJOs.

- NewFXTradeTweet

```
1  public class NewFXTradeTweet < T > extends FXTradeTweet < T > {
2   private final double stopLoss,
3   takeProfit;
4   private final TradingSignal action;
5   private final String str;
6
7   public NewFXTradeTweet(TradeableInstrument < T > instrument, double
    price,
8    double stopLoss, double takeProfit,
9    TradingSignal action) {
10   super(instrument, price);
11   this.stopLoss = stopLoss;
12   this.takeProfit = takeProfit;
13   this.action = action;
14   this.str = String.format("%s@%3.5f TP: %3.5f: SL: %3.5f %s",
15    instrument.getInstrument(), price, takeProfit,
16    stopLoss, action.name());
17   }
18
19   @Override
20   public String toString() {
21   return str;
22   }
23
24   public TradingSignal getAction() {
25   return this.action;
26   }
27
28   public double getStopLoss() {
29   return stopLoss;
30   }
31
32   public double getTakeProfit() {
33   return takeProfit;
34   }
35
36  }
```

- CloseFXTradeTweet

```
1  public class CloseFXTradeTweet < T > extends FXTradeTweet < T > {
2   private final double profit,
3   price;
4
5   public CloseFXTradeTweet(TradeableInstrument < T > instrument, double
    profit,
6    double price) {
7    super(instrument, price);
8    this.profit = profit;
9    this.price = price;
10   }
11
12   public double getProfit() {
13    return profit;
14   }
15
16   @Override
17   public double getPrice() {
18    return price;
19   }
20
21  }
```

where the base FXTradeTweet is

```
1  public abstract class FXTradeTweet < T > {
2   private final TradeableInstrument < T > instrument;
3   private final double price;
4
5   public FXTradeTweet(TradeableInstrument < T > instrument, double
    price) {
6    super();
7    this.instrument = instrument;
8    this.price = price;
9   }
10
11   public TradeableInstrument < T > getInstrument() {
12    return instrument;
13   }
14
15   public double getPrice() {
16    return price;
17   }
18
19  }
```

The concept of a well structured trade tweet indicates a set of Twitter users who consistently tweet in a given format and for which we can write a `TweetHandler`. We are only interested in their tweets that are about a new order or closing a trade. The reason for this will become clearer when we discuss a strategy based on tweets. For the time being, let's look at some examples of tweets from the `@SignalFactory`[7] and `@ZuluTrader101`[8] users as an illustration.

- Tweets from @SignalFactory are shown in Figures 8-5 through 8-8.

Figure 8-5. New trade

Figure 8-6. New trade

Figure 8-7. Close trade

Figure 8-8. Close trade

---

[7]https://twitter.com/SignalFactory
[8]https://twitter.com/ZuluTrader101

- Tweets from @ZuluTrader101 are shown in Figures 8-9 and 8-10.

Figure 8-9. *New and close trades*

Figure 8-10. *New and close trades*

Looking at the tweet examples from these two users, notice that there is certain format in which they tweet. It then becomes trivial to parse these tweets if we assign a dedicated tweet handler that parses tweets from a given user. We will come back to discussing the handlers shortly. Before that let's look at how we search for tweets from given users.

TweetHarvester Interface

The TweetHarvester interface mandates the search for Tweets for a given user that result in a collection of both new/closed trades FX Tweets. Its definition is as follows:

```
1    public interface TweetHarvester < T > {
2
3      Collection < NewFXTradeTweet < T >> harvestNewTradeTweets(String
         userId);
4
5      Collection < CloseFXTradeTweet < T >> harvestHistoricTradeTweets(Stri
         ng userId,
6        TradeableInstrument < T > instrument);
7    }
```

The first method of the interface is fairly straightforward. This method's contract is to harvest new trade tweets from a given user since the last search was done. The implementer is responsible for keeping track of the timeline and should only return the new ones.

The second method's contract is again to harvest new tweets, this time for closed trades since the last search and for a given instrument.

FXTweetHandler Interface

As discussed earlier in this chapter, as long as the user consistently tweets in a given format, a dedicated handler assigned to that FX new/close trade tweet can parse their tweets and create NewFxTradeTweet and CloseFXTradeTweet from them. This interface formulates that contract and provides a few other useful methods:

```
1    public interface FXTweetHandler < T > {
2
3      FXTradeTweet < T > handleTweet(Tweet tweet);
4
5      String getUserId();
6
7      Collection < Tweet > findNewTweets();
8
9      Collection < Tweet > findHistoricPnlTweetsForInstrument(
10       TradeableInstrument < T > instrument);
11   }
```

The first three interface methods are fairly self-explanatory. The method findHistoricPnlTweetsForInstrument requires a bit of explanation. The contract for this method is to retrieve all tweets that were posted by a given user for a given instrument. They must also be close trade tweets that resulted in a PNL figure. (For example, a positive or a negative pip figure result. Refer back to the close trade tweets of the two users discussed in this chapter.) This might not make much sense now, but it will become clear when we discuss our Twitter-based strategy in the next chapter.

AbstractFXTweetHandler Base Class

We start the discussion about the implementation of FXTweetHandler interface by defining an abstract class that implements this interface but only implements a couple of key methods of the interface—findNewTweets() and getUserId().

The implementation of the method findNewTweets() in particular presents us with the opportunity to discuss Twitter search API[9]. The API provides us with comprehensive set of query operators that enable us to build a search query and retrieve a collection of tweets in reverse chronological order. The response from Twitter is a JSON payload, but because we are using TwitterTemplate, Spring takes care of parsing the payload and converting it into a collection of org.springframework.social.twitter.api.Tweet objects, which are much easier to work with.

■ **Tip**   It is strongly recommended that you read the search API page in order to understand the operators, the constraints around the results returned, and best practices before proceeding further.

Some examples taken directly and slightly modified from the documentation and relevant to our search are as follows:

Operator	Finds Tweets
from:foo	Find tweets from user foo
from:foo since: 2015-012-01	Find tweets from user foo since 2015-012-01
from:foo since_id: 10000000	Find tweets from user foo since tweet ID 10000000
from:foo Profit: OR Loss:	Find tweets from user foo containing certain characters (Profit: OR Loss:)

---

[9]https://dev.twitter.com/rest/public/search

```
1    public abstract class AbstractFXTweetHandler < T > implements
     FXTweetHandler < T > {
2
3     @Autowired
4     protected Twitter twitter;
5     @Autowired
6     protected InstrumentService < T > instrumentService;
7     @Autowired
8     protected ProviderHelper providerHelper;
9
10    protected final DateTime startTime = DateTime.now();
11    protected final String startTimeAsStr;
12    protected volatile Long lastTweetId = null;
13    protected final String userId;
14    protected static final String CLOSED = "Closed";
15    protected static final String BOUGHT = "Bought";
16    protected static final String SOLD = "Sold";
17    protected static final Logger LOG =
18    Logger.getLogger(AbstractFXTweetHandler.class);
19    static final String FROM_USER_SINCE_TIME_TWITTER_QRY_TMPL =
20    "from:%s since:%s";
21    static final String FROM_USER_SINCE_ID_TWITTER_QRY_TMPL =
22    "from:%s since_id:%d";
23
24    protected AbstractFXTweetHandler(String userId) {
25     this.userId = userId;
26     DateTimeFormatter formatter = DateTimeFormat.forPattern("yyyy-MM-dd");
27     startTimeAsStr = formatter.print(this.startTime);
28    }
29
30    protected abstract NewFXTradeTweet < T > parseNewTrade(String
      tokens[]);
31
32    protected abstract CloseFXTradeTweet < T > parseCloseTrade(String
      tokens[]);
33
34    @Override
35    public String getUserId() {
36     return userId;
37    }
38
39    private class TweetPredicate implements Predicate < Tweet > {
40
41     @Override
42     public boolean apply(Tweet input) {
43      return startTime.isBefore(input.getCreatedAt().getTime());
44     }
```

```
45
46    }
47
48    @Override
49    public Collection < Tweet > findNewTweets() {
50     SearchResults results = null;
51     if (lastTweetId == null) { // find new tweets since the start of the
       app
52      synchronized(this) {
53       if (lastTweetId == null) { // double check locking
54        results = twitter.searchOperations().search(
55         String.format(
56          FROM_USER_SINCE_TIME_TWITTER_QRY_TMPL, getUserId(), this.
          startTimeAsStr));
57        TweetPredicate predicate = new TweetPredicate();
58        List < Tweet > filteredTweets = Lists.newArrayList();
59        for (Tweet tweet: results.getTweets()) {
60         if (predicate.apply(tweet)) {
61          if (lastTweetId == null) {
62           /*take the first one as the tweets are in reverse
                   chronological order */
63           this.lastTweetId = tweet.getId();
64          }
65          filteredTweets.add(tweet);
66         }
67        }
68        return filteredTweets;
69       }
70
71      }
72
73     }
74     results = twitter.searchOperations().search(
75      String.format(
76       FROM_USER_SINCE_ID_TWITTER_QRY_TMPL, getUserId(), lastTweetId));
77     List < Tweet > tweets = results.getTweets();
78     if (!TradingUtils.isEmpty(tweets)) {
79      lastTweetId = tweets.get(0).getId();
80     }
81     return tweets;
82
83    }
84   }
```

The meat of this class lies in the implementation of the the method findNewTweets(). The method tries to retrieve all new tweets since the last API call was made. It is assumed that there is a scheduled job that runs at regular intervals and calls this method to fetch the newest tweets. In order to retrieve the newest ones since the last call, the class has to internally keep track of the last tweet fetched. By using an ID greater than the last ID for the given user, it is able to find all the newest tweets for that user. However, when it is invoked for the first time, we need to explore another way to find the newest tweets. In this case, we use the time the class was initialized as the starting point to retrieve tweets. This is the logic that we see executed when if (lastTweetId == null). In order to make the class thread-safe, additional synchronization is provided, taking into account the double-check locking[10]. The time-based approach uses the query from:%s since:%s, where we supply the user ID in question and the startup time in the format yyyy-MM-dd. Once this search returns results, we can take the first tweet in the collection and set its ID as the latest ID to start the next search from. In that case, we use the query string from:%s since_id:%d, providing the user ID and the ID set from the last search. Just to reiterate, the search results are sorted from newest to oldest.

User-Specific TweetHandlers

■ **Warning**   The tweet format discussed for individual users can change without any notice. Therefore, it is imperative that we write defensive code as much as possible for parsing purposes.

To conclude this discussion, we will look at TweetHandlers for the users we discussed earlier in the chapter. Most of the code should center on parsing tweets, as it is very specific to that user. The functionality that is common, like searching for new tweets by a user, is abstracted in the base class AbstractFXTweetHandler, which we discussed in the previous section.

For new trades we are interested in parsing the following information:

- Trade action
- Instrument pair
- Limit price
- Stop loss price
- Take profit price

For close trades we want to parse this information:

- Instrument pair
- Close price
- Profit/loss pips

---

[10]https://en.wikipedia.org/wiki/Double-checked_locking

SignalFactoryFXTweetHandler

This tweet handler attempts to parse new/close trade related tweets published by the user @SignalFactory. Just to refresh our minds, let's look at some examples of new and close trade tweets by the user in text form:

```
1    //New Trade
2    Forex Signal | Sell USDCHF@0.91902 | SL:0.92302 | TP:0.91102 |
     2015.01.30 17:52 GMT | #fx #forex #fb
3
4    Forex Signal | Sell GBPAUD@2.03572 | SL:2.03972 | TP:2.02772 |
     2016.01.22 12:40 GMT | #fx #forex #fb
5
6    Forex Signal | Buy GBPCAD@2.03229 | SL:2.02829 | TP:2.04029 |
     2016.01.22 13:56 GMT | #fx #forex #fb
7
8    //Close Trade
9    Forex Signal | Close(SL) Buy NZDCHF@0.66566 | Loss: -40 pips |
     2015.01.30 18:16 GMT | #fx #forex #fb
10
11   Forex Signal | Close(TP) Buy GBPCHF@1.44636 | Profit: +80 pips |
     2016.01.22 11:55 GMT | #fx #forex #fb
12
13   Forex Signal | Close(SL) Sell GBPAUD@2.03972 | Loss: -40 pips |
     2016.01.22 13:03 GMT | #fx #forex #fb
```

For a new trade, we can make the following observations for this user (assuming we initially parse the whole tweet by the separator character | and get six tokens):

- The trade actions are indicated by the words "Buy" or "Sell," which are the first words of the second token.

- The instrument pair is always the first subtoken obtained from the second word of second token split by an @ character.

- The limit price is the second subtoken obtained from the second word of second token split by an @ character.

- The stop loss price is the second subtoken obtained from the third token when split by the : character.

- The take profit price is the second subtoken obtained from the fourth token when split by the : character.

For a close trade, we can make the following observations for this user (assuming we initially parse the whole tweet by the separator character | and get five tokens):

- The instrument pair is always the first subtoken obtained from the third word of the second token split by an @ character.

- The close price is always the second subtoken obtained from the third word of the second token split by an @ character.

- The profit/loss is the always the second word of the third token.

A general observation:

- A tweet relates to a new trade if the first word of the second token is either "buy" or "sell".

- A tweet relates to a close trade if the first word of the second token starts with the word "close".

Let's look at the code that implements these observations.

```
1   public class SignalFactoryFXTweetHandler
2   extends AbstractFXTweetHandler < String > {
3     private static final String BUY = "Buy";
4     private static final String SELL = "Sell";
5     private static final String CLOSE = "Close";
6     private static final String COLON = ":";
7     private static final String AT_THE_RATE = "@";
8
9     public SignalFactoryFXTweetHandler(String userid) {
10      super(userid);
11    }
12
13    @Override
14    protected NewFXTradeTweet < String > parseNewTrade(String tokens[]) {
15      String token1[] = tokens[1].trim().split(TradingConstants.SPACE_RGX);
16      String action = token1[0];
17      String tokens1spl[] = token1[1].split(AT_THE_RATE);
18      String tokens2[] = tokens[2].trim().split(COLON);
19      String tokens3[] = tokens[3].trim().split(COLON);
20
21      return new NewFXTradeTweet < String > (new TradeableInstrument <
          String > (this.providerHelper
22        .fromIsoFormat(tokens1spl[0])), Double.parseDouble(tokens1spl[1]),
23        Double.parseDouble(tokens2[1]),  Double.parseDouble(tokens3[1]),
24        BUY.equals(action) ? TradingSignal.LONG : TradingSignal.SHORT);
25    }
26
27    @Override
28    protected CloseFXTradeTweet < String > parseCloseTrade(String
      tokens[]) {
29      String token1[] = tokens[1].trim().split(TradingConstants.SPACE_RGX);
30      String tokens1spl[] = token1[token1.length - 1].split(AT_THE_RATE);
31      String token2[] = tokens[2].trim().split(TradingConstants.SPACE_RGX);
```

```
32    return new CloseFXTradeTweet < String > (new TradeableInstrument <
      String > (this.providerHelper
33      .fromIsoFormat(tokens1spl[0])), Double.parseDouble(token2[1]),
34     Double.parseDouble(tokens1spl[1]));
35    }
36
37    @Override
38    public FXTradeTweet < String > handleTweet(Tweet tweet) {
39     String tweetTxt = tweet.getText();
40     String tokens[] = StringUtils.split(tweetTxt, TradingConstants.
      PIPE_CHR);
41     if (tokens.length >= 5) {
42      String action = tokens[1].trim();
43      if (action.startsWith(BUY) || action.startsWith(SELL)) {
44       return parseNewTrade(tokens);
45      } else if (action.startsWith(CLOSE)) {
46       return parseCloseTrade(tokens);
47      }
48     }
49     return null;
50    }
51
52    @Override
53    public Collection < Tweet > findHistoricPnlTweetsForInstrument(Tradeab
      leInstrument < String > instrument) {
54     /*
55      * AND queries for the case below have suddenly stopped working.
56      * something simple like from:SignalFactory GBPNZD is not working.
57      * Check it out yourself on https://twitter.com/search-advanced.
58      * Apparently the only option is to get all tweets with phrase Profit
59      * or Loss and then use String contains to perform the step2
60      * filtering */
61
62     String query = String.format("Profit: OR Loss: from:%s", getUserId(),
      isoInstr);
63     SearchResults results = twitter.searchOperations().search(query);
64     List < Tweet > pnlTweets = results.getTweets();
65     List < Tweet > filteredPnlTweets = Lists.newArrayList();
66     for (Tweet pnlTweet: pnlTweets) {
67      if (pnlTweet.getText().contains(isoInstr)) {
68       filteredPnlTweets.add(pnlTweet);
69      }
70     }
71     return filteredPnlTweets;
72    }
73   }
```

The action starts in the handleTweet(Tweet tweet) method, which is invoked as part of parsing the search results for a given user. There is logic to decide whether the tweet relates to a new or a close trade or none. This is pretty much the "general observation" we made regarding tweets from this user. If the tweet is indeed a new or a close trade, we parse and return an instance of the NewFxTradeTweet or CloseFxTradeTweet, which are both subclasses of the FXTradeTweet class. The parsing logic is pretty much exactly what we discussed in the observations section.

The last remaining method that needs a bit more explanation is findHistoricPnlTweetsForInstrument. Here, we are looking for past close trades tweets. Since we are only looking for such tweets by this user, we must use the phrases this user uses to denote a profit or a loss. This is precisely what the query from:%s AND %s AND Profit: OR Loss: does. Looking back at the examples of close trades from this user, we can see that the words "Profit:" or "Loss:" appear as the first word of the third token.

ZuluTrader101FXTweetHandler

This tweet handler attempts to parse new/close trade-related tweets published by the user @ZuluTrader101. Just to refresh our minds, let's look at some examples of new and close trade tweets by this user in text form:

```
1   //New Trade
2   Bought 0.43 Lots #EURUSD 1.1371 | Auto-copy FREE at http://goo.gl/
    moaYzx #Forex #Finance #Money
3
4   Bought 0.69 Lots #GBPCHF 1.4614 SL 1.45817 TP 1.46617 | Auto-copy FREE
    at http://goo.gl/moaYzx #Forex #Finance #Money
5
6   Sold 0.34 Lots #EURUSD 1.13694 | Auto-copy FREE at  http://goo.gl/
    moaYzx #Forex #Finance #Money
7
8   Sold 0.43 Lots #EURUSD 1.13117 SL 1.13281 TP 1.12963 | Auto-copy FREE
    at http://goo.gl/moaYzx #Forex #Finance #Money
9
10  Bought 0.66 Lots #EURGBP 0.73532 SL 0.70534 | Auto-copy FREE at http://
    goo.gl/moaYzx #Forex #Finance #Money
11
12  //Close Trade
13  Closed Buy 0.64 Lots #USDJPY 118.773 for +17.7 pips, total for today
    -136.7 pips
14
15  Closed Sell 0.69 Lots #NZDUSD 0.75273 for +8.4 pips, total for today
    -1072.8 pips
16
17  Closed Buy 7.0 Lots #XAUUSD 1207.94 for -549.0 pips, total for today
    -1731.4 pips
```

For a new trade, we can make the following observations for this user (assuming we initially parse the whole tweet by the separator character | and get two tokens):

- The trade actions always include the words "bought" or "sold," which are the first word of the first token.

- The currency pair is always the fourth word starting with # in the first token.

- The price is always the fifth word in the first token.

- The stop loss price is optional and is only present as the next word after the keyword SL in the first token.

- The take profit price is optional and is only present as the next word after the keyword TP in the first token.

For a close trade, we can make the following observations for this user:

- The currency pair is always the fifth word starting with # in the tweet.

- The close price is always the sixth word in the tweet.

- The profit/loss figure is always the eighth word in the tweet.

A general observation:

- A tweet relates to a close trade if it starts with the word "closed".

- A tweet relates to a new trade if the tweet starts with the words "bought" or "sold".

Now let's switch our attention to the code implementation:

```java
1  public class ZuluTrader101FXTweetHandler  2    extends
   AbstractFXTweetHandler < String > {
3
4    protected ZuluTrader101FXTweetHandler(String userId) {
5      super(userId);
6    }
7
8    private int idxOfTP(String[] tokens) {
9     int idx = 0;
10   for (String token: tokens) {
11    if ("TP".equals(token)) {
12      return idx;
13    }
14    idx++;
15   }
16   return -1;
17  }
18
```

```java
19    private int idxOfSL(String[] tokens) {
20     int idx = 0;
21     for (String token: tokens) {
22     if ("SL".equals(token)) {
23      return idx;
24     }
25     idx++;
26     }
27     return -1;
28    }
29
30    @Override
31    protected NewFXTradeTweet < String > parseNewTrade(String[] tokens) {
32
33     String currencyPair = null;
34     try {
35      String ccyWithHashTag = tokens[3];
36      currencyPair = this.providerHelper.fromHashTagCurrency(ccyWithHash
       Tag);
37      double price = Double.parseDouble(tokens[4]);
38      TradingSignal signal = BOUGHT.equals(tokens[0]) ? TradingSignal.LONG :
39       TradingSignal.SHORT;
40      double stopLoss = 0.0;
41      double takeProfit = 0.0;
42      int idxTp = idxOfTP(tokens);
43      if (idxTp != -1) {
44       takeProfit = Double.parseDouble(tokens[idxTp + 1]);
45      }
46      int idxSl = idxOfSL(tokens);
47      if (idxSl != -1) {
48       stopLoss = Double.parseDouble(tokens[idxSl + 1]);
49      }
50      return new NewFXTradeTweet < String > (new TradeableInstrument <
       String > (currencyPair), price, stopLoss,
51       takeProfit, signal);
52     } catch (Exception e) {
53      LOG.info(
54       String.format(" got err %s parsing tweet tokens for new trade ",
55       e.getMessage()));
56      return null;
57     }
58
59    }
60
61    @Override
```

```
62   protected CloseFXTradeTweet < String > parseCloseTrade(String[]
     tokens) {
63
64    String currencyPair = null;
65    try {
66     String ccyWithHashTag = tokens[4];
67     currencyPair = this.providerHelper.fromHashTagCurrency(ccyWithHash
       Tag);
68     String strPnlPips = tokens[7];
69     return new CloseFXTradeTweet < String > (new TradeableInstrument <
       String > (currencyPair), Double
70       .parseDouble(strPnlPips),  Double.parseDouble(tokens[5]));
71    } catch (Exception e) {
72     LOG.info(
73      String.format(" got err %s parsing tweet tokens for close trade:",
74       e.getMessage())));
75     return null;
76    }
77
78   }
79
80   @Override
81   public FXTradeTweet < String > handleTweet(Tweet tweet) {
82    String tweetTxt = tweet.getText();
83    String tokens[] = tweetTxt.trim().split(TradingConstants.SPACE_RGX);
84    if (tweetTxt.startsWith(CLOSED)) {
85     return parseCloseTrade(tokens);
86    } else if (tweetTxt.startsWith(BOUGHT) || tweetTxt.startsWith(SOLD))
     {
87     return parseNewTrade(tokens);
88    }
89    return null;
90   }
91
92   @Override
93   public Collection < Tweet >
94    findHistoricPnlTweetsForInstrument(TradeableInstrument < String >
     instrument) {
95     String isoInstr = TradingConstants.HASHTAG +
96      this.providerHelper.toIsoFormat(instrument.getInstrument());
97     SearchResults results = twitter.searchOperations().search(
98      String.format("from:%s AND %s AND \"Closed Buy\" OR \"Closed
       Sell\"",
99       getUserId(), isoInstr));
100    return results.getTweets();
101   }
102
103  }
```

As before, the action starts in the handleTweet(Tweet tweet) method. This time around, we have a slightly different logic, based on the general observation regarding which tweet is a new or close trade or is not parsable. Assuming that it is either a new or a close trade, we proceed to parse the tweet. The parsing follows the same logic mentioned in the observations section.

The very last thing remaining to discuss is the method findHistoricPnlTweetsForInstrument for this user. Just as for the user @SignalFactory, we need to find the phrases used by this user to denote closed trades. It turns out that this user, @ZuluTrader101, from our observations about closed trades, uses the phrases "closed buy" or "closed sell". Hence, our query looks like from:%s AND %s AND "Closed Buy" OR "Closed Sell". Just a remark before we go, about the Twitter search API. If we double-quote a phrase, it means we are looking for an exact match of that phrase. And this is what we want for this user.

Try It Yourself

In this section we are going to write a demo program that harvests tweets from a given user. Recent tests show that a very simple tweet search from user @ZuluTrader101 do not show up, even on the Twitter advanced search page. We are going to use the @Forex_EA4U [11] user, who tweets in very similar format.

```
1   package com.precioustech.fxtrading.tradingbot.social.twitter.
    tweethandler;
2
3   import java.util.Collection;
4   import java.util.Iterator;
5
6   import org.apache.log4j.Logger;
7   import org.springframework.context.ApplicationContext;
8   import org.springframework.context.support.
    ClassPathXmlApplicationContext;
9
10  import com.precioustech.fxtrading.instrument.TradeableInstrument;
11  import com.precioustech.fxtrading.tradingbot.social.twitter.
    CloseFXTradeTweet;
12  import com.precioustech.fxtrading.tradingbot.social.twitter.
    NewFXTradeTweet;
13
14  public class TweetHarvesterDemo {
15    private static final Logger LOG = Logger.getLogger(TweetHarvesterDemo.
      class);
16
17    @SuppressWarnings("unchecked")
18    public static void main(String[] args) {
```

---

[11]https://twitter.com/Forex_EA4U

```
19
20     ApplicationContext appContext =
21      new ClassPathXmlApplicationContext("tweetharvester-demo.xml");
22     TweetHarvester < String > tweetHarvester = appContext.
       getBean(TweetHarvester.class);
23
24     TradeableInstrument < String > eurusd = new  TradeableInstrument
       < String > ("EUR_USD");
25     String userId = "Forex_EA4U";
26     // String userId = "SignalFactory";
27     final int tweetsToDump = 10;
28     int ctr = 0;
29
30     Collection < NewFXTradeTweet < String >> newTradeTweets =
31      tweetHarvester.harvestNewTradeTweets(userId);
32     LOG.info(
33      String.format("+++++++++ Dumping the first %d of %d new fx tweets
       for userid %s +++++++",
34       tweetsToDump, newTradeTweets.size(), userId));
35     Iterator < NewFXTradeTweet < String >> newTweetItr = newTradeTweets.
       iterator();
36     while (newTweetItr.hasNext() && ctr < tweetsToDump) {
37      NewFXTradeTweet < String > newFxTweet = newTweetItr.next();
38      LOG.info(newFxTweet);
39      ctr++;
40     }
41
42     Collection < CloseFXTradeTweet < String >> closedTradeTweets =
43      tweetHarvester.harvestHistoricTradeTweets(userId,  eurusd);
44     ctr = 0;
45     Iterator < CloseFXTradeTweet < String >> closedTweetItr =
       closedTradeTweets.iterator();
46     LOG.info(
47      String.format("+++++++++ Dumping the first %d of %d closed fx tweets
       for userid %s +++++++",
48       tweetsToDump, closedTradeTweets.size(), userId));
49     while (closedTweetItr.hasNext() && ctr < tweetsToDump) {
50      CloseFXTradeTweet < String > closeFxTweet = closedTweetItr.next();
51      LOG.info(
52       String.format("Instrument %s, profit = %3.1f, price=%2.5f ",
53        closeFxTweet.getInstrument().getInstrument(),   closeFxTweet.
        getProfit(),
54        closeFxTweet.getPrice())));
55      ctr++;
56     }
57
58     }
59
60   }
```

This is a Spring-driven demo, because we want to use the `TwitterTemplate` discussed earlier. The Spring configuration looks like this:

```
1   <?xml version="1.0" encoding="UTF-8"?>
2   <beans xmlns="http://www.springframework.org/schema/beans"
3       xmlns:xsi="http://www.w3.org/2001/XMLSchema-instance"
4       xmlns:context="http://www.springframework.org/schema/context"
5       xmlns:util="http://www.springframework.org/schema/util"
6       xmlns:task="http://www.springframework.org/schema/task"
7       xmlns:tx="http://www.springframework.org/schema/tx"
8       xsi:schemaLocation="http://www.springframework.org/schema/beans
9       http://www.springframework.org/schema/beans/spring-beans.xsd
10      http://www.springframework.org/schema/context
11      http://www.springframework.org/schema/context/spring-context.xsd
12      http://www.springframework.org/schema/util
13      http://www.springframework.org/schema/util/spring-util.xsd">
14      <context:annotation-config/>
15      <bean id="twitter" class="org.springframework.social.twitter.api.
        impl.TwitterTemplate">
16              <constructor-arg  index="0" value="#{
                systemProperties['twitter.consumerKey'] }"/>
17              <constructor-arg index="1" value="#{
                systemProperties['twitter.consumerSecret'] }"/>
18              <constructor-arg index="2" value="#{
                systemProperties['twitter.accessToken'] }"/>
19              <constructor-arg index="3" value="#{
                systemProperties['twitter.accessTokenSecret'] }"/>
20      </bean>
21      <bean id="providerHelper" class="com.precioustech.fxtrading.
        oanda.restapi.helper.OandaProviderHelper"/>
22      <bean id="instrumentDataProvider"
23              class="com.precioustech.fxtrading.oanda.restapi.
                instrument.OandaInstrumentDataProviderService">
24              <constructor-arg  index="0" value="#{
                systemProperties['oanda.url'] }"/>
25              <constructor-arg index="1" value="#{
                systemProperties['oanda.accountId'] }"/>
26              <constructor-arg index="2" value="#{
                systemProperties['oanda.accessToken'] }"/>
27      </bean>
28      <bean id="instrumentService" class="com.precioustech.fxtrading.
        instrument.InstrumentService">
29              <constructor-arg index="0" ref="instrumentDataProvider"/>
30      </bean>
```

```
31          <bean id="fxTweeterList" class="java.util.ArrayList">
32                  <constructor-arg index="0">
33                          <list>
34                                  <value>SignalFactory</value>
35                                  <value>Forex_EA4U</value>
36                          </list>
37                  </constructor-arg>
38          </bean>
39          <bean id="startTimeLine" class="org.joda.time.DateTime">
40                  <constructor-arg index="0" value="1451606400000"
                    type="long"/><!-- 01 Jan 2016 -->
41          </bean>
42          <util:map id="tweetHandlerMap">
43                  <entry key="#{fxTweeterList[0]}">
44                          <bean
45          class="com.precioustech.fxtrading.tradingbot.social.twitter.
            tweethandler.SignalFactoryFXTweetHandler">
46                          <constructor-arg index="0" value="#{
                            fxTweeterList[0]}"/>
47                          <property name="startTime" ref="startTimeLine"/>
48                          </bean>
49                  </entry>
50                  <entry key="#{fxTweeterList[1]}">
51                          <bean
52          class="com.precioustech.fxtrading.tradingbot.social.twitter.
            tweethandler.ZuluTrader101FXTweetHandler">
53                          <constructor-arg index="0" value="#{fxTweeterLi
                            st[1]}"/>
54                          <property name="startTime" ref="startTimeLine"/>
55                          </bean>
56                  </entry>
57          </util:map>
58          <bean id="orderQueue" class="java.util.concurrent.
            LinkedBlockingQueue"/>
59          <bean id="copyTwitterStrategy"
60          class="com.precioustech.fxtrading.tradingbot.strategies.
            CopyTwitterStrategy"/>
61  </beans>
```

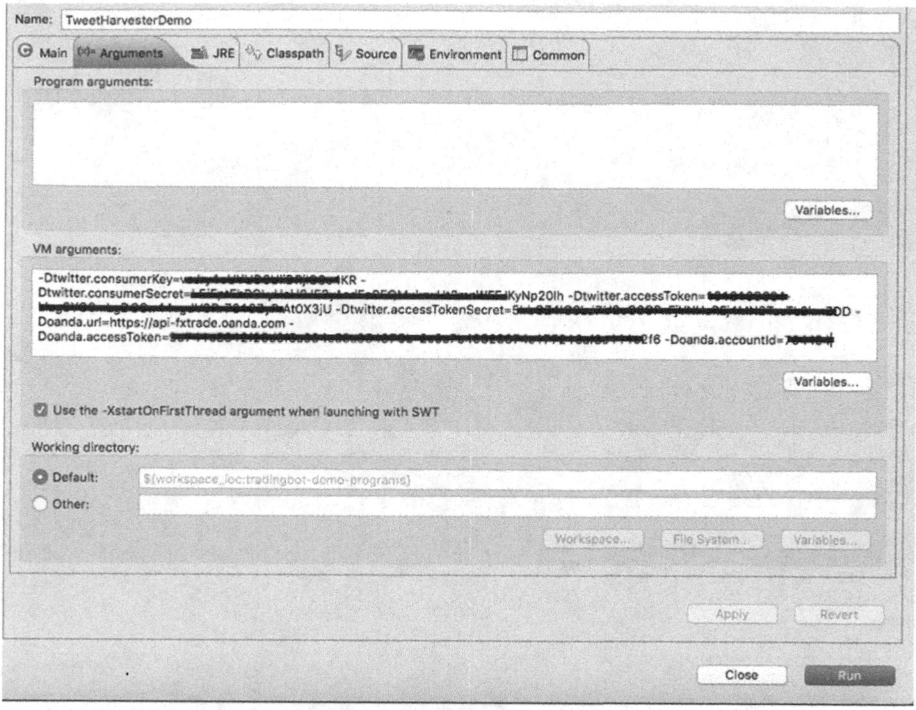

Figure 8-11. *Launch configuration with system properties*

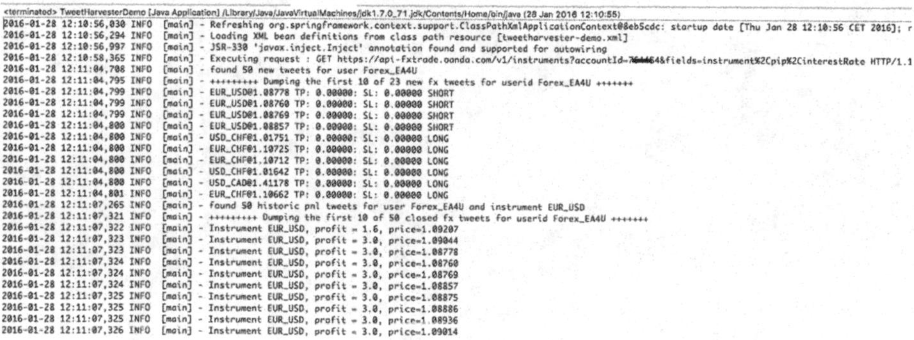

Figure 8-12. *Sample output*

CHAPTER 9

■ ■ ■

Implementing Strategies

It is now time to give our bot wings and make it fly!! Well, what I mean is that the time has come to add capabilities to our bot so that it can make decisions in terms of placing orders based on a certain set of rules that we know is a strategy. Basically, we want to add the power of analysis to our bot to determine whether to buy or sell a currency pair or to stay put and wait for the right moment. The analysis can be based on several external parameters, including:

- Market data

- News events

- Social media feeds

- Technical analysis

- Sentiment

A strategy can be based solely on technical analysis of prices over a period of time and on the other hand can be based on realtime analysis of all or a mixture of these parameters. For example, a complex strategy could be built on realtime analysis of social media feeds to ascertain the *sentiment index* (a hypothetical index based on how much positivity surrounds us) and market data to arrive at a trading decision. It can be as simple as single dimensional analysis to as complex as multivariate analysis. The possibilities are infinite!

In this chapter, we try to implement a couple of strategies, one of them based on Twitter feed analysis and the other a more popular one, used often by traders. We will program these strategies and integrate them into our trading bot in order to build capabilities to produce a trading signal, and as a result, place orders.

Before we dive into these strategies, I want to take this opportunity to discuss briefly the design of how the various strategies generate a TradingDecision that's placed in the queue. The OrderExecutionService then picks these TradingDecision messages (see Figure 9-1). Chapter 6 covers how these messages are handled.

© Shekhar Varshney 2016

S. Varshney, *Building Trading Bots Using Java*, DOI 10.1007/978-1-4842-2520-2_9

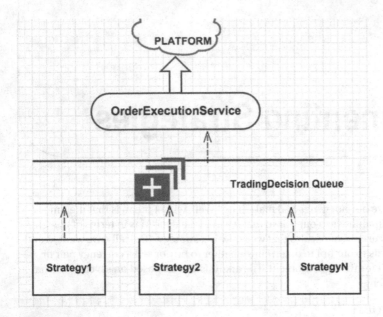

Figure 9-1. *Trading signal generation*

■ **Disclaimer** The strategies discussed in this chapter are purely for discussion and demonstration purposes. Developers must use their own reasoning/judgment before applying them in a live trading environment. In no event is the author liable for any direct, indirect, incidental, special, exemplary, or consequential damages arising from the deployment of the strategies discussed.

Copy Twitter Strategy

This strategy is aimed at blindly copying or doing the exact opposite of what the Twitter user has just tweeted. It works as follows:

- Using the tools and knowledge we developed in the last chapter, we follow a set of users on Twitter who often tweet new trade and close trade messages. We use a predefined structure, something that a handler can parse and use to create a NewFxTradeTweet or CloseFxTradeTweet object. We studied and analyzed the tweets of two such users–@SignalFactory and @ZuluTrader101.

- We create a scheduled job that searches for new tweets from these users. When a new trade tweet is found and successfully parsed into a NewFxTradeTweet object, we search historic tweets by the same user and for the instrument for which he just tweeted to go *long* or *short*.

- We parse the collection of historic tweets to create a collection of CloseFxTradeTweet objects. Each CloseFxTradeTweet, as we know, has an attribute that holds a profit/loss figure. If we cannot find one, it defaults to 0.0.

- We analyze how many previous trades were profitable and how many were loss, making the total.

- If the analysis tells us that the user recommendation for this trade in the past was more than 75% accurate, we do exactly what he has suggested in the recent trade. If, on the contrary, it suggests that he/she was wrong more than 75% of the time, we do exactly the opposite. For any other condition, we take no further decision and ignore the tweet. We also need to make sure that we are analyzing at least four historic tweets in order to give us better accuracy.

The figure of 75% and picking four tweets is arbitrary and can vary from one installation to another. Let's look at the code that tries to implement this strategy.

```
1   @TradingStrategy
2   public class CopyTwitterStrategy < T > implements TweetHarvester
    < T > {
3
4     @Resource
5     Map < String,
6     FXTweetHandler < T >> tweetHandlerMap;
7     @Resource(name = "orderQueue")
8     BlockingQueue < TradingDecision < T >> orderQueue;
9     private static final Logger LOG = Logger.
      getLogger(CopyTwitterStrategy.class);
10    private ExecutorService executorService = null;
11    private static final double ACCURACY_DESIRED = 0.75;
12    private static final int MIN_HISTORIC_TWEETS = 4;
13
14    @PostConstruct
15    public void init() {
16     this.executorService = Executors.newFixedThreadPool(tweetHandlerMap.
       size());
17    }
18
19    TradingDecision < T >
20    analyseHistoricClosedTradesForInstrument(Collection <
      CloseFXTradeTweet < T >>
21     closedTrades, NewFXTradeTweet < T > newTrade) {
22     int lossCtr = 0;
23     int profitCtr = 0;
```

```
24    for (CloseFXTradeTweet < T > closedTrade: closedTrades) {
25     if (closedTrade.getProfit() <= 0) {
26      lossCtr++;
27     } else {
28      profitCtr++;
29     }
30    }
31    TradingSignal signal = TradingSignal.NONE;
32    if ((lossCtr != 0 || profitCtr != 0) && closedTrades.size() >=
      MIN_HISTORIC_TWEETS) {
33     double profitAccuracy = profitCtr / ((profitCtr + lossCtr) * 1.0);
34     double lossAccuracy = 1.0 - profitAccuracy;
35     if (profitAccuracy >= ACCURACY_DESIRED) {
36      signal = newTrade.getAction();
37      return new TradingDecision < T > (newTrade.getInstrument(), signal,
38       newTrade.getTakeProfit(),  newTrade.getStopLoss(),
39       newTrade.getPrice(),  TradingDecision.SRCDECISION.SOCIAL_MEDIA);
40     } else if (lossAccuracy >= ACCURACY_DESIRED) {
41      /*execute an opposite trade as the loss accuracy is quite high*/
42      signal = newTrade.getAction().flip();
43      final double takeProfit = newTrade.getTakeProfit() != 0 ?
44       newTrade.getPrice() +
45       (newTrade.getPrice() - newTrade.getTakeProfit()) :
46       newTrade.getTakeProfit();
47      final double stopLoss = newTrade.getStopLoss() != 0.0 ?
48       newTrade.getPrice() +
49       (newTrade.getPrice() - newTrade.getStopLoss()) :
50       newTrade.getStopLoss();
51      return new TradingDecision < T > (newTrade.getInstrument(),
52       signal, takeProfit, stopLoss, newTrade.getPrice(),
53       TradingDecision.SRCDECISION.SOCIAL_MEDIA);
54     }
55    }
56    return new TradingDecision < T > (newTrade.getInstrument(), signal);
57   }
58
59   // called by scheduler
60   public synchronized void harvestAndTrade() {
61    for (final String userId: tweetHandlerMap.keySet()) {
62     this.executorService.submit(new  Callable < Void > () {
63
64      @Override
65      public Void call() throws Exception {
66       Collection < NewFXTradeTweet < T >> newTradeTweets =
67        harvestNewTradeTweets(userId);
```

```java
68      for (NewFXTradeTweet < T > newTradeTweet: newTradeTweets) {
69        Collection < CloseFXTradeTweet < T >> pnlTweets =
70          harvestHistoricTradeTweets(userId,  newTradeTweet.
           getInstrument());
71        TradingDecision < T > tradeDecision =
72          analyseHistoricClosedTradesForInstrument(pnlTweets,
           newTradeTweet);
73        if (tradeDecision.getSignal() != TradingSignal.NONE) {
74          orderQueue.offer(tradeDecision);
75        }
76      }
77      return null;
78      }
79    });
80   }
81 }
82
83 @Override
84 public Collection < NewFXTradeTweet < T >>
   harvestNewTradeTweets(String userId) {
85   FXTweetHandler < T > tweetHandler = tweetHandlerMap.get(userId);
86   if (tweetHandler == null) {
87    return Collections.emptyList();
88   }
89   Collection < Tweet > tweets = tweetHandler.findNewTweets();
90   if (tweets.size() > 0) {
91    LOG.info(String.format(
92      "found %d new tweets for user %s", tweets.size(), userId));
93   } else {
94    return Collections.emptyList();
95   }
96
97   Collection < NewFXTradeTweet < T >> newTradeTweets = Lists.
   newArrayList();
98   for (Tweet tweet: tweets) {
99    FXTradeTweet < T > tradeTweet = tweetHandler.handleTweet(tweet);
100   if (tradeTweet instanceof NewFXTradeTweet) {
101    newTradeTweets.add((NewFXTradeTweet < T > ) tradeTweet);
102   }
103  }
104
105  return newTradeTweets;
106 }
107
```

```
108   @Override
109   public Collection < CloseFXTradeTweet < T >>
      harvestHistoricTradeTweets(
110    String userId, TradeableInstrument < T > instrument) {
111    FXTweetHandler < T > tweetHandler = tweetHandlerMap.get(userId);
112    if (tweetHandler == null) {
113     return Collections.emptyList();
114    }
115    Collection < Tweet > tweets =
116     tweetHandler.findHistoricPnlTweetsForInstrument(instrument);
117    if (tweets.size() > 0) {
118     LOG.info(String.format(
119      "found %d historic pnl tweets for user %s and instrument %s",
120      tweets.size(), userId, instrument.getInstrument()));
121    } else {
122     return Collections.emptyList();
123    }
124    Collection < CloseFXTradeTweet < T >> pnlTradeTweets = Lists.
      newArrayList();
125    for (Tweet tweet: tweets) {
126     FXTradeTweet < T > tradeTweet = tweetHandler.handleTweet(tweet);
127     if (tradeTweet instanceof CloseFXTradeTweet) {
128      pnlTradeTweets.add((CloseFXTradeTweet < T > ) tradeTweet);
129     }
130    }
131    return pnlTradeTweets;
132   }
133   }
```

We begin by annotating the class with a custom annotation @TradingStrategy. By doing so, we are making a statement about this class, which is that this class explicitly implements a *trading strategy*. It is always a good idea to do this when certain classes are specifically written to accomplish a task but cannot be tied down to an interface definition. Pre Java 1.5, you could achieve the same effect by declaring marker interfaces.

```
1   @Retention(RetentionPolicy.RUNTIME)
2   @Target(ElementType.TYPE)
3   public @interface TradingStrategy {
4   }
```

Going back to our strategy class CopyTwitterStrategy, before we discuss the implementation, we point out the *resources* that are automatically injected by Spring and are available. These are as follows:

- *orderQueue*: The queue on which you can drop a TradingDecision, which will be picked up by the OrderExecutionService (refer back to Figure 9-1).

- *tweetHandlerMap*: The map of Twitter user IDs and the respective handlers, which we discussed in great detail in the last chapter. We use this as a starting point to find all tweets by user IDs in the map and then delegate to the respective handler to analyze them.

The init() method annotated by @PostConstruct is invoked automatically by Spring once the bean is fully initialized. Here we take the opportunity to initialize our ExecutorService, which we will come back to shortly.

All the action for this class starts in the method harvestAndTrade(). This method, as will be discussed in the following chapter, is automatically called by the Spring task scheduler after every T and is configured in the Spring configuration. This method is *synchronized* in order to make sure that we do not have more than one thread executing the method. As the name suggests, it harvests tweets for each user and generates a trading decision. Inside the method, we loop for all entries in the tweetHandlerMap and submit a Callable to the ExecutorService. This Callable has the following logic in the call() method for the given user:

- Find all tweets that relate to new trades and are successfully parsed to create a collection of NewFXTradeTweet objects. (Refer to Chapter 8, where we discuss the search API to find these tweets and parse them.)

- For each of the NewFXTradeTweet objects, harvest tweets relating to closed trades only for the given instrument.

- Delegate the analysis of these tweets to the analyseHistoricClosedTradesForInstrument method, which does the accuracy rate computation for the user and generates a TradingDecision. Recall that the accuracy rate is the percentage of time the user was correct in their previous trades. This is the gist of our strategy discussed earlier in the section.

The analyseHistoricClosedTradesForInstrument method merits a bit of explanation. At the beginning of the method we compute the accuracy rate. For this we first get a count of all trades that are loss making or in profit by looping through the collection of old closed trades. The closedTrade.getProfit() method helps us in this respect. We then go further only if the number of closed trades is greater than or equal to the minimum threshold, in this case four. Assuming

- P = Number of profit-making trades

- L = Number of loss-making trades

- N = Total number of closed trades found

such that **P + L = N**, then:

- Accuracy rate $\mathbf{R = P/N}$

- Miss rate $\mathbf{M = 1 - R}$

So if R is greater than or equal to the threshold for the desired accuracy, in this case 0.75, we do exactly what the user tweeted. For example, if the user recommends selling a currency pair at a given price, we do exactly that. On the other hand, if M is greater than or equal to the threshold, we do exactly the opposite. So for example, if the user recommends selling a currency pair, we buy the currency pair at the given price. The calculation of stop loss and take profit levels needs readjusting. Since the user initially recommended selling the currency pair and would have set a take profit at level pips P below the price, we now need to turn it around and make it at a distance of pips P above the price. The same logic applies to the stop loss levels.

This concludes our discussion of the *copy Twitter strategy*. The crux of the strategy, which is the accuracy rate calculation, is based on a very simplistic mathematical calculation. Many would argue that it's too simple and circumvents the statistical analysis that might be required to arrive at a more accurate decision. This may be very true but again I would like to reiterate that it's for demonstration purposes only. The key aim of the chapter was to demonstrate:

- Integrate with Twitter and analyze tweets.

- Use simplistic code/algorithm to do some mathematical analysis of the tweets and arrive at a trading signal.

- Queue this signal in the order queue to be processed further by OrderExecutionService, which ultimately has the responsibility of placing the order.

Fade the Move Strategy

In this section, we are going to discuss and implement a very simplistic version of the *fade the move*[1] strategy. Our implementation of the strategy works as follows:

- After the strategy is initialized, we create a subscription for tick data for predefined instruments injected via the configuration.

- After every period of time T, let's say 15 minutes (the value in the current configuration), we check if the the absolute value of the difference of pips between the price at the start of interval and at the end of the period has exceeded a configured value V pips, let's say 45 (the value in the current configuration).

- If the value has exceeded V pips, we then place a limit order in the opposite direction of current market trend, at a distance D pips, let's say 25 (the value in the current configuration), from the current price. For example, if EURUSD has jumped by 55 pips from 1.0815 (start price) to 1.087 (current price) in the last 15 minutes, we place a limit order to sell EURUSD at price 1.0895 (1.087+0.0025).

---

[1]http://www.investopedia.com/articles/forex/08/pure-fade-trade.asp

- We set a take profit target of 10 pips (take profit at 1.0885 if limit order filled at 1.0895).

Now let's jump directly to the source code to see how the strategy is implemented.

```
1    @TradingStrategy
2    public class FadeTheMoveStrategy < T > {
3
4      @Autowired
5      TradingConfig tradingConfig;
6      @Autowired
7      InstrumentService < T > instrumentService;
8      @Resource(name = "orderQueue")
9      BlockingQueue < TradingDecision < T >> orderQueue;
10     private final Collection < TradeableInstrument < T >> instruments;
11
12     private final Map < TradeableInstrument < T > ,
13     Cache < DateTime,
14     MarketDataPayLoad < T >>> instrumentRecentPricesCache = Maps
15      .newHashMap();
16
17     public FadeTheMoveStrategy(Collection < TradeableInstrument < T >>
       instruments) {
18       this.instruments = instruments;
19     }
20
21     @PostConstruct
22     public void init() {
23       for (TradeableInstrument < T > instrument: instruments) {
24        Cache < DateTime, MarketDataPayLoad < T >> recentPricesCache =
25         CacheBuilder.newBuilder().expireAfterWrite(
26          tradingConfig.getFadeTheMovePriceExpiry(),  TimeUnit.MINUTES)
27     .    < DateTime, MarketDataPayLoad < T >> build();
28        instrumentRecentPricesCache.put(instrument,  recentPricesCache);
29       }
30     }
31
32     @Subscribe
33     @AllowConcurrentEvents
34     public void handleMarketDataEvent(MarketDataPayLoad < T >
       marketDataPayLoad) {
35       if (instrumentRecentPricesCache.containsKey(
36         marketDataPayLoad.getInstrument())) {
37        instrumentRecentPricesCache.get(marketDataPayLoad.getInstrument())
38         .put(marketDataPayLoad.getEventDate(),  marketDataPayLoad);
39       }
40     }
41
```

```
42    // called by scheduler
43    public void analysePrices() {
44     for (Map.Entry < TradeableInstrument < T > , Cache < DateTime,
45      MarketDataPayLoad < T >>> entry: instrumentRecentPricesCache.
        entrySet()) {
46      SortedMap < DateTime, MarketDataPayLoad < T >> sortedByDate =
47       ImmutableSortedMap.copyOf(entry.getValue().asMap());
48      if (sortedByDate.isEmpty()) {
49       continue;
50      }
51      Double pipJump = calculatePipJump(sortedByDate.values(), entry.
        getKey());
52      Double absPipJump = Math.abs(pipJump);
53      if (absPipJump >= tradingConfig.getFadeTheMoveJumpReqdToTrade()) {
54       MarketDataPayLoad < T > lastPayLoad =
55        sortedByDate.get(sortedByDate.lastKey());
56       Double pip = this.instrumentService.getPipForInstrument(entry.
        getKey());
57       double takeProfitPrice;
58       double limitPrice;
59       TradingSignal signal = null;
60       if (Math.signum(pipJump) > 0) { // Short
61        signal = TradingSignal.SHORT;
62        limitPrice = lastPayLoad.getBidPrice() +
63         tradingConfig.getFadeTheMoveDistanceToTrade() * pip;
64        takeProfitPrice = limitPrice -
65         tradingConfig.getFadeTheMovePipsDesired() * pip;
66       } else {
67        signal = TradingSignal.LONG;
68        limitPrice = lastPayLoad.getAskPrice() -
69         tradingConfig.getFadeTheMoveDistanceToTrade() * pip;
70        takeProfitPrice = limitPrice +
71         tradingConfig.getFadeTheMovePipsDesired() * pip;
72       }
73       this.orderQueue.offer(new TradingDecision < T > (entry.getKey(),
        signal,
74        takeProfitPrice, 0.0, limitPrice,
75        TradingDecision.SRCDECISION.FADE_THE_MOVE));
76       entry.getValue().asMap().clear();
77       /*clear the prices so that we do not keep working on old decision*/
78      }
79     }
80    }
81
```

```
82    private double calculatePipJump(Collection < MarketDataPayLoad < T >>
      prices,
83      TradeableInstrument < T > instrument) {
84      List < MarketDataPayLoad < T >> priceList = Lists.
        newArrayList(prices);
85      MarketDataPayLoad < T > startPrice = priceList.get(0);
86      MarketDataPayLoad < T > lastPrice = priceList.get(priceList.size()
        - 1);
87      Double pip = this.instrumentService.getPipForInstrument(instrument);
88      Double pipJump = (lastPrice.getBidPrice() - startPrice.
        getBidPrice()) / pip;
89      return pipJump;
90    }
91  }
```

We start our discussion by looking at the dependencies autowired into the strategy class. The resource orderQueue is the obvious inclusion that we discussed in the beginning of the chapter. The instrumentService class in the strategy is called upon to provide a pip value for each instrument. The pip, from our discussion in Chapter 3, is the lower precision value for a price tick. For example, for all JPY pairs (with majors), it is 0.001 and for instruments like EURUSD, GBPUSD it is 0.00001. We need this information to calculate how many pips the price has jumped in the given observation interval. This is pretty much also captured in the calculatePipJump method. The last price of the observation interval minus the first price and the result divided by this pip value for the instrument gives us the pips, how much the currency pair rose or dipped. The last dependency injected, tradingConfig, gives us the parameters that we have configured in the Spring config, for our strategy:

- The minimum pip jump or dip required to consider fading the move is stored in the method getfade-TheMoveJumpReqdToTrade().

- The distance in pips from the current price the limit order should be placed in the opposite direction of the trend is stored in the method getFadeTheMoveDistanceToTrade().

- The session length for observation interval in minutes is stored in the method getFadeTheMovePrice- Expiry().

- The profit desired in pips, which helps set the take profit price for the limit order, is stored in the method getFadeTheMovePipsDesired().

The constructor of the class accepts a list of instruments that we must apply this strategy to and is a constructor injected by Spring.

We also have a @PostConstruct annotated method init() where we initialize a guava[2] *cache* for each instrument injected. The cache is keyed by DateTime of the tick data

---

[2]https://github.com/google/guava/wiki/CachesExplained

event and the value is the MarketDataPayLoad. We also set the expireAfterWrite value T provided by tradingConfig.getFadeTheMovePriceExpiry() to automatically expire the entries from the cache after T minutes.

The handleMarketDataEvent() method is annotated by the @Subscribe annotation, which means it receives all tick data events that have been parsed into the MarketDataPayLoad object and disseminated by the EventBus. Once received, the instance of MarketDataPayload is accepted only if it relates to the instrument that we configured the cache for and then put in the cache for that instrument.

The main action in the strategy happens in the method analysePrices(). This method is called by the task scheduler after every T minutes, the value of which is configured in the Spring configuration. This should normally be the same as tradingConfig.getFadeTheMovePriceExpiry(). We start by looping through all instruments configured in the cache. For each of them, we calculate the pip jump in absolute value in the given time period. If the pip jump is not above the minimum threshold (> getfadeTheMoveJumpReqdToTrade()), we ignore this. If the pip jump is above this threshold, we try to ascertain the market trend by looking at the sign of the pip jump. If its negative, we know that the trend is downward; otherwise, it's upward. For an upward trend, we place a SHORT trade or use LONG for a downward trend. We then calculate the limit price of the order using tradingConfig.getFadeTheMoveDistanceToTrade() and the take profit price using tradingConfig.getFadeTheMovePipsDesired().

This concludes our discussion of this strategy. It is a well known strategy and seems to work. Don't use a large number for the take profit pips. It seems to work most of the time if this value is around 10-12 pips. That seems to be the general observation of many market participants.

Try It Yourself

In this section, we are going to write a Spring-driven program that test drives FadeTheMoveStrategy. We will use an array of prices to simulate increasing prices for the currency pair AUD_CHF over a period of a few minutes. When the analysePrices() is invoked, the jump in prices should result in a SHORT signal being generated on the orderQueue. Let's look at the code and the Spring configuration:

```
1    package com.precioustech.fxtrading.tradingbot.strategies;
2
3    import java.util.concurrent.BlockingQueue;
4
5    import org.joda.time.DateTime;
6    import org.springframework.context.ApplicationContext;
7    import org.springframework.context.support.
     ClassPathXmlApplicationContext;
8
9    import com.google.common.eventbus.EventBus;
10   import com.precioustech.fxtrading.TradingDecision;
11   import com.precioustech.fxtrading.instrument.TradeableInstrument;
12   import com.precioustech.fxtrading.marketdata.MarketDataPayLoad;
13
```

```
14   public class FadeTheMoveStrategyDemo {
15
16     private static double precision = 0.0001;
17
18     @SuppressWarnings("unchecked")
19     public static void main(String[] args) throws InterruptedException {
20
21       ApplicationContext appContext =
22         new ClassPathXmlApplicationContext("fadethemove-demo.xml");
23       FadeTheMoveStrategy < String > fadeTheMoveStrategy = appContext.
         getBean(FadeTheMoveStrategy.class);
24       BlockingQueue < TradingDecision < String >> orderQueue =
         appContext.getBean(BlockingQueue.class);
25       EventBus eventBus = new EventBus();
26       eventBus.register(fadeTheMoveStrategy);
27
28       TradeableInstrument < String > audchf = new  TradeableInstrument
         < String > ("AUD_CHF");
29       final double[] audchfPrices = {
30         0.7069,
31         0.7070,
32         0.7073,
33         0.7076,
34         0.7077,
35         0.7078,
36         0.708,
37         0.7082,
38         0.7084,
39         0.7085,
40         0.7086,
41         0.7089,
42         0.7091,
43         0.7093,
44         0.7094,
45         0.7098,
46         0.71,
47         0.7102,
48         0.7105,
49         0.7104,
50         0.7103,
51         0.7105,
52         0.7109,
53         0.7111,
54         0.7112,
55         0.7115,
56         0.7118
57       };
```

```
58    DateTime eventStartaudchf = DateTime.now().minusMinutes(10);
59    for (double price: audchfPrices) {
60     eventStartaudchf = eventStartaudchf.plusSeconds(5);
61     eventBus.post(new MarketDataPayLoad < String > (audchf,
62       price - precision, price + precision, eventStartaudchf));
63    }
64    fadeTheMoveStrategy.analysePrices();
65    TradingDecision < String > decision = orderQueue.take();
66    System.out.println(String.format(
67     "The strategy signaled to go %s on instrument %s at limit price
       %2.5f and take profit %2.5f ",
68     decision.getSignal().name(), decision.getInstrument().
       getInstrument(),
69     decision.getLimitPrice(),  decision.getTakeProfitPrice()));
70    }
71  }
```

Here is the Spring configuration:

```
1   <?xml version="1.0" encoding="UTF-8"?>
2   <beans xmlns="http://www.springframework.org/schema/beans"
3       xmlns:xsi="http://www.w3.org/2001/XMLSchema-instance"
4       xmlns:context="http://www.springframework.org/schema/context"
5       xmlns:tx="http://www.springframework.org/schema/tx"
6       xsi:schemaLocation="http://www.springframework.org/schema/beans
7       http://www.springframework.org/schema/beans/spring-beans.xsd
8       http://www.springframework.org/schema/context
9       http://www.springframework.org/schema/context/spring-context.xsd">
10      <context:annotation-config/>
11      <bean id="tradeableInstrumentList" class="java.util.ArrayList">
12                   <constructor-arg index="0">
13                         <list>
14                               <bean class="com.precioustech.
                                 fxtrading.instrument.
                                 TradeableInstrument">
15                                     <constructor-arg  index="0"
                                        value="AUD_CHF"/>
16                               </bean>
17                         </list>
18                   </constructor-arg>
19      </bean>
20      <bean id="fadeTheMoveStrategy"
21                   class="com.precioustech.fxtrading.tradingbot.
                       strategies.FadeTheMoveStrategy">
22              <constructor-arg index="0" ref="tradeableInstrumentList"/>
23      </bean>
```

```
24      <bean id="tradingConfig"
25                  class="com.precioustech.fxtrading.tradingbot.
                    TradingConfig">
26              <property name="minReserveRatio" value="0.1"/>
27              <property name="maxAllowedQuantity" value="10"/>
28              <property name="maxAllowedNetContracts" value="5"/>
29              <property name="minAmountRequired" value="10.0"/>
30              <property name="mailTo" value="foobar@gmail.com"/>
31              <property name="max10yrWmaOffset" value="0.1"/>
32              <property name="fadeTheMoveJumpReqdToTrade" value="45"/>
33              <property name="fadeTheMoveDistanceToTrade" value="25"/>
34              <property name="fadeTheMovePipsDesired" value="10"/>
35              <property name="fadeTheMovePriceExpiry" value="15"/>
36      </bean>
37      <bean  id="orderQueue" class="java.util.concurrent.
        LinkedBlockingQueue"/>
38      <bean id="instrumentService" class="com.precioustech.fxtrading.
        instrument.InstrumentService">
39              <constructor-arg index="0" ref="instrumentDataProvider"/>
40      </bean>
41      <bean id="instrumentDataProvider"
42  class="com.precioustech.fxtrading.oanda.restapi.instrument.
    OandaInstrumentDataProviderService">
43              <constructor-arg index="0" value="#{
                systemProperties['oanda.url'] }"/>
44              <constructor-arg index="1" value="#{
                systemProperties['oanda.accountId'] }"/>
45              <constructor-arg index="2" value="#{
                systemProperties['oanda.accessToken'] }"/>
46      </bean>
47  </beans>
```

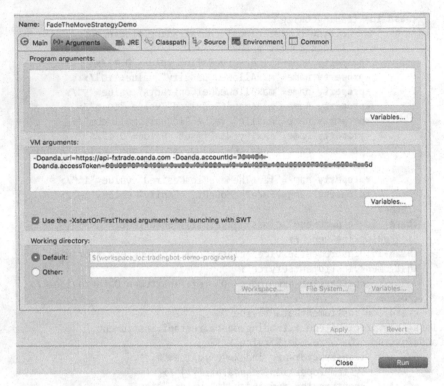

Figure 9-2. *Launch configuration*

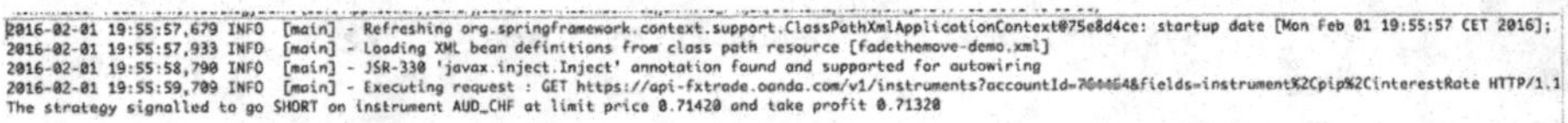

2016-02-01 19:55:57,679 INFO [main] - Refreshing org.springframework.context.support.ClassPathXmlApplicationContext@75e8d4ce: startup date [Mon Feb 01 19:55:57 CET 2016];
2016-02-01 19:55:57,933 INFO [main] - Loading XML bean definitions from class path resource [fadethemove-demo.xml]
2016-02-01 19:55:58,790 INFO [main] - JSR-330 'javax.inject.Inject' annotation found and supported for autowiring
2016-02-01 19:55:59,709 INFO [main] - Executing request : GET https://api-fxtrade.oanda.com/v1/instruments?accountId=7044648&fields=instrument%2Cpip%2CinterestRate HTTP/1.1
The strategy signalled to go SHORT on instrument AUD_CHF at limit price 0.71420 and take profit 0.71320

Figure 9-3. *Output of trade signal*

■ ■ ■

CHAPTER 10

Heartbeating

Heartbeats are a crucial element of any trading system. Any streaming or persistent connection over a long period of time must send a heartbeat down the pipe to let the consumer know that all is well and alive. Ours is no exception. In short, the heartbeat indicates the health of a system.

The bot, in theory, should receive frequent heartbeats to be assured that all is well. If the heartbeat is irregular or exceeds the wait period for an expected heartbeat, it will try to reconnect and restore the passive event stream.

In this chapter we discuss heartbeats, including how to process them and what to do if we stop receiving them.

HeartBeatPayLoad

Every persistent/streaming connection potentially can have different payloads to communicate the state of the connection. In order to accommodate for this wide range of payload types, we define the following POJO that models this characteristic:

```
1   public class HeartBeatPayLoad < T > {
2
3     private final T payLoad;
4     private final String source;
5
6     public HeartBeatPayLoad(T payLoad) {
7       this(payLoad, StringUtils.EMPTY);
8     }
9
10    public HeartBeatPayLoad(T payLoad, String source) {
11      this.payLoad = payLoad;
12      this.source = source;
13    }
14
15    public T getHeartBeatPayLoad() {
16      return this.payLoad;
17    }
18
```

S. Varshney, *Building Trading Bots Using Java*, DOI 10.1007/978-1-4842-2520-2_10

```
19    public String getHeartBeatSource() {
20     return this.source;
21    }
22  }
```

The source attribute identifies the source of the heartbeat. This is to distinguish between different heartbeat sources in the system. For example in the trading bot system, we have at least two heartbeat streams, one for the tick data and the other for the trade/order/account events.

Streaming the Heartbeat Interface

We begin, as we did for other streaming interfaces, with the interface definition that stipulates the minimum set of methods required to support heartbeat streaming. We have exactly the same design pattern as before:

- A method to start the streaming
- A method to stop the streaming
- An infinite event loop to process the heartbeats
- A callback interface to disseminate the event to downstream consumers

Let's look at the interface definition that defines this contract:

```
1   /**
2    * A service that provides streaming heartbeats from the trading
3    * platform. The service provided in the end by the platform may not
4    * be streaming at all but some sort of regular callbacks in order to
5    * indicate that the connection is alive. A loss of heartbeats may
6    * indicate a general failure to receive any trade/order events and/or
7    * market data from the trading platform. Therefore any monitoring of
8    * the application may involve directly interacting with this service to
9    * raise alerts/notifications.
10   *
11   */
12  public interface HeartBeatStreamingService {
13
14   /**
15    * Start the service in order to receive heartbeats from the trading
16    * platform. Ideally the implementation would make sure that
17    * multiple heartbeat connections/handlers are not created for the
18    * same kind of service. Depending on the trading platform, there
19    * may be a single heartbeat for all services or a dedicated one for
20    * services such as market data, trade/order events etc.
21    */
```

```
22    void startHeartBeatStreaming();
23
24    /**
25     * Stop the service in order to stop receiving heartbeats. The
26     * implementation must dispose any resources/connections in a
27     * suitable manner so as not to cause any resource leaks.
28     */
29    void stopHeartBeatStreaming();
30
31    /**
32     *
33     * @return heartBeat source id which identifies the source for which
34     * this service is providing heartbeats. This is useful to keep track all
35     * sources which are heartbeating and can be individually monitored
36     * on a regular basis. On some platforms there may be a dedicated
37     * single heartbeat service for ALL in which case this may not be as
38     * useful.
39     */
40    String getHeartBeatSourceId();
41  }
```

This interface, unlike the other streaming interfaces, includes an additional method that stipulates the implementation to provide a unique source ID for the heartbeat stream implementation.

A Concrete Implementation for HeartBeatStreamingService

OANDA pushes the heartbeat events via the same stream, i.e., it uses the market data and trade/order/account event streams to intermittently push a heartbeat payload to communicate the well-being of the respective streams. An example heartbeat payload looks like this:

```
1    {"heartbeat":{"time":"1443968021000000"}}
```

Since both the OANDA streams push the same heartbeat payload, the abstract class OandaStreamingService, which is the base class for OandaEventsStreamingService and OandaMarketDataStreamingService, implements the interface and provides the plumbing to handle these heartbeats. Let's look specifically at the implementation of the three interface methods in this abstract class. Additionally, we will also look at the method that parses out the JSON payload and the constructor.

```
1    public abstract class OandaStreamingService
2    implements HeartBeatStreamingService {
3      protected OandaStreamingService(String accessToken,
```

```
4       HeartBeatCallback < DateTime > heartBeatCallback, String
        heartbeatSourceId) {
5       this.hearbeatSourceId = heartbeatSourceId;
6       this.heartBeatCallback = heartBeatCallback;
7       ...
8       }
9
10      protected void handleHeartBeat(JSONObject streamEvent) {
11      Long t = Long.parseLong(((JSONObject) streamEvent.get(heartbeat)).
        get(time).toString());
12      heartBeatCallback.onHeartBeat(new HeartBeatPayLoad < DateTime >
        (new DateTime(TradingUtils.toMillisFromNanos(t)), hear\
13      beatSourceId));
14      }
15
16      @Override
17      public void stopHeartBeatStreaming() {
18       stopStreaming();
19      }
20
21      @Override
22      public void startHeartBeatStreaming() {
23      if (!serviceUp) {
24        startStreaming();
25      }
26      }
27
28      @Override
29      public String getHeartBeatSourceId() {
30       return this.hearbeatSourceId;
31      }
32      ...
33      ...
34      ...
35      }
```

The methods startHeartBeatStreaming() and stopHeartBeatStreaming()
delegate to startStreaming() and stopStreaming() respectively, which further
delegates to the underlying methods to start/stop the main streams. So in the case
of market data streaming, the methods that start and stop the main stream are
startMarketDataStreaming() and stopMarketDataStreaming(). This makes sense
because the heartbeats are coupled with the main stream events and the two coexist.
Stopping the heartbeat stream must stop the main stream and vice versa.

The method handleHeartBeat parses the JSON payload and creates an instance
of the HeartBeat-PayLoad<DateTime>. This is then passed on to an instance of
HeartBeatCallback, which we discuss later in this chapter, to disseminate to downstream
consumers. The timestamp in the heartbeat payload is the heartbeat timestamp and, as
we will see later, it's used later to figure out if the stream is still alive or dead.

HeartBeatCallback Interface

Like the other *callback* that we have looked at so far, the HeartBeatCallback is no different. It is directly invoked by the provider implementation that is directly receiving streaming events from the platform. After parsing the event and creating a HeartBeatPayLoad instance, the onHeartBeat method is invoked. Let's jump directly to how the source code looks.

```
1  public interface HeartBeatCallback<T> {
2
3    void onHeartBeat(HeartBeatPayLoad<T> payLoad);
4  }
```

The implementation for this interface is similar to other *callback* interfaces we have discussed previously. The HeartBeatPayLoad is disseminated to downstream consumers via the EventBus:

```
1  public class HeartBeatCallbackImpl < T > implements HeartBeatCallback
   < T > {
2
3    private final EventBus eventBus;
4
5    public HeartBeatCallbackImpl(EventBus eventBus) {
6      this.eventBus = eventBus;
7    }
8
9    @Override
10   public void onHeartBeat(HeartBeatPayLoad < T > payLoad) {
11     this.eventBus.post(payLoad);
12   }
13
14 }
```

DefaultHeartBeatService

We are now ready to discuss the service that uses heartbeat payloads to keep track of the health of various streaming connections and tries to revive them if they stop sending heartbeats. The DefaultHeartBeatService service, which extends from AbstractHeartBeatService, consumes the heartbeat payloads posted by the HeartBeatCallback via the EventBus. Every heartbeat received for the given source helps the service keep track of the health of the given stream.

We first look at the constructor that is injected into all the instances of HeartBeatStreamingService in a collection that it must keep track of.

223

```
1   protected abstract boolean isAlive(HeartBeatPayLoad < T > payLoad);
2   protected static final long MAX_HEARTBEAT_DELAY = 60000 L;
3   private final Map < String, HeartBeatStreamingService >
    heartBeatProducerMap =
4    Maps.newHashMap();
5   private final Map < String, HeartBeatPayLoad < T >> payLoadMap =
6    Maps.newConcurrentMap();
7   volatile boolean serviceUp = true;
8   protected final Collection < HeartBeatStreamingService >
9    heartBeatStreamingServices;
10  protected final long initWait = 2000 L;
11  long warmUpTime = MAX_HEARTBEAT_DELAY;
12
13  public AbstractHeartBeatService(Collection < HeartBeatStreamingService >
14   heartBeatStreamingServices) {
15   this.heartBeatStreamingServices = heartBeatStreamingServices;
16   for (HeartBeatStreamingService heartBeatStreamingService:
17    heartBeatStreamingServices) {
18    this.heartBeatProducerMap.put(
19     heartBeatStreamingService.getHeartBeatSourceId(),
20     heartBeatStreamingService);
21   }
22  }
```

The constructor also populates the heartBeatProducerMap with each instance of HeartBeatStreamingService keyed by its source ID inside the map. The payLoadMap is a map that has the last HeartBeatPayLoad object for the given heartbeat source. It constantly gets heartbeats for various sources via the EventBus subscriber method.

```
1   @Subscribe
2   @AllowConcurrentEvents
3   public void handleHeartBeats(HeartBeatPayLoad<T> payLoad) {
4           this.payLoadMap.put(payLoad.getHeartBeatSource(), payLoad);
5   }
```

What we need now is a background thread to periodically check the last time a payload was received. If it breaches the threshold limit for delay allowed for heartbeats, we try to revive it by calling the startHeartBeatStreaming() method.

```
1   @PostConstruct
2   public void init() {
3    this.heartBeatsObserverThread.start();
4   }
5
6   final Thread heartBeatsObserverThread = new Thread(new Runnable() {
7
```

```
8    private void sleep() {
9     try {
10      Thread.sleep(warmUpTime); /*let the streams start naturally*/
11     } catch (InterruptedException e1) {
12      LOG.error(e1);
13     }
14    }
15
16   @Override
17   public void run() {
18    while (serviceUp) {
19     sleep();
20     for (Map.Entry < String, HeartBeatStreamingService > entry:
21      heartBeatProducerMap.entrySet()) {
22      long startWait = initWait; // start with 2secs
23      while (serviceUp && !isAlive(payLoadMap.get(entry.getKey()))) {
24       entry.getValue().startHeartBeatStreaming();
25       LOG.warn(String
26        .format("heartbeat source %s was not responding." +
27        " Just restarted it and will listen for heartbeat after %d ms",
28        entry.getKey(), startWait));
29       try {
30        Thread.sleep(startWait);
31       } catch (InterruptedException e) {
32        LOG.error(e);
33       }
34       //double the sleep time but not more than MAX_HEARTBEAT_DELAY
35       startWait = Math.min(MAX_HEARTBEAT_DELAY, 2 * startWait);
36      }
37     }
38    }
39   }
40  }, "HeartBeatMonitorThread");
```

The @PostConstruct annotated method init() launches the heartBeatsObserverThread background thread. This thread periodically wakes up and loops through the heartBeatProducerMap for each of the entries in the map, and then checks if the streaming service is alive. The isAlive method that does the check is implemented by the DefaultHeartBeatService.

```
1   public class DefaultHeartBeatService
2   extends AbstractHeartBeatService < DateTime > {
3
4    public DefaultHeartBeatService(Collection < HeartBeatStreamingService >
5     heartBeatStreamingServices) {
6     super(heartBeatStreamingServices);
7    }
8
```

```
9    @Override
10   protected boolean isAlive(HeartBeatPayLoad < DateTime > payLoad) {
11    return payLoad != null && (DateTime.now().getMillis() -
12     payLoad.getHeartBeatPayLoad().getMillis()) < MAX_HEARTBEAT_DELAY;
13   }
14
15  }
```

This service, as you see from this code, expects a HeartBeatPayLoad<DateTime>. The isAlive implementation uses the payload that has a DateTime and then does some date calculations to figure out if the time since the last payload was received has breached the MAX_HEARTBEAT_DELAY. If it hasn't, the streaming connection is deemed to be alive; otherwise, it's not. Going back to the background thread code, if isAlive returns false, we then try to restart the streaming connection via invocation to startHeartBeatStreaming(). If the streaming connection restarts successfully, the posts to the handleHeartBeats method resume and isAlive then returns true.

There may be cases where other platforms might send a dummy object or a string down the pipe to communicate that it is heartbeating. In such cases, the DefaultHeartBeatService may be inadequate. For these, we may have to create a wrapper payload that includes the original payload and the time it was received by the handleHeartBeats method. The wrapper payload may have to be then passed on to another implementation, which extends the AbstractHeartBeatService and implements isAlive accordingly.

This concludes our discussion of the heartbeat mechanism of the bot. The heartbeats are an extremely important functionality of the bot because they tell us the health of the streams that are core to the functioning of the bot. A lot of the strategies might depend on the tick data stream and hence we cannot afford to have it down for a long period of time. Similarly we need to have the trade/order/account stream up and running so that the caches are in sync with the platform.

Try It Yourself

In this section we are going to write a demo program that demonstrates how the DefaultheartBeatService revives a dead stream once it detects that it has died.

```
1    package com.precioustech.fxtrading.heartbeats;
2
3    import java.util.Collection;
4
5    import org.apache.commons.lang3.StringUtils;
6    import org.apache.log4j.Logger;
7    import org.joda.time.DateTime;
8
9    import com.google.common.collect.Lists;
10   import com.google.common.eventbus.AllowConcurrentEvents;
11   import com.google.common.eventbus.EventBus;
```

```
12   import com.google.common.eventbus.Subscribe;
13   import com.precioustech.fxtrading.instrument.TradeableInstrument;
14   import com.precioustech.fxtrading.marketdata.MarketEventCallback;
15   import com.precioustech.fxtrading.marketdata.MarketEventHandlerImpl;
16   import com.precioustech.fxtrading.oanda.restapi.streaming.marketdata.
     OandaMarketDataStreamingService;
17   import com.precioustech.fxtrading.streaming.heartbeats.
     HeartBeatStreamingService;
18
19   public class DefaultHeartBeatServiceDemo {
20
21     private static final Logger LOG = Logger.getLogger(DefaultHeartBeatSe
       rviceDemo.class);
22
23     private static void usageAndValidation(String[] args) {
24       if (args.length != 3) {
25         LOG.error("Usage: DefaultHeartBeatServiceDemo <url> <accountid>
           <accesstoken>");
26         System.exit(1);
27       } else {
28         if (!StringUtils.isNumeric(args[1])) {
29           LOG.error("Argument 2 should be numeric");
30           System.exit(1);
31         }
32       }
33     }
34
35     private static class DataSubscriber {
36
37       @Subscribe
38       @AllowConcurrentEvents
39       public void handleHeartBeats(HeartBeatPayLoad < DateTime > payLoad) {
40         LOG.info(
41           String.format("Heartbeat received @ %s from source %s",
42             payLoad.getHeartBeatPayLoad(),  payLoad.getHeartBeatSource())));
43       }
44
45     }
46
47     @SuppressWarnings("unchecked")
48     public static void main(String[] args) throws Exception {
49       usageAndValidation(args);
50       final String url = args[0];
51       final Long accountId = Long.parseLong(args[1]);
52       final String accessToken = args[2];
53       final String heartbeatSourceId="DEMO_MKTDATASTREAM";
54
```

227

```
55    TradeableInstrument < String > eurusd = new TradeableInstrument
      < String > ("EUR_USD");
56
57    Collection < TradeableInstrument < String >> instruments = Lists.
      newArrayList(eurusd);
58
59    EventBus eventBus = new EventBus();
60
61    MarketEventCallback < String > mktEventCallback =
62     new MarketEventHandlerImpl < String > (eventBus);
63    HeartBeatCallback < DateTime > heartBeatCallback =
64     new HeartBeatCallbackImpl < DateTime > (eventBus);
65
66    OandaMarketDataStreamingService mktDataStreaminService =
67     new OandaMarketDataStreamingService(url, accessToken,
68      accountId, instruments, mktEventCallback, heartBeatCallback,
        heartbeatSourceId);
69     mktDataStreaminService.startMarketDataStreaming();
70     Collection < HeartBeatStreamingService > heartbeatstreamingLst =
       Lists.newArrayList();
71     heartbeatstreamingLst.add(mktDataStreaminService);
72     DefaultHeartBeatService heartBeatService = new
       DefaultHeartBeatService(heartbeatstreamingLst);
73     eventBus.register(heartBeatService);
74     eventBus.register(new DataSubscriber());
75     heartBeatService.init();
76
77     heartBeatService.warmUpTime = 5000 L;
78     Thread.sleep(30000 L);
79     mktDataStreaminService.stopMarketDataStreaming();
80     Thread.sleep(20000 L);
81    }
82
83  }
```

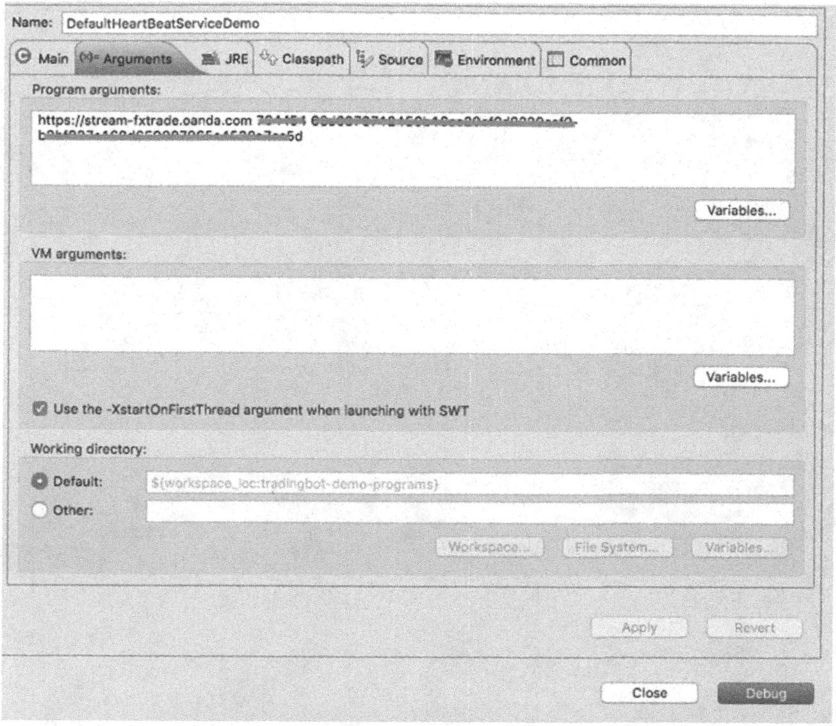

Figure 10-1. *Launch configuration*

Figure 10-2. *Sample output*

After a bit of time, the market data stream is stopped. The heartBeatService then tries to revive it and is successful in doing so. We see heartbeats being received again after the connection is successfully reestablished.

CHAPTER 11

■ ■ ■

E-Mail Notifications

In this chapter we discuss e-mail notifications that are extremely useful to notify users when certain events are triggered inside the bot. These notifications are closely coupled to the trade/order/account events discussed in the Chapter 7. As a result, the e-mail notification component has the same input payload, delivered by the EventBus, as the other handlers we discussed in that chapter. These notifications can be very useful when a user action is urgently warranted. For example, a MARGIN_CALL_ENTER[1] might be triggered on the OANDA platform, which suggests that the account faces an urgent margin call. On the other hand, these notifications serve as a useful tool to keep track of what the automated trading bot is up to. By switching on notifications for trade/order and account events, users can have a useful appreciation of the state of things happening inside the bot.

Notification Design

As discussed, the event that is handled by the trade/order and account event handlers is also posted to the e-mail notification service. This service, EventEmailNotifier, handles this event and generates an e-mail if an appropriate EmailContentGenerator is configured for that event. The EmailContentGenerator implementation is responsible for generating subject and body, aka the EmailPayLoad, and it can vary from event to event.

Let's first look at the POJO EmailPayLoad that holds the result of the e-mail content generation.

EmailPayLoad POJO

```
1   public class EmailPayLoad {
2     private final String subject;
3     private final String body;
4
```

---

[1] http://fxtrade.oanda.com/help/policies/margin-rules

© Shekhar Varshney 2016
S. Varshney, *Building Trading Bots Using Java*, DOI 10.1007/978-1-4842-2520-2_11

```
5    public EmailPayLoad(String subject, String body) {
6    super();
7    this.subject = subject;
8    this.body = body;
9    }
10
11   public String getSubject() {
12   return subject;
13   }
14
15   public String getBody() {
16   return body;
17   }
18
19   }
```

The EmailPayLoad has the subject and the body of the e-mail that is sent out using the JavaMail API and configured inside the Spring configuration.

EmailContentGenerator Interface

```
1    public interface EmailContentGenerator<T> {
2
3      EmailPayLoad generate(EventPayLoad<T> payLoad);
4
5    }
```

Sample Implementations

In this section, we discuss some sample implementations of the EmailContentGenerator interface. First, we look at an implementation that sends an e-mail out if the following trade events are generated by the platform

- Trade closed

- Stop loss triggered

- Take profit triggered

When a take profit level is hit, for example, we can expect a JSON response like the following one:

```
1    {
2      "id":10003,
3      "accountId":234567,
4      "time":"1443968061000000",
5      "type":"TAKE_PROFIT_FILLED",
```

```
6    "tradeId":1800805337,
7    "instrument":"USD_CHF",
8    "units":3000,
9    "side":"sell",
10   "price":1.00877,
11   "pl":3.48,
12   "interest":0.0002,
13   "accountBalance":5912.5829
14  }
```

The TradeEventHandler that handled the trade events from the OANDA platform also implements the EmailContentGenerator interface. As a result, the method that generates the EmailPayLoad looks like this:

```
1   @Override
2   public EmailPayLoad generate(EventPayLoad < JSONObject > payLoad) {
3     JSONObject jsonPayLoad = payLoad.getPayLoad();
4     TradeableInstrument < String > instrument = new TradeableInstrument
      < String > (jsonPayLoad.get(
5       OandaJsonKeys.instrument).toString());
6     final String type = jsonPayLoad.get(OandaJsonKeys.type).toString();
7     final long accountId = (Long) jsonPayLoad.get(OandaJsonKeys.
      accountId);
8     final double accountBalance = ((Number) jsonPayLoad.get(OandaJsonKeys.
      accountBalance)).doubleValue();
9     final long tradeId = (Long) jsonPayLoad.get(OandaJsonKeys.tradeId);
10    final double pnl = ((Number) jsonPayLoad.get(OandaJsonKeys.pl)).
      doubleValue();
11    final double interest = ((Number) jsonPayLoad.get(OandaJsonKeys.
      interest)).doubleValue();
12    final long tradeUnits = (Long) jsonPayLoad.get(OandaJsonKeys.units);
13    final String emailMsg = String
14      .format("Trade event %s received for account %d. " + "Trade id=%d.
        Pnl=%5.3f, Interest=%5.3f, Trade Units=%d. " + "Acc\
15  ount balance after the event=%5.2f",
16        type, accountId, tradeId, pnl, interest, tradeUnits,
        accountBalance);
17    final String subject = String.format(
18      "Order event %s for %s", type, instrument.getInstrument());
19    return new EmailPayLoad(subject, emailMsg);
20  }
```

This code extracts key pieces of information such as the following from the JSONObject:

- PNL
- Interest

- Account ID

- Account balance

It then creates the following body for the e-mail for our JSON response:

```
1  Trade event TAKE_PROFIT_FILLED received for account 234567.
2  Trade id=1800805337. Pnl=3.48, Interest=0, Trade Units=3000.
3  Account balance after the event=5912.58
```

The subject generated is

```
1  Order event TAKE_PROFIT_FILLED for USD_CHF
```

The next example covers an order filled event. When such an event happens, you could expect a JSON like this one from the OANDA platform:

```
1  {
2    "id": 10002,
3    "accountId": 123456,
4    "time": "1443968041000000",
5    "type": "ORDER_FILLED",
6    "instrument": "EUR_USD",
7    "units": 10,
8    "side": "sell",
9    "price": 1,
10   "pl": 1.234,
11   "interest": 0.034,
12   "accountBalance": 10000,
13   "orderId": 0,
14   "tradeReduced": {
15     "id": 54321,
16     "units": 10,
17     "pl": 1.234,
18     "interest": 0.034
19   }
20 }
```

The OrderFilledEventHandler handled the order filled events from the OANDA platform, and it also implements the EmailContentGenerator interface. As a result, the method that generates the EmailPayLoad looks like this:

```
1  @Override
2  public EmailPayLoad generate(EventPayLoad < JSONObject > payLoad) {
3    JSONObject jsonPayLoad = payLoad.getPayLoad();
4    TradeableInstrument < String > instrument = new TradeableInstrument
       < String > (jsonPayLoad
```

```
5      .containsKey(OandaJsonKeys.instrument) ? jsonPayLoad.
       get(OandaJsonKeys.instrument).toString() : "N/A");
6  final String type = jsonPayLoad.get(OandaJsonKeys.type).toString();
7  final long accountId = (Long) jsonPayLoad.get(OandaJsonKeys.
       accountId);
8  final double accountBalance = jsonPayLoad.
9  containsKey(OandaJsonKeys.accountBalance) ? ((Number) jsonPayLoad
10     .get(OandaJsonKeys.accountBalance)).doubleValue() : 0.0;
11 final long orderId = (Long) jsonPayLoad.get(OandaJsonKeys.id);
12 final String emailMsg = String.format(
13     "Order event %s received on account %d. Order id=%d. " + "Account
       balance after the event=%5.2f", type,
14     accountId, orderId, accountBalance);
15 final String subject = String.format(
16     "Order event %s for %s", type, instrument.getInstrument());
17 return new EmailPayLoad(subject, emailMsg);
18 }
```

This code like the previous example. It extracts some key bits of information to prepare the e-mail body. These include

- Account ID
- Account balance
- Order ID

For this example, the following body would be produced.

```
1  Order event ORDER_FILLED received on account 123456. Order id=10002.
2  Account balance after the event=10000.00
```

and the subject would be

```
1  Order event ORDER_FILLED for EUR_USD
```

EventEmailNotifier Service

The EventEmailNotifier is a simple service that has a eventEmailContentGeneratorMap that is injected by Spring and configured inside the app Spring configuration file. The map is keyed by an instance of the Event interface and the value is an implementation of the EmailContentGenerator interface. When an EventPayLoad is received by the EventBus inside the notifyByEmail method, this map is searched for an appropriate instance of EmailContentGenerator that could handle this payload. If found, this instance then generates an EmailPayLoad instance. This is then used to construct a SimpleMailMessage and sent out by the mailSender.

```
1   public class EventEmailNotifier < T > {
2
3   private static final Logger LOG = Logger.getLogger(EventEmailNotifier.
    class);
4
5   @Autowired
6   JavaMailSender mailSender;
7   @Resource
8   Map < Event,
9   EmailContentGenerator < T >> eventEmailContentGeneratorMap;
10  @Autowired
11  TradingConfig tradingConfig;
12
13  @Subscribe
14  @AllowConcurrentEvents
15  public void notifyByEmail(EventPayLoad < T > payLoad) {
16   Preconditions.checkNotNull(payLoad);
17   EmailContentGenerator < T > emailContentGenerator =
18    eventEmailContentGeneratorMap.get(payLoad.getEvent());
19   if (emailContentGenerator != null) {
20    EmailPayLoad emailPayLoad = emailContentGenerator.generate(payLoad);
21    SimpleMailMessage msg = new SimpleMailMessage();
22    msg.setSubject(emailPayLoad.getSubject());
23    msg.setTo(tradingConfig.getMailTo());
24    msg.setText(emailPayLoad.getBody());
25    this.mailSender.send(msg);
26   } else {
27    LOG.warn("No email content generator found for event:" + payLoad.
     getEvent().name());
28   }
29  }
30  }
```

We gain a better appreciation if we take a quick look at the Spring config file where we configure the events that we want to send notifications out for.

```
1   <bean id="orderEventHandler"
2   class="com.precioustech.fxtrading.oanda.restapi.events.
    OrderFilledEventHandler">
3                   <constructor-arg index="0" ref="tradeInfoService"/>
4       </bean>
5   <bean id="tradeEventHandler"
6   class="com.precioustech.fxtrading.oanda.restapi.events.
    TradeEventHandler">
7                   <constructor-arg index="0" ref="tradeInfoService"/>
8   </bean>
9
```

```
10    <util:map id="eventEmailContentGeneratorMap" key-type="com.
      precioustech.fxtrading.events.Event">
11            <entry key="#{T(com.precioustech.fxtrading.oanda.restapi.
                  events.OrderEvents).MARKET_ORDER_CREATE}"
12    value-ref="orderEventHandler"/>
13            <entry key="#{T(com.precioustech.fxtrading.oanda.restapi.
                  events.OrderEvents).LIMIT_ORDER_CREATE}"
14    value-ref="orderEventHandler"/>
15            <entry key="#{T(com.precioustech.fxtrading.oanda.restapi.
                  events.OrderEvents).ORDER_CANCEL}"
16    value-ref="orderEventHandler"/>
17            <entry key="#{T(com.precioustech.fxtrading.oanda.restapi.
                  events.OrderEvents).ORDER_FILLED}"
18    value-ref="orderEventHandler"/>
19            <entry key="#{T(com.precioustech.fxtrading.oanda.restapi.
                  events.TradeEvents).TRADE_CLOSE}"
20    value-ref="tradeEventHandler"/>
21            <entry key="#{T(com.precioustech.fxtrading.oanda.restapi.
                  events.TradeEvents).STOP_LOSS_FILLED}"
22    value-ref="tradeEventHandler"/>
23            <entry key="#{T(com.precioustech.fxtrading.oanda.restapi.
                  events.TradeEvents).TAKE_PROFIT_FILLED}"
24    value-ref="tradeEventHandler"/>
25    </util:map>
```

In this config, we first configure the two handlers—OrderFilledEventHandler and TradeEventHandler—that would handle events of type OrderEvents and TradeEvents respectively, both being the implementations of the Event interface. We then pick our events we want the send notifications out for and configure them here.

This concludes our short discussion of the e-mail notifications.

Try It Yourself

In this section we are going to write a sample Spring configured demo program in which we simulate the posting of a trade event using the EventBus and see the actual notifications turn up in the mailbox. First let's look at the code.

```
1    package com.precioustech.fxtrading.tradingbot.events.notification.email;
2
3    import java.util.Map;
4
5    import org.json.simple.JSONObject;
6    import org.springframework.context.ApplicationContext;
7    import org.springframework.context.support.
     ClassPathXmlApplicationContext;
8
```

```
9   import com.google.common.collect.Maps;
10  import com.google.common.eventbus.EventBus;
11  import com.precioustech.fxtrading.events.EventPayLoad;
12  import com.precioustech.fxtrading.oanda.restapi.OandaJsonKeys;
13  import com.precioustech.fxtrading.oanda.restapi.events.TradeEvents;
14
15  public class EventEmailNotifierDemo {
16
17  @SuppressWarnings("unchecked")
18  public static void main(String[] args) {
19   ApplicationContext appContext =
20    new ClassPathXmlApplicationContext("emailnotify-demo.xml");
21   EventEmailNotifier < JSONObject > emailNotifier =
22    appContext.getBean(EventEmailNotifier.class);
23   EventBus eventBus = new EventBus();
24   eventBus.register(emailNotifier);
25
26   Map < String, Object > payload = Maps.newHashMap();
27   payload.put(OandaJsonKeys.instrument,  "GBP_USD");
28   payload.put(OandaJsonKeys.type, TradeEvents.TAKE_PROFIT_FILLED.name());
29   payload.put(OandaJsonKeys.accountId, 123456 l);
30   payload.put(OandaJsonKeys.accountBalance,  127.8);
31   payload.put(OandaJsonKeys.tradeId, 234567 l);
32   payload.put(OandaJsonKeys.pl,  11.8);
33   payload.put(OandaJsonKeys.interest,  0.27);
34   payload.put(OandaJsonKeys.units, 2700 l);
35
36   JSONObject jsonObj = new JSONObject(payload);
37   eventBus.post(new EventPayLoad < JSONObject > (TradeEvents.TAKE_
       PROFIT_FILLED, jsonObj));
38   }
39
40  }
```

In the following code, we create an instance of JSONObject by hand and post it to the EventBus. The configuration that drives this program looks like this:

```
1   <?xml version="1.0" encoding="UTF-8"?>
2   <beans xmlns="http://www.springframework.org/schema/beans"
3       xmlns:xsi="http://www.w3.org/2001/XMLSchema-instance"
4       xmlns:context="http://www.springframework.org/schema/context"
5       xmlns:util="http://www.springframework.org/schema/util"
6       xmlns:task="http://www.springframework.org/schema/task"
7       xmlns:tx="http://www.springframework.org/schema/tx"
8       xsi:schemaLocation="http://www.springframework.org/schema/beans
9       http://www.springframework.org/schema/beans/spring-beans.xsd
10      http://www.springframework.org/schema/context
11      http://www.springframework.org/schema/context/spring-context.xsd
```

```
12        http://www.springframework.org/schema/util
13        http://www.springframework.org/schema/util/spring-util.xsd">
14        <context:annotation-config/>
15        <bean id="mailSender" class="org.springframework.mail.javamail.
          JavaMailSenderImpl">
16             <property name="host" value="#{ systemProperties['mail.host']
               }"/>
17             <property name="port" value="#{ systemProperties['mail.port']
               }"/>
18             <property name="username" value="#{ systemProperties['mail.
               user'] }"/>
19             <property name="password" value="#{ systemProperties['mail.
               password'] }"/>
20             <property name="javaMailProperties">
21                  <props>
22                       <prop key="mail.transport.protocol">smtps</prop>
23                       <prop key="mail.smtp.auth">true</prop>
24                       <prop key="mail.smtp.starttls.enable">true</prop>
25                       <prop key="mail.smtp.socketFactory.class">javax.net.
                         ssl.SSLSocketFactory</prop>
26                       <prop key="mail.debug">false</prop>
27                       <prop key="mail.smtp.socketFactory.fallback">false
                         </prop>
28                  </props>
29             </property>
30        </bean>
31        <bean id="tradingConfig"
32                       class="com.precioustech.fxtrading.tradingbot.
                         TradingConfig">
33                  <property name="minReserveRatio" value="0.1"/>
34                  <property name="maxAllowedQuantity" value="10"/>
35                  <property name="maxAllowedNetContracts" value="5"/>
36                  <property name="minAmountRequired" value="10.0"/>
37                  <property name="mailTo" value="#{
                     systemProperties['mail.to'] }"/>
38                  <property name="max10yrWmaOffset" value="0.1"/>
39                  <property name="fadeTheMoveJumpReqdToTrade"
                     value="45"/>
40                  <property name="fadeTheMoveDistanceToTrade"
                     value="25"/>
41                  <property name="fadeTheMovePipsDesired" value="10"/>
42                  <property name="fadeTheMovePriceExpiry" value="15"/>
43        </bean>
44        <bean id="eventEmailNotifier"
45                       class="com.precioustech.fxtrading.tradingbot.
                         events.notification.email.EventEmailNotifier"/>
46        <bean id="tradeEventHandler"
```

239

```
47                             class="com.precioustech.fxtrading.oanda.restapi.
                               events.TradeEventHandler">
48                 <constructor-arg index="0">
49                     <null/>
50                 </constructor-arg>
51         </bean>
52
53     <util:map id="eventEmailContentGeneratorMap" key-type="com.
       precioustech.fxtrading.events.Event">
54             <entry key="#{T(com.precioustech.fxtrading.oanda.
                   restapi.events.TradeEvents).TRADE_CLOSE}"
55                             value-ref="tradeEventHandler"/>
56         <entry key="#{T(com.precioustech.fxtrading.oanda.restapi.
           events.TradeEvents).STOP_LOSS_FILLED}"
57                             value-ref="tradeEventHandler"/>
58         <entry key="#{T(com.precioustech.fxtrading.oanda.restapi.
           events.TradeEvents).TAKE_PROFIT_FILLED}"
59                             value-ref="tradeEventHandler"/>
60     </util:map>
61 </beans>
```

Since all the e-mail account credentials are passed in system properties, let's look at the launch configuration shown in Figure 11-1.

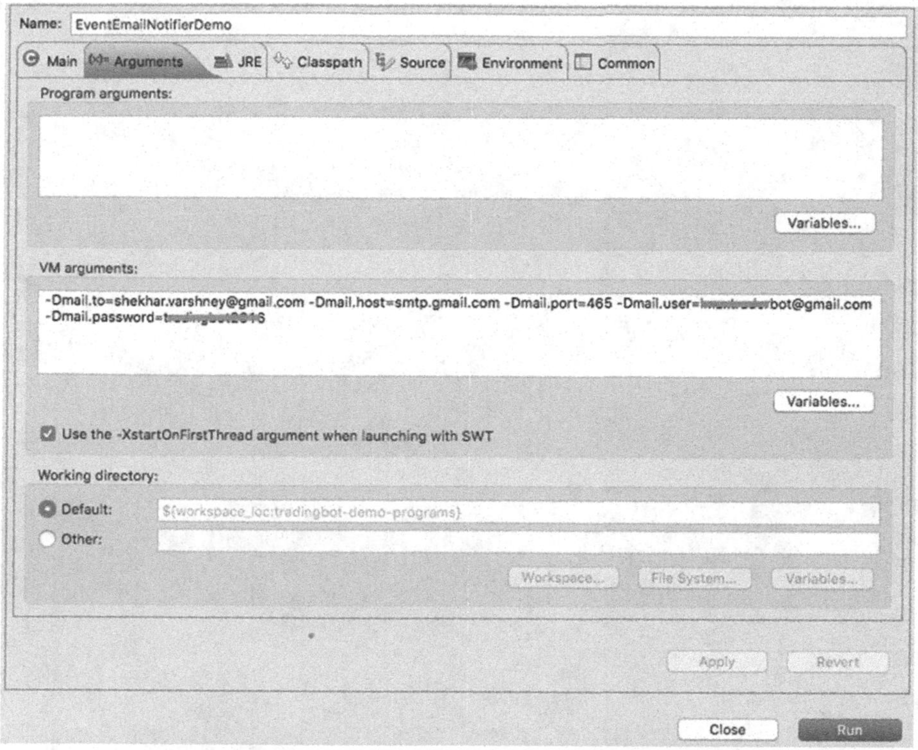

Name:	EventEmailNotifierDemo

⊙ Main ⋈= Arguments ≡\ JRE ⊙ Classpath ⋤ Source ▦ Environment ▭ Common

Program arguments:

Variables...

VM arguments:

-Dmail.to=shekhar.varshney@gmail.com -Dmail.host=smtp.gmail.com -Dmail.port=465 -Dmail.user=~~lmextradev~~bot@gmail.com -Dmail.password=~~tradingbot2016~~

Variables...

☑ Use the -XstartOnFirstThread argument when launching with SWT

Working directory:

⦿ Default: ${workspace_loc:tradingbot-demo-programs}

◯ Other:

Workspace...   File System...   Variables...

Apply   Revert

Close   Run

Figure 11-1. Launch configuration

After the program is successfully run, we see the e-mail turning up in the `mail.to` address with the values we used in our test program, as shown in Figure 11-2.

Figure 11-2. E-mail notification arrives in the inbox

CHAPTER 12

■ ■ ■

Configuration, Deployment, and Running the Bot

We are now all set to put the bot into action. All that remains before pressing the button is the configuration and deployment. Configuration of the bot involves the following steps:

- Spring configuration of the core services and API, i.e., `tradingbot-app.xml`.

- Property file for the core Spring configuration, i.e., `tradingbot.properties`.

- Spring configuration of the runtime provider (OANDA in our case), i.e., `tradingbot-oanda.xml`.

- Property file for the runtime provider Spring configuration, i.e., `tradingbot-oanda.properties`.

Just like the JAR files, we also have a separate configuration file for the runtime provider. As we will see later in the chapter, the name of the provider configuration file is passed in as a program argument in order to easily pick the provider at runtime. Without further ado, let's jump into the configuration of the bot.

Configuring the Trading Bot

We start by creating the main configuration file in the `tradingbot-app` project in the `src/main/resources` folder, which is automatically included in the build and as a result ends up inside the `tradingbot-app.jar` file. The name of the file is `tradingbot-app.xml`. We also create the properties file, called `tradingbot.properties`, that has the values for various placeholders referenced in this Spring configuration file.

We also use the cool *SpEL*[1] in our configuration, the reason for which will become clear as we progress through this chapter.

---

[1] http://docs.spring.io/spring/docs/current/spring-framework-reference/html/expressions.html

S. Varshney, *Building Trading Bots Using Java*, DOI 10.1007/978-1-4842-2520-2_12

Core Beans Configuration

In this section, we configure all the core beans that are part of the core API except the services which we will configure later. These beans include e-mail, queues, trading config, etc. which are central to the functioning of the bot.

Since all our dependency beans are @Autowired, we switch on annotation processing by including <context:annotation-config/> in the configuration file. This will ensure that all the dependencies we have injected via @Autowired will be processed correctly. We also switch on property file processing by including the following in the configuration file and also specify where to find the properties file:

```
1  <context:property-placeholder location="classpath:tradingbot.properties"
   ignore-unresolvable="true"/>
```

The trading.properties has the following properties. We added some sample values to demonstrate how they look:

```
1  mail.to=tradingbot@gmail.com
2  mail.host=smtp.gmail.com
3  mail.port=465
4  mail.user=foobar@gmail.com
5  mail.password=foobar123
6  twitter.consumerKey=veJerryUYUDHUliDXjlC6o4KR
7  twitter.consumerSecret=L5iFptFbLKMyUoH8NB3yAodEeOEQMukriUt3mnNICEKy
   Np2OIh
8  twitter.accessToken=0123456789-LISP3YOOmLgDOSw44vgdVORr7313Zy
   PrAtOX3jU
9  twitter.accessTokenSecret=5IrbOYUlGOLd7UPeG6GPxFjVNWHREj4MN2
   TaoTL2kmVTT
```

We have already discussed the Twitter integration properties in Chapter 8. The mail properties are used to configure the JavaMailSender bean in the Spring configuration except mail.to, which actually is the TO address of the user who gets all the notifications generated by the bot.

We now turn our attention to the configuration of the core *beans* that make up the bot. The first is the configuration of the TradingConfig class. This class must be configured correctly for other services to work. We must also be careful to configure some of the values as they might affect the orders that are placed. For example, the maxAllowedQuantity is the maximum size of an order placed. In our case, it is just 5, but changing this value to, say, 50000 will place a huge order, which might lead to a margin call if the trade goes in the opposite direction.

Let's briefly discuss each of the config params in the TradingConfig class:

- minReserveRatio is the ratio of the amount available to trade to the total amount in the account. A value of 0.1 stipulates that if this amount falls below 10%, the bot stops putting in new orders.

- `maxAllowedNetContracts` is the maximum net the bot will go long or short on a given currency. This setting was inspired by the event on Jan 15, 2015, when SNB[2] unexpectedly ended the CHF peg versus EUR of 1.2 and CHF soured by nearly 30%. Anyone who was massively short CHF ended up losing huge amounts of money.

- `minAmountRequired` is the minimum balance in the designated currency of the account required to allow the bot to place orders. If the balance falls below this threshold, no further order placement is possible.

- `max10yrWmaOffset` defines the safe zone of a currency pair. We discussed it in detail while discussing `PreOrderValidationService`.

- `fadeTheMovePriceExpiry` is the time in minutes, the observation interval, for the `FadeTheMove` strategy.

- `fadeTheMoveJumpReqdToTrade` is the net jump in pips required during the `fadeTheMovePriceExpiry` that will create a scenario to place limit orders in the opposite direction of the market move.

- `fadeTheMoveDistanceToTrade` is the distance from the current price in pips when the limit order placed by the `FadeTheMoveStrategy` will be filled.

- `fadeTheMovePipsDesired` is the profit desired in pips for the `FadeTheMove` strategy.

```
1   <bean id="tradingConfig"
2          class="com.precioustech.fxtrading.tradingbot.TradingConfig">
3                  <property name="minReserveRatio" value="0.1"/>
4                  <property name="maxAllowedQuantity" value="10"/>
5                  <property name="maxAllowedNetContracts" value="5"/>
6                  <property name="minAmountRequired" value="10.0"/>
7                  <property name="mailTo" value="${mail.to}"/>
8                  <property name="max10yrWmaOffset" value="0.1"/>
9                  <property name="fadeTheMoveJumpReqdToTrade" value="45"/>
10                 <property name="fadeTheMoveDistanceToTrade" value="25"/>
11                 <property name="fadeTheMovePipsDesired" value="10"/>
12                 <property name="fadeTheMovePriceExpiry" value="15"/>
13  </bean>
```

Next we configure the Google EventBus and all the callback handlers that use the EventBus to disseminate the event payloads. We also configure the bean post processor `FindEventBusSubscribers`, which we discussed in the first chapter. It finds all

---

[2]https://www.snb.ch/en/mmr/reference/pre_20150115/source/pre_20150115.en.pdf

classes with methods annotated by @Subscriber and registers them with the EventBus automatically.

```
1  <bean id="eventBus" class="com.google.common.eventbus.EventBus"/>
2  <bean id="findEventBusSubscribers"
3    class="com.precioustech.fxtrading.tradingbot.spring.
     FindEventBusSubscribers"/>
4  <bean id="eventCallback"
5    class="com.precioustech.fxtrading.events.EventCallbackImpl">
6    <constructor-arg index="0" ref="eventBus"/>
7  </bean>
8  <bean id="heartBeatCallback"
9    class="com.precioustech.fxtrading.heartbeats.HeartBeatCallbackImpl">
10   <constructor-arg index="0" ref="eventBus"/>
11 </bean>
12 <bean id="marketEventCallback"
13   class="com.precioustech.fxtrading.marketdata.MarketEventHandlerImpl">
14   <constructor-arg index="0" ref="eventBus"/>
15 </bean>
```

For the JavaMailSender bean, the configuration looks like this:

```
1  <bean id="mailSender" class="org.springframework.mail.javamail.
     JavaMailSenderImpl">
2          <property name="host" value="${mail.host}"/>
3          <property name="port" value="${mail.port}"/>
4          <property name="username" value="${mail.user}"/>
5          <property name="password" value="${mail.password}"/>
6          <property name="javaMailProperties">
7            <props>
8                <prop key="mail.transport.protocol">smtps</prop>
9                <prop key="mail.smtp.auth">true</prop>
10               <prop key="mail.smtp.starttls.enable">true</prop>
11               <prop key="mail.smtp.socketFactory.class">javax.net.ssl.
                 SSLSocketFactory</prop>
12               <prop key="mail.debug">false</prop>
13               <prop key="mail.smtp.socketFactory.fallback">false</prop>
14           </props>
15         </property>
16     </bean>
```

The placeholders for this bean are defined in the tradingbot.properties file. A related service that uses the JavaMailSender bean to send out notifications is configured as follows:

```
1  <bean id="eventEmailNotifier"
2      class="com.precioustech.fxtrading.tradingbot.events.notification.
       email.EventEmailNotifier"/>
```

The orderQueue is used to place orders and has a very simple configuration.

```
1   <bean id="orderQueue" class="java.util.concurrent.LinkedBlockingQueue"/>
```

We use the built-in Spring Task Scheduler [^sprsched] to schedule our jobs. An example job is polling new tweets for our configured Twitter accounts.

```
1   <task:scheduler id="taskScheduler" pool-size="5"/>
```

Twitter-Related Beans Configuration

We first configure TwitterTemplate, which enables all interaction with Twitter and is part of Spring Social.

```
1   <bean id="twitter" class="org.springframework.social.twitter.api.impl.
    TwitterTemplate">
2                   <constructor-arg index="0" value="${twitter.
                    consumerKey}"/>
3                   <constructor-arg index="1" value="${twitter.
                    consumerSecret}"/>
4                   <constructor-arg index="2" value="${twitter.
                    accessToken}"/>
5                   <constructor-arg index="3" value="${twitter.
                    accessTokenSecret}"/>
6   </bean>
```

The placeholders for the configuration are all defined in the tradingbot.properties file, which we discussed in the previous section. It's pretty self-explanatory.

Next we configure a bean that is a list of all Twitter accounts for which we want to process the tweets. Although not a dependency for other beans, it is used by SpEL to inject values. For example:

```
1   <bean id="fxTweeterList" class="java.util.ArrayList">
2                   <constructor-arg index="0">
3                           <list>
4                                   <value>SignalFactory</value>
5                                   <value>Forex_EA4U</value>
6                           </list>
7                   </constructor-arg>
8   </bean>
9   <util:map id="tweetHandlerMap">
10      <entry key="#{fxTweeterList[0]}">
11              <bean class=
12  "com.precioustech.fxtrading.tradingbot.social.twitter.tweethandler.
    SignalFactoryFXTweetHandler">
```

```
13                              <constructor-arg index="0" value="#{fxTweeter
                                  List[0]}"/>
14                      </bean>
15          </entry>
16      <entry key="#{fxTweeterList[1]}">
17              <bean class=
18      "com.precioustech.fxtrading.tradingbot.social.twitter.
        tweethandler.ZuluTrader101FXTweetHandler">
19                              <constructor-arg index="0" value="#{fxTweeter
                                  List[1]}"/>
20                      </bean>
21          </entry>
22  </util:map>
```

The SpEL enables us to define all the Twitter accounts in once place and then reference the list via expressions and inject the value of these expressions into other beans.

If we need to listen to more Twitter accounts for tweets, we just create or reuse existing handlers (if applicable) and configure them here.

Provider Beans Configuration

In this section, we configure all the beans that implement the Provider interfaces and are provider-specific. Since our discussion throughout the book has been based on the OANDA REST API, we define it inside its own configuration called tradingbot-oanda.xml and which has all its properties defined in the tradingbot-oanda.properties file.

It is important that the ID given to the beans in this OANDA config file be reused in other provider implementations, since the main configuration references this ID to configure the core services bean.

We begin by looking at the properties file:

```
1  oanda.url=https://api-fxtrade.oanda.com
2  oanda.accessToken=7d741c1234f25d9f5a094e53a356789b-2c9a7b49578904
   e177210af8e111c2f6
3  oanda.userName=foo
4  oanda.accountId=123456
5  oanda.streaming.url=https://stream-fxtrade.oanda.com
```

- oanda.url is the URL we want to point our trading bot to. Remember we have the live, practice, and sandbox environments provided by OANDA.

- oanda.streaming.url is the streaming URL for tick data and platform events.

- oanda.accessToken is the token that was generated in the environment pointed by oanda.url.

- oanda.userName is a valid username in the environment pointed by oanda.url.

- oanda.accountId is a valid account belonging to the value configured for oanda.userName in the environment pointed by oanda.url. A valid account ID is required to start a market data stream, for example.

We provide the location of this properties file, as usual as a *classpath* location, and turn on the annotation processing, like we did for the main configuration file.

```
1  <context:annotation-config/>
2  <context:property-placeholder location="classpath:tradingbot-oanda.
   properties"
3              ignore-unresolvable="true"/>
```

We now list the configurations for all the OANDA provider services.

AccountDataProviderService

```
1  <bean id="accountDataProvider" class=
2    "com.precioustech.fxtrading.oanda.restapi.account.
   OandaAccountDataProviderService">
3                      <constructor-arg index="0" value="${oanda.url}"/>
4                      <constructor-arg index="1" value="${oanda.userName}"/>
5                      <constructor-arg index="2" value="${oanda.accessToken}"/>
6  </bean>
```

ProviderHelper

```
1  <bean id="providerHelper"
2      class="com.precioustech.fxtrading.oanda.restapi.helper.
   OandaProviderHelper"/>
```

InstrumentDataProvider

```
1  <bean id="instrumentDataProvider"
2      class="com.precioustech.fxtrading.oanda.restapi.instrument.
   OandaInstrumentDataProviderService">
3                      <constructor-arg index="0" value="${oanda.url}"/>
4                      <constructor-arg index="1" value="${oanda.accountId}"/>
5                      <constructor-arg index="2" value="${oanda.
   accessToken}"/>
6  </bean>
```

CurrentPriceInfoProvider

```
1    <bean id="currentPriceInfoProvider"
2      class="com.precioustech.fxtrading.oanda.restapi.marketdata.
     OandaCurrentPriceInfoProvider">
3                        <constructor-arg index="0" value="${oanda.url}"/>
4                        <constructor-arg index="1" value="${oanda.
     accessToken}"/>
5    </bean>
```

HistoricMarketDataProvider

```
1    <bean id="historicMarketDataProvider"
2      class="com.precioustech.fxtrading.oanda.restapi.marketdata.historic.
     OandaHistoricMarketDataProvider">
3                        <constructor-arg index="0" value="${oanda.url}"/>
4                        <constructor-arg index="1" value="${oanda.
     accessToken}"/>
5    </bean>
```

OrderManagementProvider

```
1    <bean id="orderManagementProvider"
2      class="com.precioustech.fxtrading.oanda.restapi.order.
     OandaOrderManagementProvider">
3                        <constructor-arg index="0" value="${oanda.url}"/>
4                        <constructor-arg index="1" value="${oanda.
     accessToken}"/>
5                        <constructor-arg index="2" ref="accountDataProvider"/>
6    </bean>
```

TradeManagementProvider

```
1    <bean id="tradeManagementProvider"
2      class="com.precioustech.fxtrading.oanda.restapi.trade.
     OandaTradeManagementProvider">
3                        <constructor-arg index="0" value="${oanda.url}"/>
4                        <constructor-arg index="1" value="${oanda.
     accessToken}"/>
5            </bean>
```

PositionManagementProvider

```
1   <bean id="positionManagementProvider"
2     class="com.precioustech.fxtrading.oanda.restapi.position.
      OandaPositionManagementProvider">
3                 <constructor-arg index="0" value="${oanda.url}"/>
4                 <constructor-arg index="1" value="${oanda.
                    accessToken}"/>
5   </bean>
```

EventStreamingService

```
1   <bean id="eventsStreamingService"
2     class="com.precioustech.fxtrading.oanda.restapi.streaming.events.
      OandaEventsStreamingService">
3                 <constructor-arg index="0" value="${oanda.streaming.
                    url}"/>
4                 <constructor-arg index="1" value="${oanda.
                    accessToken}"/>
5                 <constructor-arg index="2" ref="accountDataProvider"/>
6                 <constructor-arg index="3" ref="eventCallback"/>
7                 <constructor-arg index="4" ref="heartBeatCallback"/>
8                 <constructor-arg index="5" value="EVENTSTREAM"/>
9   </bean>
```

We assign the source ID EVENTSTREAM as a heartbeat source ID, since the same class is responsible for handling the event heartbeats.

Platform Event Handlers

```
1   <bean id="orderEventHandler"
2     class="com.precioustech.fxtrading.oanda.restapi.events.
      OrderFilledEventHandler">
3           <constructor-arg index="0" ref="tradeInfoService"/>
4   </bean>
5   <bean id="tradeEventHandler"
6     class="com.precioustech.fxtrading.oanda.restapi.events.
      TradeEventHandler">
7         <constructor-arg index="0" ref="tradeInfoService"/>
8   </bean>
```

These event handlers need to be assigned to platform events that they will handle:

```
1   <util:map id="eventEmailContentGeneratorMap" key-type="com.
    precioustech.fxtrading.events.Event">
2           <entry
3       key="#{T(com.precioustech.fxtrading.oanda.restapi.events.
        OrderEvents).MARKET_ORDER_CREATE}"
4       value-ref="orderEventHandler"/>
5           <entry
6       key="#{T(com.precioustech.fxtrading.oanda.restapi.events.
        OrderEvents).LIMIT_ORDER_CREATE}"
7       value-ref="orderEventHandler"/>
8           <entry
9       key="#{T(com.precioustech.fxtrading.oanda.restapi.events.
        OrderEvents).ORDER_CANCEL}"
10      value-ref="orderEventHandler"/>
11          <entry
12      key="#{T(com.precioustech.fxtrading.oanda.restapi.events.
        OrderEvents).ORDER_FILLED}"
13      value-ref="orderEventHandler"/>
14          <entry
15      key="#{T(com.precioustech.fxtrading.oanda.restapi.events.
        TradeEvents).TRADE_CLOSE}"
16      value-ref="tradeEventHandler"/>
17          <entry
18      key="#{T(com.precioustech.fxtrading.oanda.restapi.events.
        TradeEvents).STOP_LOSS_FILLED}"
19      value-ref="tradeEventHandler"/>
20          <entry
21      key="#{T(com.precioustech.fxtrading.oanda.restapi.events.
        TradeEvents).TAKE_PROFIT_FILLED}"
22      value-ref="tradeEventHandler"/>
23  </util:map>
```

We configure the eventEmailContentGeneratorMap map to express interest in notifications that we want the bot to generate when the platform event is generated. The corresponding handlers are responsible for generating the content for the e-mail. as discussed in the previous chapter.

MarketDataStreamingService

```
1   <bean id="marketDataStreamingService"
2       class="com.precioustech.fxtrading.oanda.restapi.streaming.marketdata.
        OandaMarketDataStreamingService">
3               <constructor-arg index="0" value="${oanda.streaming.
                url}"/>
```

```
 4                         <constructor-arg index="1" value="${oanda.
                           accessToken}"/>
 5                         <constructor-arg index="2" value="${oanda.accountId}"/>
 6                         <constructor-arg index="3" ref="tradeableInstrument
                           List"/>
 7                         <constructor-arg index="4" ref="marketEventCallback"/>
 8                         <constructor-arg index="5" ref="heartBeatCallback"/>
 9                         <constructor-arg index="6" value="MKTDATASTREAM"/>
10     </bean>
```

We assign the source ID MKTDATASTREAM as a heartbeat source ID, since the same class is responsible to tick data heartbeats.

The tradeableInstrumentList is the list of instruments for which we want to subscribe tick data from the OANDA platform. The list is configured as follows:

```
 1    <bean id="tradeableInstrumentList" class="java.util.ArrayList">
 2            <constructor-arg index="0">
 3                    <list>
 4                            <bean class="com.precioustech.fxtrading.
                               instrument.TradeableInstrument">
 5            <constructor-arg index="0" value="USD_CAD"/>
 6            </bean>
 7                            <bean class="com.precioustech.fxtrading.
                               instrument.TradeableInstrument">
 8            <constructor-arg index="0" value="GBP_USD"/>
 9            </bean>
10                            <bean class="com.precioustech.fxtrading.
                               instrument.TradeableInstrument">
11            <constructor-arg index="0" value="AUD_JPY"/>
12            </bean>
13                            <bean class="com.precioustech.fxtrading.
                               instrument.TradeableInstrument">
14            <constructor-arg index="0" value="EUR_NZD"/>
15            </bean>
16                            <bean class="com.precioustech.fxtrading.
                               instrument.TradeableInstrument">
17            <constructor-arg index="0" value="GBP_CHF"/>
18            </bean>
19                            <bean class="com.precioustech.fxtrading.
                               instrument.TradeableInstrument">
20            <constructor-arg index="0" value="EUR_JPY"/>
21            </bean>
22                    </list>
23            </constructor-arg>
24    </bean>
```

This concludes our discussion of the configuration of all the *provider* beans for the OANDA implementation.

Strategies Configuration

In this book we discussed a couple of strategies that happen to get activated via a scheduler-based invocation. In this section we configure them and show how they are invoked.

```
1   <bean id="fadeTheMoveStrategy"
2       class="com.precioustech.fxtrading.tradingbot.strategies.
        FadeTheMoveStrategy">
3           <constructor-arg index="0" ref="tradeableInstrumentList"/>
4   </bean>
5   <bean id="copyTwitterStrategy"
6       class="com.precioustech.fxtrading.tradingbot.strategies.
        CopyTwitterStrategy"/>
```

The configuration is fairly straightforward. The FadeTheMove strategy has an additional constructor dependency that gets injected with a list of instruments to observe and place an order if the given conditions are met.

Now we look at the scheduler configuration that invokes a given strategy bean method after every time interval T:

```
1   <task:scheduled-tasks scheduler="taskScheduler">
2                   <task:scheduled ref="fadeTheMoveStrategy"
                    method="analysePrices"
3               fixed-delay="60000"/>
4                   <task:scheduled ref="copyTwitterStrategy"
                    method="harvestAndTrade"
5               fixed-delay="300000"/>
6   </task:scheduled-tasks>
```

The scheduler invokes every 60000ms the analysePrices() method of the fadeTheMoveStrategy bean. It also invokes every 300000ms the harvestAndTrade() method of the copyTwitterStrategy bean.

Services Configuration

In this concluding section on configuration, we discuss how to configure the core services of the bot. These services could be considered the public API of the bot if there were a GUI client or for that matter any other client interacting with the bot. Most of the demo programs in this book directly interact with these services.

AccountInfoService

```
1   <bean id="accountInfoService"
2       class="com.precioustech.fxtrading.account.AccountInfoService">
3           <constructor-arg index="0" ref="accountDataProvider"/>
```

```
4              <constructor-arg index="1" ref="currentPriceInfoProvider"/>
5              <constructor-arg index="2" ref="tradingConfig"/>
6              <constructor-arg index="3" ref="providerHelper"/>
7      </bean>
```

InstrumentService

```
1      <bean id="instrumentService"
2          class="com.precioustech.fxtrading.instrument.InstrumentService">
3                      <constructor-arg index="0" ref="instrumentDataProvider"/>
4      </bean>
```

MovingAverageCalculationService

```
1      <bean id="movingAverageCalculationService"
2          class="com.precioustech.fxtrading.marketdata.historic.
       MovingAverageCalculationService">
3                      <constructor-arg index="0" ref="historicMarketData
                       Provider"/>
4      </bean>
```

OrderInfoService

```
1      <bean id="orderInfoService"
2          class="com.precioustech.fxtrading.order.OrderInfoService">
3          <constructor-arg index="0" ref="orderManagementProvider"/>
4      </bean>
```

TradeInfoService

```
1      <bean id="tradeInfoService"
2          class="com.precioustech.fxtrading.trade.TradeInfoService">
3          <constructor-arg index="0" ref="tradeManagementProvider"/>
4          <constructor-arg index="1" ref="accountInfoService"/>
5      </bean>
```

PreOrderValidationService

```
1      <bean id="preOrderValidationService"
2          class="com.precioustech.fxtrading.order.PreOrderValidationService">
3          <constructor-arg index="0" ref="tradeInfoService"/>
4          <constructor-arg index="1" ref="movingAverageCalculationService"/>
```

255

```
5            <constructor-arg index="2" ref="tradingConfig"/>
6            <constructor-arg index="3" ref="orderInfoService"/>
7    </bean>
```

OrderExecutionService

```
1    <bean id="orderExecutionService"
2        class="com.precioustech.fxtrading.order.OrderExecutionService">
3            <constructor-arg index="0" ref="orderQueue"/>
4            <constructor-arg index="1" ref="accountInfoService"/>
5            <constructor-arg index="2" ref="orderManagementProvider"/>
6            <constructor-arg index="3" ref="tradingConfig"/>
7            <constructor-arg index="4" ref="preOrderValidationService"/>
8            <constructor-arg index="5" ref="currentPriceInfoProvider"/>
9    </bean>
```

DefaultHeartBeatService

```
1    <bean id="heartBeatService"
2        class="com.precioustech.fxtrading.heartbeats.
         DefaultHeartBeatService">
3            <constructor-arg index="0">
4                    <list>
5                            <ref bean="eventsStreamingService"/>
6                            <ref bean="marketDataStreamingService"/>
7                    </list>
8            </constructor-arg>
9    </bean>
```

Building the Bot

The bot can easily be built using maven. Since there are three projects that need to be built in a given order, we can script the actions, instead of having to remember the build order. If you have cloned the code repository from GitHub, there is a buildbot.bsh file in the <repo-code>/java directory that will build the bot using maven. Figure 12-1 shows my bash terminal after having cloned the repository.

```
[ShekharMacBook:java shekhar$ pwd
/Volumes/05/git/book-code/java
[ShekharMacBook:java shekhar$ ls -l
 total 8
-rwxr-xr-x   1 shekhar  staff  324 31 Jan 16:43 buildbot.bsh
drwxr-xr-x   9 shekhar  staff  306 31 Jan 17:32 oanda-restapi
drwxr-xr-x  11 shekhar  staff  374 31 Jan 17:32 tradingbot-app
drwxr-xr-x   9 shekhar  staff  306 31 Jan 17:32 tradingbot-core
drwxr-xr-x  10 shekhar  staff  340 27 Jan 20:10 tradingbot-demo-programs
ShekharMacBook:java shekhar$
```

Figure 12-1. Code repo structure

Before running the code, it is assumed that maven and Java 1.7 are installed and configured. When you type the mvn --version is typed command on the command line, you'll see output similar to what's shown in Figure 12-2.

```
ShekharMacBook:java shekhar$ mvn --version
Apache Maven 3.2.5 (12a6b3acb947671f89b81f49094c53f426d8cea1; 2014-12-14T18:29:23+01:00)
Maven home: /usr/local/Cellar/maven/3.2.5/libexec
Java version: 1.7.0_71, vendor: Oracle Corporation
Java home: /Library/Java/JavaVirtualMachines/jdk1.7.0_71.jdk/Contents/Home/jre
Default locale: en_US, platform encoding: UTF-8
OS name: "mac os x", version: "10.11", arch: "x86_64", family: "mac"
ShekharMacBook:java shekhar$ ▌
```

Figure 12-2. mvn –version output

If this is not the case, make sure maven is properly installed[3].

We are now ready to run the buildbot.bsh script. Before that, let's take a quick look at the script code:

```
1   function buildmodule {
2       cd $SCRIPT_DIR/$1
3       mvn clean install
4       if [[ "$?" -ne 0 ]]; then
5          echo "ERROR: $1 project build failed. BUILD FAILED"; exit -1;
6       fi
7   }
8   SCRIPT_DIR=`pwd`
9   buildmodule tradingbot-core
10  buildmodule oanda-restapi
11  buildmodule tradingbot-app
12
13  echo "TRADING BOT built successfully"
```

---

[3]https://maven.apache.org/install.html

```
drwxr-xr-x  10 shekhar  staff   340 27 Jan 20:10 tradingbot-demo-programs
ShekharMacBook:java shekhar$ ./buildbot.bsh
[INFO] Scanning for projects...
[WARNING]
[WARNING] Some problems were encountered while building the effective model for com.precioustech:tradingbot-core:jar:1.0
[WARNING] 'build.plugins.plugin.version' for org.apache.maven.plugins:maven-compiler-plugin is missing. @ line 78, column 19
[WARNING]
[WARNING] It is highly recommended to fix these problems because they threaten the stability of your build.
[WARNING]
[WARNING] For this reason, future Maven versions might no longer support building such malformed projects.
[WARNING]
[INFO]
[INFO] ------------------------------------------------------------------------
[INFO] Building tradingbot-core 1.0
[[INFO] ------------------------------------------------------------------------
[WARNING] The artifact org.apache.commons:commons-io:jar:1.3.2 has been relocated to commons-io:commons-io:jar:1.3.2
[[INFO]
[INFO] --- maven-clean-plugin:2.5:clean (default-clean) @ tradingbot-core ---
[[INFO] Deleting /Volumes/05/git/book-code/java/tradingbot-core/target
[INFO]
[INFO] --- maven-resources-plugin:2.6:resources (default-resources) @ tradingbot-core ---
[INFO] Using 'UTF-8' encoding to copy filtered resources.
[INFO] skip non existing resourceDirectory /Volumes/05/git/book-code/java/tradingbot-core/src/main/resources
[INFO]
[INFO] --- maven-compiler-plugin:3.1:compile (default-compile) @ tradingbot-core ---
[INFO] Changes detected - recompiling the module!
[[INFO] Compiling 50 source files to /Volumes/05/git/book-code/java/tradingbot-core/target/classes
[INFO]
[[INFO] --- maven-resources-plugin:2.6:testResources (default-testResources) @ tradingbot-core ---
[INFO] Using 'UTF-8' encoding to copy filtered resources.
[INFO] Copying 2 resources
[INFO]
[[INFO] --- maven-compiler-plugin:3.1:testCompile (default-testCompile) @ tradingbot-core ---
[[INFO] Changes detected - recompiling the module!
[INFO] Compiling 11 source files to /Volumes/05/git/book-code/java/tradingbot-core/target/test-classes
[INFO]
[INFO] --- maven-surefire-plugin:2.12.4:test (default-test) @ tradingbot-core ---
[[INFO] Surefire report directory: /Volumes/05/git/book-code/java/tradingbot-core/target/surefire-reports
[
 -------------------------------------------------------
 T E S T S
```

Figure 12-3. *Start build at the command line*

We call the function buildmodule for each of the three modules we want to build.
The function first does a cd to the appropriate source code directory and then issues a
mvn clean install command to build the artifacts (i.e., the *jar* file). If there are unit
tests failure or compilation issues, mvn clean install will exit with a non-zero code. We
check this code set in the $? variable, and if it's non-zero, we exit the script straightaway.
See Figure 12-4.

```
Results :

Tests in error:
  findHistoricPnlTweetsForInstrumentTest(com.precioustech.fxtrading.tradingbot.social.twitter.tweethandler.SignalFactoryFXTweetHandlerTest)
  findHistoricPnlTweetsForInstrumentTest(com.precioustech.fxtrading.tradingbot.social.twitter.tweethandler.ZuluTrader161FXTweetHandlerTest)

Tests run: 11, Failures: 0, Errors: 2, Skipped: 0

[INFO] -----------------------------------------------------------------------
[INFO] BUILD FAILURE
[INFO] -----------------------------------------------------------------------
[INFO] Total time: 7.459 s
[INFO] Finished at: 2016-01-31T16:41.14+01:00
[INFO] Final Memory: 19M/222M
[INFO] -----------------------------------------------------------------------
[ERROR] Failed to execute goal org.apache.maven.plugins:maven-surefire-plugin:2.12.4:test (default-test) on project tradingbot-app: There are test failur
es.
[ERROR]
[ERROR] Please refer to /Volumes/05/git/code-repo/java/tradingbot-app/target/surefire-reports for the individual test results.
[ERROR] -> [Help 1]
[ERROR]
[ERROR] To see the full stack trace of the errors, re-run Maven with the -e switch.
[ERROR] Re-run Maven using the -X switch to enable full debug logging.
[ERROR]
[ERROR] For more information about the errors and possible solutions, please read the following articles:
[ERROR] [Help 1] http://cwiki.apache.org/confluence/display/MAVEN/MojoFailureException
tradingbot-app project build failed
[ShekharMacBook:java shekhar$ vim buildbot.bsh
```

Figure 12-4. *Build failure*

If the build succeeds, we should see the output in Figure 12-5.

```
T E S T S
------------------------------------------------------------
Running com.precioustech.fxtrading.tradingbot.events.notification.email.EventEmailNotifierTest
2016-01-31 17:32:44,100 WARN  [main] - No email content generator found for event:null
Tests run: 1, Failures: 0, Errors: 0, Skipped: 0, Time elapsed: 0.744 sec
Running com.precioustech.fxtrading.tradingbot.social.twitter.tweethandler.SignalFactoryFXTweetHandlerTest
Tests run: 3, Failures: 0, Errors: 0, Skipped: 0, Time elapsed: 0.409 sec
Running com.precioustech.fxtrading.tradingbot.social.twitter.tweethandler.ZuluTrader101FXTweetHandlerTest
Tests run: 2, Failures: 0, Errors: 0, Skipped: 0, Time elapsed: 0.01 sec
Running com.precioustech.fxtrading.tradingbot.strategies.CopyTwitterStrategyTest
2016-01-31 17:32:44,643 INFO  [main] - found 2 new tweets for user foo
2016-01-31 17:32:44,655 INFO  [pool-1-thread-1] - found 1 new tweets for user foo
2016-01-31 17:32:44,656 INFO  [pool-1-thread-1] - found 8 historic pnl tweets for user foo and instrument EUR_AUD
2016-01-31 17:32:44,661 INFO  [main] - found 2 historic pnl tweets for user foo and instrument GBP_USD
Tests run: 4, Failures: 0, Errors: 0, Skipped: 0, Time elapsed: 0.098 sec
Running com.precioustech.fxtrading.tradingbot.strategies.FadeTheMoveStrategyTest
Tests run: 1, Failures: 0, Errors: 0, Skipped: 0, Time elapsed: 0.164 sec

Results :

Tests run: 11, Failures: 0, Errors: 0, Skipped: 0

[INFO]
[INFO] --- maven-jar-plugin:2.4:jar (default-jar) @ tradingbot-app ---
[INFO] Building jar: /Volumes/85/git/book-code/java/tradingbot-app/target/tradingbot-app-1.0.jar
[INFO]
[INFO] --- maven-install-plugin:2.4:install (default-install) @ tradingbot-app ---
[INFO] Installing /Volumes/85/git/book-code/java/tradingbot-app/target/tradingbot-app-1.0.jar to /Users/shekhar/.m2/repository/com/precioustech/f
/1.0/tradingbot-app-1.0.jar
[INFO] Installing /Volumes/85/git/book-code/java/tradingbot-app/pom.xml to /Users/shekhar/.m2/repository/com/precioustech/fxtrading/tradingbot-ap
0.pom
[INFO] ------------------------------------------------------------
[INFO] BUILD SUCCESS
[INFO] ------------------------------------------------------------
[INFO] Total time: 10.904 s
[INFO] Finished at: 2016-01-31T17:32:45+01:00
[INFO] Final Memory: 18M/229M
[INFO] ------------------------------------------------------------
TRADING BOT built successfully  ⟵
ShekharMacBook:java shekhar$ pwd
```

Figure 12-5. Build success

Running the Bot

■ **Warning**   Serious losses can be incurred if some of the configuration values used to run the bot are extremely high. The author has taken every opportunity to highlight those throughout the book. In no event is the author liable for any consequential damages arising from the configuration values the user deems fit for his/her risk appetite.

Now that the bot is fully built, we are ready to run it. But before we really push the button, we need to make sure the following config params have been adapted and a build is done so that these changes are in the JAR file for the given user. Here is the full checklist of changes:

- All OANDA-specific parameters in tradingbot-oanda. properties belong to the user of a valid live or practice account.

- All Twitter-specific access tokens in tradingbot.properties are correctly populated. These valid tokens are generated for a Twitter app or for a Twitter account to which the user has full access.

- Double-check that the values for the TradingConfig bean are within comfortable limits, especially maxAllowedQuantity, minReserveRatio, and maxAllowedNetContracts.

- Configure a valid mail account in tradingbot.properties. The credentials are used to send e-mail notifications to the mail.to e-mail address.

- Configure log4j.properties in the tradingbot-app resources directory if required.

- Execute buildbot.sh again to rebuild the bot with the new set of parameters.

To run the bot with the strategies discussed in the book and OANDA implementation, we simply do the following

```
1   $ ./runbot-oanda.bsh
```

If all goes well, you should see the output shown in Figure 12-6 coming from the bot.

Figure 12-6. *Running the bot*

While the bot is running, we should see it harvesting the tweet shown in Figure 12-7 from time to time.

```
INFO  2016-01-25 17:20:00.807 [pool-1-thread-1] com.precioustech.fxtrading.tradingbot.strategies.CopyTwitterStrategy(harvestNewTradeTweets): found 1 new tweets for user SignalFactory
```

Figure 12-7. *New tweet harvested*

That is it. Our bot is now fully up and running. We should see that FadeTheMove strategy is very busy, especially around market moving currency events such as FOMC decision or GDP data from various countries. One point to bear in mind is that this strategy maintains an internal cache for the last 15 minutes. The more instruments you configure for subscription to tick the data stream, the more memory footprint you will have. Therefore, it may be imperative to run with a higher memory value. Since the bot runs inside maven, you would have to change the MAVEN_OPTS params.

CHAPTER 13

■■■

Unit Testing

In this chapter we discuss a very important topic, unit testing our code. Proper unit testing coverage of our bot will ensure that we do not create many regressions when we make changes or add enhancements to the existing code. For some of the target audience of this book, the trading bot may be deployed to place real orders with a live account where huge sums of money could be involved. Making sure that we have enough test coverage will ensure that a code bug would be unlikely to place bad orders. We briefly summarize the immense benefits of unit testing here. Proper unit tests:

- Eliminate most of the unlikely surprises in the production environment.

- Help document the code.

- Force a developer to develop and think in a way that leads to better design, code, and architecture of the system components.

- Help developers write more maintainable code because they adopt the test-driven development approach. We are forced to write smaller classes so that they can be unit tested easily.

- Help developers write loosely coupled components. Having many dependencies to mock forces us to think this way.

Keeping these issues in mind, we will discuss some of the concepts and techniques of unit testing the bot in this chapter.

Using Mockito as a Mocking Framework

For writing unit tests for the bot, we are going to use Mockito[1] extensively to create mocks for our objects. The mock for an object like TwitterTemplate helps to simulate the behavior of this object without having to instantiate it fully. In order to harvest tweets using a real TwitterTemplate, we have to provide valid tokens in order to authenticate with Twitter. This is not the real problem actually. The real problem is getting the same deterministic results every time we do a search query. This is impossible with the real

---

[1]http://mockito.org/

© Shekhar Varshney 2016
S. Varshney, *Building Trading Bots Using Java*, DOI 10.1007/978-1-4842-2520-2_13

TwitterTemplate, as the tweets are constantly getting created and as a result the search results too. We cannot write deterministic *asserts* to unit test our code. To get around this problem, we use mocks and get deterministic results. The same applies to getting the deterministic order of price tick data from the provider, which is impossible in the real world.

Mocking HTTP Interaction

We need to be able to mock HTTP interaction in order to test our OANDA provider implementations. The concept is that this mock method, which we are going to explore shortly, returns an InputStream that is an instance of FileInputStream instead of a real-world instance of org.apache.http.client.entity.LazyDecompressingInputStream. Therefore, all of our interaction with OANDA comes from files of JSON payloads that we create instead of going to the OANDA platform. Let's take a quick look at the code of this method:

```
1  public static final void mockHttpInteraction(String fname, HttpClient
   mockHttpClient) throws Exception {
2    CloseableHttpResponse mockResp = mock(CloseableHttpResponse.class);
3    when(mockHttpClient.execute(any(HttpUriRequest.class))).
     thenReturn(mockResp);
4
5    HttpEntity mockEntity = mock(HttpEntity.class);
6
7    when(mockResp.getEntity()).thenReturn(mockEntity);
8
9    StatusLine mockStatusLine = mock(StatusLine.class);
10
11   when(mockResp.getStatusLine()).thenReturn(mockStatusLine);
12   when(mockStatusLine.getStatusCode()).thenReturn(HttpStatus.SC_OK);
13   when(mockEntity.getContent()).thenReturn(new FileInputStream(fname));
14 }
```

The mockHttpInteraction method accepts a filename and a mock HttpClient as an argument. The last line of the method is where the magic happens after we have mocked all the interactions to get to this line. The HttpEntity object, which has the content returned from the OANDA REST API in the real world, is mocked to return the content of the file instead.

This is a very useful concept that we just discussed. Now we are in a position to just about mock any interaction by mimicking the response in a file. Let's look at an example of a unit test that does this interaction.

```
1  @Test
2  public void accountIdTest() throws Exception {
3    final OandaAccountDataProviderService service = new
4    OandaAccountDataProviderService(url, userName, accessToken);
```

```
5     assertEquals("https://api-fxtrade.oanda.com/v1/accounts/123456",
6       service.getSingleAccountUrl(accountId));
7
8     OandaAccountDataProviderService spy =
9       createSpyAndCommonStuff("src/test/resources/account123456.txt",
      service);
10    Account < Long > accInfo = spy.getLatestAccountInfo(accountId);
11    assertNotNull(accInfo);
12    assertEquals("CHF",  accInfo.getCurrency());
13    assertEquals(0.05,  accInfo.getMarginRate(), OandaTestConstants.
      precision);
14    assertEquals(-897.1,  accInfo.getUnrealisedPnl(), OandaTestConstants.
      precision);
15    }
16
17    private OandaAccountDataProviderService createSpyAndCommonStuff(String
      fname,
18      OandaAccountDataProviderService service) throws Exception {
19      OandaAccountDataProviderService spy = spy(service);
20
21      CloseableHttpClient mockHttpClient = mock(CloseableHttpClient.class);
22      when(spy.getHttpClient()).thenReturn(mockHttpClient);
23
24      OandaTestUtils.mockHttpInteraction(fname,  mockHttpClient);
25
26      return spy;
27    }
```

Before looking at the code in detail, let's first look at the contents of the src/test/resources/account123456.txt file used in this unit test case.

```
1     {
2         "accountId" : 123456,
3         "accountName" : "main",
4         "balance" : 20567.9,
5         "unrealizedPl" : -897.1,
6         "realizedPl" : 1123.65,
7         "marginUsed" : 89.98,
8         "marginAvail" : 645.3,
9         "openTrades" : 5,
10        "openOrders" : 0,
11        "marginRate" : 0.05,
12        "accountCurrency"  : "CHF"
13    }
```

The test begins by creating a real instance of the AccountDataProvider, in this case OandaAccountDataProviderService. We then create a *spy*[2] on this object in the private method createSpyAndCommonStuff. Also inside this method we associate a mock HttpClient object that is used by the mockHttpInteraction method previously discussed to interact with the file that is passed as an argument to the method.

So what happens when spy.getLatestAccountInfo(accountId) is invoked?

```
1    private Account < Long > getLatestAccountInfo(final Long accountId,
2    CloseableHttpClient httpClient) {
3    try {
4    HttpUriRequest httpGet = new HttpGet(getSingleAccountUrl(accountId));
5    httpGet.setHeader(authHeader);
6
7    LOG.info(TradingUtils.executingRequestMsg(httpGet));
8    HttpResponse httpResponse = httpClient.execute(httpGet);
9    String strResp = TradingUtils.responseToString(httpResponse);
10   ...
11   ...
```

- The code HttpResponse httpResponse = httpClient. execute(httpGet) returns a mock CloseableHttpResponse object (refer to method mockHttpInteraction).

- When TradingUtils.responseToString is invoked with this mock httpResponse object, the call to entity.getContent inside this method returns an InputStream object which is actually an instance of FileInputStream that has a handle on the src/test/ resources/account123456.txt file used in the unit test.

- When this InputStream method is read, the underlying file is read and the contents returned from the method.

- This response is then parsed in the normal way, as is done from the actual OANDA platform when the HTTP 200 code is returned.

For reference, TradingUtils.responseToString is as follows:

```
1    /**
2     * A utility method that tries to toString an HttpResponse object. Only
3     * when HTTP status 200 is returned by the server, will this method
4     * attempt to process the response.
5     *
6     * @param response
7     * @return a String representation of the response if possible else an
8     *   empty string.
9     * @throws IOException
10    */
```

---

[2]http://docs.mockito.googlecode.com/hg/1.9.5/org/mockito/Spy.html

```
11  public static final String responseToString(HttpResponse response)
    throws IOException {
12   HttpEntity entity = response.getEntity();
13   if ((response.getStatusLine().getStatusCode() == HttpStatus.SC_OK ||
14     response.getStatusLine().getStatusCode() == HttpStatus.SC_CREATED)
       && entity != null) {
15    InputStream stream = entity.getContent();
16    String line;
17    BufferedReader br = new BufferedReader(new InputStreamReader(stream));
18    StringBuilder strResp = new  StringBuilder();
19    while ((line = br.readLine()) != null) {
20     strResp.append(line);
21    }
22    IOUtils.closeQuietly(stream);
23    IOUtils.closeQuietly(br);
24    return strResp.toString();
25   } else {
26    return StringUtils.EMPTY;
27   }
28  }
```

Mocking Streams

In this section, we discuss how we can unit test streams discussed in the book, i.e., the market data stream and trade/order/account event stream. We are going to use exactly the same technique, i.e., using the mocking techniques described in the previous section to unit test them. Like before, we switch the InputStream available from the HttpGet to that of a FileInputStream, each line of which is an event in a JSON format. An extract from our unit test file looks like this:

```
1  {"tick":{"instrument":"AUD_CAD","time":"1401919213548144",
   "bid":1.01479,"ask":1.01498}}
2  {"tick":{"instrument":"NZD_SGD","time":"1401919213548822",
   "bid":1.07979,"ask":1.07998}}
3  {"heartbeat":{"time":"1401919213548226"}}
4  {"tick":{"instrument":"AUD_CAD","time":"1401919217201682",
   "bid":1.01484,"ask":1.01502}}
5  {"tick":{"instrument":"NZD_SGD","time":"1401919217201500",
   "bid":1.07984,"ask":1.08002}}
6  {"tick":{"instrument":"AUD_CAD","time":"1401919217206100",
   "bid":1.01484,"ask":1.01504}}
7  {"tick":{"instrument":"NZD_SGD","time":"1401919217206465",
   "bid":1.07984,"ask":1.08004}}
8  {"heartbeat":{"time":"1401919217206269"}}
9  {"tick":{"instrument":"AUD CAD","time":"1401919221292441",
   "bid":1.0149,"ask":1.01505}}
```

```
10   {"tick":{"instrument":"NZD_SGD","time":"1401919221292791",
     "bid":1.07990,"ask":1.08005}}
11   {"tick":{"instrument":"AUD_CAD","time":"1401919221297498",
     "bid":1.01484,"ask":1.01505}}
12   {"tick":{"instrument":"NZD_SGD","time":"1401919221297233",
     "bid":1.07984,"ask":1.08005}}
13   {"heartbeat":{"time":"1401919221297319"}}
14   {"tick":{"instrument":"AUD_CAD","time":"1401919224790916",
     "bid":1.01489,"ask":1.01505}}
15   {"tick":{"instrument":"NZD_SGD","time":"1401919224790630",
     "bid":1.07989,"ask":1.08005}}
16   {"tick":{"instrument":"AUD_CAD","time":"1401919224795379",
     "bid":1.01489,"ask":1.01506}}
17   {"tick":{"instrument":"NZD_SGD","time":"1401919224795198",
     "bid":1.07989,"ask":1.08006}}
18   {"heartbeat":{"time":"1401919224795130"}}
19   {"tick":{"instrument":"AUD_CAD","time":"1401919224800549",
     "bid":1.01489,"ask":1.01508}}
20   {"tick":{"instrument":"NZD_SGD","time":"1401919224800275",
     "bid":1.07989,"ask":1.08008}}
```

This file tries to mimic a live environment when there is a constant stream of tick data for instruments AUD_CAD and NZD_SGD. These ticks are interspersed with heartbeats, also mimicking the fact that the stream is alive. Let's look at the actual test case that tests the OandaMarketDataStreamingService. We want to test that this service handles the tick data and heartbeats coming in correctly and calls the relevant callback handlers to disseminate the events downstream via EventBus. The test will have one of the asserts being that the count of events in the file matches the events pushed downstream. Let's look at the code and see how we can accomplish one of these asserts.

```
1    private static final int expectedPriceEvents = 668; // 1 for each
2    private static final TradeableInstrument < String > AUDCAD =
3     new TradeableInstrument < String > ("AUD_CAD");
4    private static final TradeableInstrument < String > NZDSGD =
5     new TradeableInstrument < String > ("NZD_SGD");
6    @Test
7    public void marketDataStreaming() throws Exception {
8     Collection < TradeableInstrument < String >> instruments = Lists.
       newArrayList();
9     EventBus eventBus = new EventBus();
10    MarketEventCallback < String > mktEventCallback = new
      MarketEventHandlerImpl < String > (eventBus);
11    HeartBeatCallback < DateTime > heartBeatCallback = new
      HeartBeatCallbackImpl < DateTime > (eventBus);
12    eventBus.register(this);
13    instruments.add(AUDCAD);
14    instruments.add(NZDSGD);
```

```
15   OandaStreamingService service =
16     new OandaMarketDataStreamingService(OandaTestConstants.streaming_url,
17      OandaTestConstants.accessToken, OandaTestConstants.accountId,
18        instruments, mktEventCallback, heartBeatCallback, "TESTMKTSTREAM");
19   assertEquals("https://stream-fxtrade.oanda.com/v1/prices" + "?accoun
     tId=123456&instruments=AUD_CAD%2CNZD_SGD",
20     service.getStreamingUrl());
21   OandaStreamingService spy =
22     setUpSpy(service, "src/test/resources/marketData123456.txt");
23   assertEquals(expectedPriceEvents / 2, audcadCt);
24   assertEquals(expectedPriceEvents / 2, nzdsgdCt);
25   assertEquals(expectedPriceEvents / 4, heartbeatCt);
26   MarketDataPayLoad < String > audcadPayLoad = audcadLastRef.get();
27   assertEquals(1.0149, audcadPayLoad.getBidPrice(), OandaTestConstants.
     precision);
28   assertEquals(1.0151, audcadPayLoad.getAskPrice(), OandaTestConstants.
     precision);
29   assertEquals(1401920421958 L, audcadPayLoad.getEventDate().
     getMillis());
30   MarketDataPayLoad < String > nzdsgdPayLoad = nzdsgdLastRef.get();
31   assertEquals(1.0799, nzdsgdPayLoad.getBidPrice(), OandaTestConstants.
     precision);
32   assertEquals(1.0801, nzdsgdPayLoad.getAskPrice(), OandaTestConstants.
     precision);
33   assertEquals(1401920421958 L, nzdsgdPayLoad.getEventDate().
     getMillis());
34   verify(spy, times(1)).handleDisconnect(disconnectmsg);
35 }
36
37 private OandaStreamingService setUpSpy(OandaStreamingService service,
38   String fname) throws Exception {
39   OandaStreamingService spy = spy(service);
40   CloseableHttpClient mockHttpClient = mock(CloseableHttpClient.class);
41   when(spy.getHttpClient()).thenReturn(mockHttpClient);
42   when(spy.isStreaming()).thenReturn(service.isStreaming());
43   OandaTestUtils.mockHttpInteraction(fname, mockHttpClient);
44   spy.startStreaming();
45   do {
46     Thread.sleep(2 L);
47   } while (spy.streamThread.isAlive());
48   return spy;
49 }
```

The setUpSpy method performs the usual setup of the streaming service by first creating a *spy* on the underlying instance of OandaStreamingService, in this case it's OandaMarketDataStreamingService. It then sets up the mockHttpInteraction whereby the src/test/resources/marketData123456.txt file will be set up as the source of all events for the market data stream when the underlying service starts streaming by invoking spy.startStreaming().

Once the streaming starts, we wait for all the tick data and heartbeat events to be fully streamed. We set up a do-while loop with a sleep of 2ms as a wait mechanism for this to fully complete. The stream automatically stops once it receives a disconnect message, which is the last event in the file. The streams automatically stop once such a message arrives. This can happen sometimes when the OANDA platform detects that the number of streaming connections has been exceeded. The disconnect message looks like this:

```
1   {"disconnect":{"code":64,"message":"bye","moreInfo":"none"}}
```

The disconnect message leads to the termination of the stream and the background thread streamThread, which was set up as a quasi-infinite loop, also terminates. The method then returns to the caller.

Now we must test that all the events were successfully delivered to the downstream subscribers via the EventBus. For the purposes of this test case, the test class itself is the end consumer of all these events. This was shown to be the case in our test case marketDataStreaming(), where we set this up while setting up the main service itself. Since we want to want to subscribe to the MarketDataPayLoad and HeartBeatPayLoad events, we set up the following dummy methods in the test class, which just count the events received.

```
1    private volatile int audcadCt;
2    private volatile int nzdsgdCt;
3    private AtomicReference < MarketDataPayLoad < String >> audcadLastRef =
4      new AtomicReference < MarketDataPayLoad < String >> ();
5    private AtomicReference < MarketDataPayLoad < String >> nzdsgdLastRef =
6      new AtomicReference < MarketDataPayLoad < String >> ();
7    @Subscribe
8    public void dummyMarketDataSubscriber(MarketDataPayLoad < String >
     payLoad) {
9    if (payLoad.getInstrument().equals(AUDCAD)) {
10     this.audcadCt++;
11     this.audcadLastRef.set(payLoad);
12   } else {
13     this.nzdsgdCt++;
14     this.nzdsgdLastRef.set(payLoad);
15   }
16   }
17   @Subscribe
18   public void dummyHeartBeatSubscriber(HeartBeatPayLoad < DateTime >
     payLoad) {
19     heartbeatCt++;
20   }
```

All the events from the file are directed at these methods, which keep a counter of events received belonging to the currency pair AUD_CAD and NZD_SGD in addition to the heartbeat events. The *asserts* then ensure that the count and order of events received were proper.

The Versatile verify Mockito

So far we have focused on the HttpGet aspect of the interaction where reading from the file was fairly easy. However, to mock the opposite—i.e. inserting (HttpPost) a row, modifying a row (HttpPatch), and deleting a row (Httpdelete) from a file—is much more difficult, if not impossible. So how do we unit tests these interactions? The mockito verify comes to our rescue. The command helps verify interactions of a method and can optionally verify how many times it was invoked. Let's explore the use case in more detail.

To place a new order with the OANDA platform, we do the following at a high level:

- Pass the fully populated *Order* POJO along with the *account ID* to the placeOrder method of the OandaOrderManagementProvider bean.

- The placeOrder method internally delegates to the createPostCommand method, which creates a new instance of the HttpPost command and using the *Order* POJO getters. It populates the NameValuePair list on this post command. Once it's fully populated, the command can then be posted to create an order.

- Once the HttpPost succeeds, we get a response back. It is a JSON payload of the new order details if the command was successful.

During unit testing, we do not want to post a real order to the OANDA platform and just want to validate that a valid HttpPost command was created, and verify can validate this for us. Since the creation of a valid HttpPost command pretty much invokes all getters of the *Order* POJO, the fact that verify reports a getter interaction one time (and more for some others) for each getter validates our code. Similarly, assuming a valid command was posted, we must then receive details of the new order as a JSON payload, which must then be read from a file as part of mockHttpInteraction, which we discussed earlier.

Let's look at the code that tests this case:

```
1   @Test
2   @SuppressWarnings("unchecked")
3   public void createOrderTest() throws Exception {
4     OandaOrderManagementProvider service =
5       new OandaOrderManagementProvider(OandaTestConstants.url,
6         OandaTestConstants.accessToken, null);
7     TradeableInstrument < String > eurjpy = new TradeableInstrument
      < String > ("EUR_JPY");
8
9     OandaOrderManagementProvider spy =
10      doMockStuff("src/test/resources/newOrder.txt",  service);
11    Order < String, Long > orderMarket = mock(Order.class);
12    when(orderMarket.getInstrument()).thenReturn(eurjpy);
13    when(orderMarket.getSide()).thenReturn(TradingSignal.SHORT);
14    when(orderMarket.getType()).thenReturn(OrderType.MARKET);
15    when(orderMarket.getUnits()).thenReturn(150 1);
```

```
16    when(orderMarket.getTakeProfit()).thenReturn(132.65);
17    when(orderMarket.getStopLoss()).thenReturn(136.00);
18    // when(order.getPrice()).thenReturn(133.75);
19    Long orderId =
20     spy.placeOrder(orderMarket, OandaTestConstants.accountId);
21    assertNotNull(orderId);
22    verify(spy, times(1))
23     .createPostCommand(orderMarket, OandaTestConstants.accountId);
24    verify(orderMarket, times(1)).getInstrument();
25    verify(orderMarket, times(3)).getType();
26    verify(orderMarket, times(1)).getTakeProfit();
27    verify(orderMarket, times(1)).getStopLoss();
28    // verify(order, times(2)).getPrice();
29    verify(orderMarket, times(1)).getUnits();
30    verify(orderMarket, times(1)).getSide();
31
32    spy = doMockStuff("src/test/resources/newOrderLimit.txt", service);
33    Order < String, Long > orderLimit = mock(Order.class);
34    TradeableInstrument < String > eurusd =
35     new TradeableInstrument < String > ("EUR_USD");
36    when(orderLimit.getInstrument()).thenReturn(eurusd);
37    when(orderLimit.getSide()).thenReturn(TradingSignal.SHORT);
38    when(orderLimit.getType()).thenReturn(OrderType.LIMIT);
39    when(orderLimit.getUnits()).thenReturn(10 l);
40    when(orderLimit.getTakeProfit()).thenReturn(1.09);
41    when(orderLimit.getStopLoss()).thenReturn(0.0);
42    when(orderLimit.getPrice()).thenReturn(1.10);
43
44    orderId = spy.placeOrder(orderLimit, OandaTestConstants.accountId);
45    assertNotNull(orderId);
46    verify(spy, times(1))
47     .createPostCommand(orderLimit, OandaTestConstants.accountId);
48    verify(orderLimit, times(1)).getInstrument();
49    verify(orderLimit, times(3)).getType();
50    verify(orderLimit, times(1)).getTakeProfit();
51    verify(orderLimit, times(1)).getStopLoss();
52    verify(orderLimit, times(2)).getPrice();
53    verify(orderLimit, times(1)).getUnits();
54    verify(orderLimit, times(1)).getSide();
55    }
56
57    private OandaOrderManagementProvider doMockStuff(String fname,
58     OandaOrderManagementProvider service)
59    throws Exception {
60     OandaOrderManagementProvider spy = spy(service);
61     CloseableHttpClient mockHttpClient = mock(CloseableHttpClient.class);
62     when(spy.getHttpClient()).thenReturn(mockHttpClient);
```

```
63      OandaTestUtils.mockHttpInteraction(fname,  mockHttpClient);
64      return spy;
65  }
```

In this test case, we test a new market and limit order; however, the mechanics are exactly the same. We create a mock *Order* POJO and, to create a successful HttpPost command, all the getters must be invoked on this mock object that defines a new order. The verify does exactly that—it verifies the getter interactions performed inside the createPostCommand.

Mocking Twitter Interaction

Mockito makes interacting with Twitter extremely easy. The only thing to bear in mind is that the search queries might differ for various user accounts when it comes to finding historic PNL tweets. Therefore, for every new user account handler we introduce, this test should be catered to its specific needs.

To get mock tweets from Twitter that can be parsed for new trades or PNL tweets for all users, we must prepare the groundwork of the mock objects. That includes the following:

- Creating a mock for Twitter interface (which is implemented by TwitterTemplate as part of Spring Social).

- Creating a mock for the SearchOperations class, which is used to search for tweets given a search query.

- Creating a mock for SearchResults that returns the mocked tweets when getTweets() is called on this object.

- The invocation of the getTweets() method returns a list of tweet objects that can be a list of mocked tweet objects. The key is to intercept the getText() method on the individual mocked tweet object and return the text that we want.

Let's look at an example where we try to test the findHistoricPnlTweets method for the @SignalFactory user:

```
1   @Test
2   public void findHistoricPnlTweetsForInstrumentTest() {
3       AbstractFXTweetHandler < String > tweetHandler = new SignalFactory
        FXTweetHandler(userId);
4       ProviderHelper providerHelper = mock(ProviderHelper.class);
5       Twitter twitter = mock(Twitter.class);
6       tweetHandler.providerHelper = providerHelper;
7       tweetHandler.twitter = twitter;
8
9       SearchOperations searchOperations = mock(SearchOperations.class);
10      when(twitter.searchOperations()).thenReturn(searchOperations);
11
```

273

```
12    TradeableInstrument < String > nzdusd = new TradeableInstrument
      < String > ("NZD_USD");
13    when(providerHelper.toIsoFormat(eq("NZD_USD"))).thenReturn("NZDUSD");
14    SearchResults searchResults = returnHistoricPnlSearchResults();
15    String query = "Profit: OR Loss: from:SignalFactory";
16    when(searchOperations.search(eq(query))).thenReturn(searchResults);
17    Collection < Tweet > tweets = tweetHandler.findHistoricPnlTweetsForIn
      strument(nzdusd);
18    assertEquals(1, tweets.size());
19    }
20
21    private SearchResults returnHistoricPnlSearchResults() {
22    SearchResults searchResults = mock(SearchResults.class);
23    List < Tweet > tweets = Lists.newArrayList();
24    when(searchResults.getTweets()).thenReturn(tweets);
25    Tweet tweet = mock(Tweet.class);
26    when(tweet.getText()).thenReturn(
27    "Forex Signal | Close(SL) Sell NZDUSD@0.7744 | Loss: -40 pips |
      2015.02.06 11:26 GMT | #fx #forex #fb");
28    tweets.add(tweet);
29    return searchResults;
30    }
```

After setting up the mocks to return the list of tweets, we want to make sure that these tweets are returned only if the query that we expect to be fired is sent to the SearchOperations mock:

```
1    String query = "Profit: OR Loss: from:SignalFactory";
2    when(searchOperations.search(eq(query))).thenReturn(searchResults);
```

The other important aspect of tweet handling for a given user is parsing new and closed trade tweets. The parsing is done on the actual tweet text returned from the getText() method. We want to make sure that we write test cases to cover all aspects of parsing new and closed trades tweets for a given Twitter user.

EclEmma Code Coverage Tool for Eclipse IDE

The EclEmma[3] plug-in for the Eclipse IDE is an excellent tool for reporting code coverage for a Java project. You can run this tool for an individual test case or a suite of tests.

Once EclEmma has been installed successfully, you can launch a test suite via the plug-in using the button shown in Figure 13-1.

---

[3]http://eclemma.org/

Figure 13-1. Launch Test using EclEmma tool

The results appear in the Coverage view, as shown in Figure 13-2.

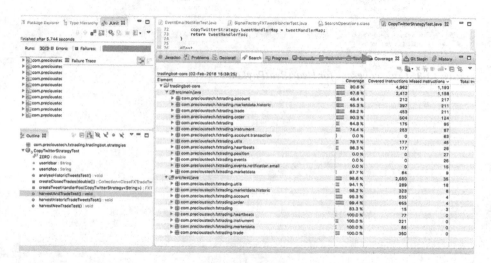

Figure 13-2. Summary of results for the tradingbot-core project

You can then drill down into individual classes and determine the exact lines of code that were executed as part of the unit test and which ones were left out.

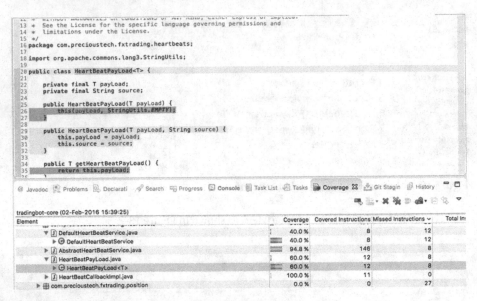

Figure 13-3. *Code coverage for HeartBeatPayLoad*

Index

Get the eBook for only $4.99!

Why limit yourself?

Now you can take the weightless companion with you wherever you go and access your content on your PC, phone, tablet, or reader.

Since you've purchased this print book, we are happy to offer you the eBook for just $4.99.

Convenient and fully searchable, the PDF version enables you to easily find and copy code—or perform examples by quickly toggling between instructions and applications.

To learn more, go to http://www.apress.com/us/shop/companion or contact support@apress.com.

Printed in the United States
By Bookmasters